Elites

Elites

Choice, Leadership and Succession

Edited by

João de Pina-Cabral
and
Antónia Pedroso de Lima

Oxford · New York

First published in 2000 by
Berg
Editorial offices:
150 Cowley Road, Oxford, OX4 1JJ, UK
70 Washington Square South, New York, NY 10012, USA

Berg is the imprint of Oxford International Publishers Ltd.

Library of Congress Cataloguing-in-Publication Data

A catalogue record for this book is available from the Library of Congress.

British Library Cataloguing-in-Publication Data

A catalogue record for this book is available from the British Library.

ISBN   1 85973 394 8 (Cloth)
        1 85973 399 9 (Paper)

Printed in the United Kingdom by Biddles Ltd, Kings Lynn

Contents

Acknowledgements

This volume comes out of a research seminar entitled 'Leadership and Succession in Elite Contexts' that took place at the Palace of Fronteira, Lisbon, in October 1997. It was only made possible due to the support of the Institute of Social Sciences of the University of Lisbon. To this, we were fortunate to add the support of the Fundação Luso-Americana para o Desenvolvimento, whose interest in our project allowed us to transform it into a genuinely international event; and the good luck of finding the support of Dr Fernando de Mascarenhas, the present Marquis of Fronteira, who took on our project with the grand hospitality and intellectual refinement for which he has become famed. Apart from these three organizing bodies, we must also express our gratitude for the generous support of the Ministry of Science and Technology, of the Universidade Atlântica and of Grafismos - whose director, Luis Martins, offered his skills when we most needed them. We are also grateful to Eugénia Rodrigues and Maria Goretti Matias for their kind assistance and to Elvira Costa for her marvellous editorial support. Jackie Waldren, in Oxford, was also a great source of encouragement and help. Not all the colleagues that participated in the discussion prepared chapters for this volume. The contributions of Robert Rowland, Maria das Dores Guerreiro and Michel Bauer were particularly valuable.

Notes on Contributors

Nana Arhin Brempong (Kwame Arhin) (Ph.D. London, D.Litt. Oxford) is Chairman of the National Commision on Culture of Ghana and was formerly Professor and Director at the Institute of African Studies, University of Ghana, Legon. His areas of academic interest are the History of Asante and the transformations in African political and social institutions. Among his publications are *Traditional Rule in Ghana: Past and Present* (Accra, 1985) and *The City of Kumasi Handbook* (Cambridge, 1992).

Michael Herzfeld, D.Phil. (Oxon. 1976, D.Litt. (Birmingham 1989) is Professor of Anthropology (and Curator of European Ethnology in the Peabody Museum) at Harvard University. Recent lectures include the inaugural Distinguished Lecture in European Anthropology at the University of Massachusetts, Amherst (1996) and the Munro Lecture at the University of Edinburgh (1997). A past President of both the Modern Greek Studies Association and the Society for the Anthropology of Europe, he is currently editor of *American Ethnologist*. He is the author of *Ours Once More* (1982), *The Poetics of Manhood* (1985), *Anthropology through the Looking-Glass* (1987), *A Place in History* (1991), *The Social Production of Indifference* (1992), *Cultural Intimacy: Social Poetics in the Nation-State* (1997), and *Portrait of a Greek Imagination* (1997). He was a co-winner of the Chicago Folklore Prize for 1981. He has also been awarded the J. B. Donne Prize on the Anthropology of Art (1989) and the Rivers Memorial Medal (1994) (both from the Royal Anthropological Institute, London), and the J. I. Staley Prize (School of American Research, 1994). In 1997 he was elected a Fellow of the American Academy of Arts and Sciences.

Jean Lave (Ph.D. Harvard) is an anthropologist and Professor of Education at the University of California, Berkeley. She is the author of *Cognition in Practice: Mind, Mathematics, and Culture in Everyday Life* (Cambridge, 1988) and, with E. Wenger, *Situated Learning: Legitimate Peripheral Participation* (Cambridge, 1991). She was recepient of the American Educational Research Association's 1994 Sylvia Scribner Award.

Carola Lentz (D.Phil. Hannover 1987, Habil. Berlin 1996) is Professor of Social Anthropology and African Studies at the Johann Wolfgang Goethe University, Frankfurt-am-Main (Germany). In the 1980s she has conducted fieldwork on labour migration and ethnicity in Ecuador, resulting in numerous articles and several books (among others: *Migración e Identidad Étnica*, Quito, 1997). Later, her research interest changed to West Africa, where she studied questions of ethnicity, traditional and modern elites, the impact of colonial rule on northern Ghana and the settlement histories and politics of land rights among the Dagara of Ghana and Burkina Faso. Recently published were *Die Konstruktion von Ethnizität: Eine politische Geschichte Nord-West Ghanas, 1870-1990* (Cologne, 1998) and, edited together with Paul Nugent, *Ethnicity in Ghana* (London, 1999). Carola Lentz is on the editorial boards of *Paideuma, Ethnos and Food and Foodways* and a member of the scientific committee of the European Association of Social Anthropology.

Antónia Pedroso de Lima is Assistant Professor at the Department of Anthropology, ISCTE (Lisbon), specializing in Kinship Theory and Contemporary Family Relations. She has published on the Portuguese urban family, focusing both on working-class neighbourhoods of Lisbon and on the Portuguese economic elite. She is currently working on a project about major family enterprises and their dynastic families.

George E. Marcus is professor and chair of the Department of Anthropology at Rice University. He is co-editor with James Clifford of *Writing Culture: the Poetics and Politics of Ethnography*, co-author with Michael Fischer of *Anthropology as Cultural Critique*, and most recently author of *Ethnography Through Thick and Thin*. His long-term work on dynastic elites in the United States is reported in the volume, *Lives in Trust: the Fortunes of Dynastic Families in Late Twentieth Century America* (Boulder, Colorado, 1992). During this fin-de-siècle he has edited a series of annuals, entitled *Late Editions* and published by the University of Chicago Press. This series probes contemporary change and transformation on a wide range of topics through the presentation of ethnographic interviews. The most recent volumes are *Corporate Futures: The Diffusion of the Culturally Sensitive; Corporate Form at Century's End* and *Paranoia Within Reason: A Casebook on Conspiracy as Explanation*.

Nuno Gonçalo Monteiro (Ph.D. Lisbon) is Senior Research Fellow at the Institute of Social Sciences of the University of Lisbon and Professor of History at ISCTE (Lisbon). His publications include *O Crepúsculo dos Grandes: 1750-1832* (Lisbon 1998). His research interests are in the area of Social History, with particular emphasis on Portuguese elite groups from the sixteenth to the nineteenth centuries.

João de Pina-Cabral (D.Phil. Oxford) is Senior Research Fellow and President of the Scientific Board of the Institute of Social Sciences of the University of Lisbon. He was co-founder and Rector of the Universidade Atlântica (1996-1997). He was founding President of the Portuguese

Association of Anthropology. He is an Honorary Member of the European Association of Social Anthropologists, having organized its first Conference (Coimbra 1990) and been its Secretary and Treasurer (1995-1996). His publications include *Sons of Adam, Daughters of Eve* (Oxford, 1986), *Os contextos da antropologia* (Lisbon, 1991) and *Em Terra de Tufões* (Macao, Portuguese edn, 1993; Chinese edn, 1995). He was co-editor of *Death in Portugal* (Oxford, 1984) and *Europe Observed* (London, 1992). He has been Malinowski Memorial Lecturer (London School of Economics, 1992) and Distinguished Lecturer of the Society for the Anthropology of Europe (San Francisco, 1992).

José Manuel Sobral (Ph.D. Lisbon) is Senior Research Fellow at the Institute of Social Sciences of the University of Lisbon. He has published a number of works in the area of the history of ideas in contemporary Portugal, as well as in the social anthropology of rural society in Central Portugal, including *Trajectos: o Presente e o Passado na Vida de uma Freguesia da Beira* (Lisboa, 1999).

Christina Toren has a B.Sc. (Hons) in Psychology from University College London and a Ph.D. in Social Anthropology from London School of Economics. She is currently Senior Lecturer in Anthropology and Psychology at Brunel University. She is the author of numerous papers and two books: *Making Sense of Hierarchy: Cognition as Social Process in Fiji* (London, 1990) and *Mind, Materiality and History: Explorations in Fijian Ethnography* (London, 1999).

Sylvia Yanagisako (Ph.D. Washington) is Professor of Anthropology at Standard University and Chair of the Department of Social and Cultural Anthropology. She was Director of the Program in Feminist Studies at that University. She is the author of *Transforming the Past* (Stanford, 1985) and with Jane Collier of *Gender and Kinship* (Stanford, 1987) and with Carol Delaney of *Naturalizing Power* (London, 1995).

Introduction

João de Pina-Cabral

For years Antónia Pedroso de Lima and myself have collaborated in the undergraduate teaching of kinship and family. As our mutual research interests evolved we were increasingly drawn to the issue of the relation between family and power - both in authority as constitutive of familial relations and in familial relations as transmitting positions of authority. Over the past decade, as we witnessed an increased interest on the part of anthropologists in the study of elite contexts, a discussion of succession seemed to us to be long overdue.

We decided to convene a research seminar to which we invited colleagues from Europe, Africa and North America who were working with elites. We wanted to enlarge the basis of the debate, not only with materials originating from different cultural backgrounds, but also from different anthropological perspectives. We could not fail to bring in also an historical viewpoint, particularly since the meeting was to take place in the palatial home of one of the principal *Ancien Régime* families of Portugal. The dedicated interest and warm hospitality of the present scion of the House of Fronteira and Alorna was a decisive contribution. The beautiful blue and white tiles (*azulejos*) depicting brave battles that surrounded us during our meetings, and the stucco figures of glorious ancestors that looked down upon our debates, could not fail to impress us with a sense of how insinuating can be the process of reproduction of social privilege.

Succession

In Fortes's classical formulations, succession appears as a corollary of 'corporateness'. As he puts it: 'succession ... is the instrument for ensuring corporate continuity, given the principle of the corporate identity of organised pluralities, not the formulation of this principle ...' (1969: 305).

Considering the ethnographic material we had at hand, such a dependence on a notion of corporateness seemed to reduce the operational value of the concept of succession. We had familial entities of very distinct kinds, and they could seldom be fitted into the Fortesian mould of corporateness - that is, 'the perpetuation of an aggregate by exclusive recruitment to restricted membership that carries actual or potential equality of status and neutrality of interests and obligations in its internal affairs' (1969: 306).

1

The divergence is largely one of perspective: while Fortes presumed the existence of the social group (with its jural principles, its constituent parts, its organizational structure) as the starting-point of any sociological analysis, we approach it from the contrary angle of seeing social relations as a permanent flux within which, through the exercise of forms of power, entities arise that are never finally fixed nor ever permanent, remaining always dependent on the constant interplay of hegemonic and counter-hegemonic forces (cf. Pina-Cabral 1998b).

Thus, the problem of succession was no longer the traditional one of social reproduction: that is, seeing how groups invested persons with specific authority in order to survive. Rather, it was necessary to capture the processes by which personal and supra-personal entities formed and reformed each other through an interplay of power relations.

Elites

In particular, we became interested in elite contexts - that is, groups that control specific resources by means of which they acquire political power and material advantage. In such contexts, the transmission across generations of the benefits resulting from control over these resources often depends on the maintenance of structures of authority. These may manifest themselves either by unitary succession to previously defined posts of authority or by a more general production of successors out of which figures of authority will emerge. In either case, there is choice to be exercised among those who might be eligible. The nature of the exercise of this choice, in turn, is a major factor in the future development of the relations between the members and their descendants.

We wanted to find out more about how succession and leadership interplay with each other, particularly in contexts where such leadership is the very basis for the continuation of the group. That is, where the group does not exist *per se*, but is a function of the control of the resource that grants it elite status (whether it be family-held assets or community or ethnic monopolies, as in my own discussion of Macao's Eurasian community).

We wanted to bring together scholars whose personal and research experience was deeply divergent from an ethnographic viewpoint but who faced similar questions about the issue of succession, so as to suggest the possibility of some form of comparative approach.

Choice

Reading through the draft versions of the papers, we soon concluded that the original title of our meeting - 'Leadership and Succession in Elite Contexts' - needed to be changed to one that better represented these concerns: 'Choice Leadership and Succession'. 'Choice' appears to be one of the central topics that most chapters address - the issue of the nature of the choice of successor, of the means to make the choice and the legal, political and economic constraints behind that choice.

Here a major aspect seems to be the confrontation between out-group factors versus in-group factors of candidate suitability. The compliance with external factors is indispensable for the preservation of the resource that keeps the group together. At the same time, however, this compliance challenges the groups's internal coherence, by distorting the factors of in-group suitability.

The other side of the coin is the conflict between what Abner Cohen would have called *universalistic* and *particularistic* interests. The successful heir has to demonstrate that he is a successful leader in out-group terms. Yanagisako's paper exemplifies clearly this quandary.

Even in cases such as Nuno Monteiro's aristocratic houses (*casas*) of seventeenth-century Portugal, where there seemed to be practically no choice as to who should be the heir, there always remained a margin for manipulation and for negotiation as to who succeeded to the leadership roles. Whether it is formal or informal, whether it is largely biologically determined or practically a form of election, whether it confers total authority or only limited seniority - succession seems to be a central preoccupation whenever the resources that are transferred across generations demand for their preservation some form of collective action. The success of collective action depends on the legitimation of authority. In the case of elites, however, this authority must apply beyond the boundaries of the immediate group. Thus, elite succession always seems to have a contradictory element: for, while out-group factors demand universalistically legitimate candidates, in-group factors tend to favour particularistically well-placed members of the group.

Production of Successors and a Stake in the Future

Another of the common themes that emerge from the chapters is that of the actual production of successors - sometimes, as in Jean Lave's case, the production of the successors appears to be even more important than the actual resource that they will succeed to. Here, the element of personal versus group identity is of major importance, and Marcus's comments on the 'uncanny' strike a chord in my own interest in understanding the interplay between personal and suprapersonal identities and how they mutually produce each other. We go well beyond Fortes's opposition between individual and group - both seen as closed and self-sufficient entities.

Finally, all the chapters converge on the notion that, for there to be succession, there have to be shared views of the future - familial life is seen as a project. In terms of the in-group there is a production of family legends that, in turn, are used to produce correct heirs. But these are managed through the manipulation of out-group resources, such as schooling or political or financial carreers. Both the chapters of Nana Arhin and Carola

Lentz show how this confrontation can lead to internal conflict and to diverging manipulations of what is 'traditional'. Segmentary logics start to arise that have their manifestations in different re-writings of the family history. This is as true for Asante traditional chiefly families as it is for Portuguese banking families.

Outline of the Book

Part I - 'Dynastic Sentiments' - comprises three chapters dealing with the transmission and preservation of power in urban upper-class contexts. The uniting theme is Marcus's concept of 'dynasty' and the way it shapes sentiments. The chapters explore the complex relation between subjectivity and the transmission of leadership positions by relation to highly demanding technical constraints, in the United States, in Northern Italy and in Portugal.

Part II - 'Choice and Tradition' - brings together a series of essays on the succession to self-avowedly 'traditional' roles of leadership. These chapters deal with forms of political power that find their legitimation in a pre-colonial past, but are formed by the colonial experience. Here, the issue of choice becomes central, ranging from situations such as Christina Toren's Fijian case, where leaders are elected from among a group of peers, to the Ghanaian examples presented by Carola Lentz and Nana Arhin Brempong, where politics and economic success intermingle with descent in legitimating succession.

Part III - 'House and Heir' - integrates two chapters that deal with the way in which the Iberian institution of primogeniture evolved in Portugal since its heyday in the seventeenth century. These historical chapters were particularly relevant to our discussion, not only in the light of the actual conference that brought us together, and that took place in the palatial home of one of these seventeenth-century families - the Fronteiras. Rather, as Nuno Monteiro points out, the Iberian model of aristocratic succession became the stereotype of dynastic succession throughout Europe. If we look back at the chapters by Toren, Arhin and Lentz, and at their comments about how the colonial presence imposed on the local cultures Eurocentric notions of aristocratic succession, Monteiro's example assumes a particular relevance.

Sobral's chapter on the relation between local power and landed property integrates the volume under two distinct aspects. On the one hand, it shows how the model of aristocratic succession evolved and was finally destroyed by the onset of the modern state. On the other hand, it prepares us for the concerns of the last section with the preservation of the means to elite status.

In Part IV - 'Monopolies and Successors' - Jean Lave and I present two very distinct situations where unitary succession is not possible or desirable, but where the preservation of a monopoly demands that the group produce suitable successors.

Introduction

Michael Herzfeld's conclusion brings us back to one of the original pre-occupations that were behind the convening of this conference. One of our aims was to bring together contributions from North American and European colleagues focusing on a topic of common interest. The past decade has witnessed an increase in communication between social scientists across the Atlantic. Often, however, this contact has failed to be a genuine dialogue, as the guiding theoretical horizons continue to be very divergent. The present collection turned out to be very telling in this sense. If we read Marcus's and Yanagisako's chapters in this perspective and compare them with those of Lentz or Toren or my own, for example, we come up with a clear notion that the horizons of reference continue to differ significantly. The choice of inviting Michael Herzfeld as the overall discussant for the conference thus seems to be vindicated – as is quite patent from reading his concluding remarks, where he is suggesting ways that allow for a convergence of perspectives. For instance, his emphasis on the question of 'intimacy' rather than on 'sentiment' could prove a valuable guideline. The debate here is hardly that of psychological reductionism versus anti-reductionism. To many of us, this kind of preoccupation has long lost its relevance (cf. Kuper 1990). More to the point is the fact that our theoretical agendas are marked by vague interests that have at their roots culturally specific horizons.

To have recourse to an example again, Marcus's discussion of the sense of the uncanny that preoccupies American heirs when they see themselves re-creating the identities of other persons cannot be taken for granted in Europe. When Antónia Pedroso de Lima's bankers experience this same sense of unwilled identification with an ancestor, they feel it is uncanny, but it does not disturb them. Rather, they are prone to cherish the experience and to dwell on it with relish. What is perhaps at stake is a greater European situation-centredness as opposed to an American individual-centredness concerning expectations as to what it is to be a person (to borrow Francis Hsu's famous concepts for differentiating Chinese from American attitudes towards the person, 1981: 12). In short, as has often happened in the history of anthropology, we find our theoretical discussions being enriched by our pre-theoretical differences.

Part I

Dynastic Sentiments

1

The Deep Legacies of Dynastic Subjectivity: The Resonances of a Famous Family Identity in Private and Public Spheres

George E. Marcus

When I have spoken of my research on American dynastic fortunes and families with European colleagues, I often receive encouraging responses until they learn that I am dealing with subjects of only a hundred years in depth, families of 'old' wealth who have risen and declined since the Civil War of the 1860s, whose experience with organized dynastic relations is over within two to four generations. Such a short cycle hardly seems dynastic in the context of European histories of aristocracy, or even of *haute bourgeoisie*. Yet there is immense respect for a family's revealed dynastic impulse and achievement in the imagination of Americans; but this regard is rooted not in any sense of aristocratic honour, tradition, or endurance, but rather in an ambivalent envy of and Social Darwinist liking for a relatively scarce 'good' that only certain of the upwardly mobile and successful can achieve - a prolonged enjoyment of success within and in the name of the family. 'Shirtsleeves to shirtsleeves in three generations' - the well-known saying that ensures democracy through a retarded, but certain, turnover of private wealth - indeed captures the fluidity of the American class system. Yet, this three- to four-generation interval of accumulation and achievement is a rare commodity that inspires a popular adulation for those of good family that is nearly as strong and perhaps more heartfelt than that exhibited in a ritual, formal way for those of ancient lineage in European societies.

Far from its having a vague or relatively unmarked class system, what is remarkable about the United States is how quickly and superficially class distinctions are established. Unlike what occurs in European societies, it takes only one generational transition of distinction to establish a widespread veneration, and even reverence, for the claims of being of good family.[1] As early as the second generation, and still more markedly in the third, the distinction of dynastic continuity takes on weight. Of course this hallowed temporal marking of a family's status could not be established if such an identity were only of value to the family itself. Indeed, the dynastic impulse played out as family drama must also appeal to more widespread longings among Americans as well as being an ornament and an asset for operators within the major economic and political institutions that have defined the constraints in law and regulation by which dynastic families can even persist in modern capitalist societies. And without a prominent history of aristocratic distinction or the encumbrance of control by long-entrenched upper classes, America's short-term dynastic cycles produce identities that can be readily appropriated and unexpectedly revived even as the fortunes, businesses, and fame on which a family's standing initially rested recede. The dynastic formation is thus a pause or hesitation in the long-term circulation of elites in the United States. It creates moral family value that is set loose in the regular dissolution of accumulations of wealth, political power, and professional fame for various kinds of appropriation that make the play of politics and economics appear less raw.

In the European context, then, Americans have experienced mini-dynastic dramas, hardly worth the title 'dynastic'; but that experience merits this designation nonetheless if it is understood as embedded in the culturally specific American making of middle-class desire and subjectivity, especially over the past century. Given how quickly the dynastic effect is established in the United States and the fluidity with which the resulting identity travels and is claimed in a society where self-making and the nurturance of the individual as the bearer of rights and human potential is paramount, the key issue in sustaining dynastic continuity is not so much the tangible strategies of keeping collective wealth, power, and organization together - these are bound to fail in predictable and programmed ways. Rather, it concerns the intimate psychocultural processes that shape subjecitvities among descendants, and how these subjectivities remain vivid in relations among descendants as the hold of dynastic organizations lessens.

Of course, the legacy of dynastic subjectivity among descendants and those who have worked for such families is of general importance wherever dynasties have established themselves, even in societies with histories of aristocratic honour and temporally deep lineage organization, and where forebears have been ancestors in the distant past.[2] But I am arguing here that, in the American context, the strength of continuity depends more centrally and intensely upon the psychocultural processes of person-making, both because the other levers of institutional and material control for insuring open-ended dynastic continuity are so attenuated and because the shallowness of lineage in American dynastic cycles makes the psychological pressures more direct and routine between descendant and forebear, the latter being not so much the venerated ancestor of many generations back as the figure of the parent, or the relatively recent grandparent and great-grandparent.

While much of my analysis below is couched in general terms, the reader should keep in mind, then, for comparative purposes the specifically American inflection and reference of my arguments. Yet I would also not want this analysis to be taken as applicable merely to the case of the United States. With globalization, there is an increasing movement toward larger and larger economic actors, and these have continued to encroach upon sectors of enterprise that until just a decade or two ago had typically been the preserves of dynastic family businesses - for example in agriculture, energy, publishing, finance, retailing and real estate - holdovers from the nineteenth-century era of family capitalism in the United States and Europe. Here conglomerates absorb family businesses, and appropriate and even commodify their hallowed names and identities.[3] Occasionally, families remain at the head of these conglomerates; but even in such cases the tempo of succession struggles and dissolution has markedly increased. What remains, if anything, of the dynastic impulse and potential for the longer term is the ironic power of the family name and identity, circulating both in private and public circles, to be renewed under various opportunistic circumstances. This has long been true in the United States, and is apparently increasingly the case for places where temporally deep lineage organizations of elites once reigned over politics, business, and culture.

Human Capital and the Shaping of Dynastic Subjectivity

For over two centuries in the West, and during the latter years of the twentieth century on an increasingly global scale, the significance of dynastic organizations in the performance of elite social functions in governance and commerce has been on the decline, in favour of more formal bureaucratic organizations. This does not mean that dynastic organizations have not been very important from time to time and from place to place; but the variety of ways that they have been important has not been very well registered because of the dominance of a certain narrative that unfolds the dynasty as a family drama - the passing of power, wealth, and status amid contestations among kin over legacies that pass lineally across generations.

The point of much of my previous writing on dynastic formations of families and fortunes (mostly in the United States over the past century) has been to qualify, nuance, and even remake this mythic narrative. I have been interested to see how dynastic families interact with institutions that are historically related to them and that they have spun off or competed with. I have been interested in the very important consequences for the operations of power, wealth, and status in society of the decline and dissolution of dynasties and dynastic motivations in elite families, rather than their reproduction, since the latter has clearly not been the historic trend in the West, nor is it now globally. In short, dynasties - elite lineages of power, wealth, and status in relation to defined institutional spheres - remain a social fact, but not in the mythic sense, evoking kings, patriarchs, etc.

Besides looking at how dynastic motivation is eventually displaced onto organizations and institutions that serve dynastic families, I have been especially interested in probing how, in terms of models of personhood and character, deep legacies of subjectivity are passed on in families that are otherwise in the process of decline in relation to performing certain elite functions outside the family.

In an important 1988 article, the legal historian John Longbein identified what he regarded as fundamental shifts in the contemporary ethos and practice of wealth transmission in America. Longbein wrote:

> Whereas of old, wealth transmission from parents to children tended to center upon major items of patrimony such as the family farm or the family firm, today for the broad middle-classes, wealth transmission centers on a radically different kind of asset: the investment in skills. In consequence, intergenerational wealth transmission no longer occurs primarily upon the death of the parents, but rather, when the children are growing up, hence during the parents' lifetimes (quoted in Hall and Marcus 1997: 22).

This shift from testamentary to *inter vivos* transfers has been due not only to changes in the nature of wealth itself, from land assets or shares in family firms to financial assets (stocks, bonds, bank deposits, mutual fund shares, insurance contracts, and the like), but also, and more significantly, to human capital - the skills and knowledge that are the foundation of advanced technological societies.

Now the concept of human capital is a very economistic way of characterizing what are in fact subtly cultural and psychological processes within elite families. For investments in human capital to work at all in relation to family purposes of reproducing leaders for both themselves and others who would carry the name and reputation of the family into the future, they would have to occur in milieux where familial authority over descendants remains strong despite the lessening of traditional, obvious means to discipline, force, intimidate and cajole descendants into certain career and behavioural paths. The imponderable, seemingly psychocultural pressures and factors, always present, but difficult to grasp, become much more independently important in arriving at an understanding of succession and inheritance in contemporary elite families.

For me, at the heart of understanding transactions in so-called human capital in dynasties in literal decline and dissolution are the psychocultural processes that I term the 'dynastic uncanny'. The capacity of an elite family to create leaders, not only in its own family succession, but also, as the result of the investment in human capital (concerns with descendants educations, attitudes, tastes, personal habits), in other institutional spheres as well, depends much on these processes that deal with the intergenerational legacy of personhood, submissive to family distinction.

On the Dynastic Uncanny[4]

> I have come to see family history as similar to architecture in certain ways. Like architecture, it is quiet. It encompasses, but does not necessarily demand attention. You might not even notice that it's there. Like architecture, too, family history can suddenly loom into consciousness. For example, you can sit in the New York Public Library at Forty-Second Street - designed by Carriere and Hastings, and perhaps the greatest building in New York - with your nose in a book, or busy with the catalogue and transactions with clerks, all the while oblivious of the splendid interior around you. You can forget it utterly, or perhaps not have noticed it at all that day, and then, casually looking up, be astonished, even momentarily disoriented, by what you see. So it is with family history. One can go about one's life with no thought of the past, and then, as if waking from a dream, be astonished to see that one is living within its enclosure.
>
> I was in my thirties when I began to perceive that my own life was encompassed in this way. At first this seemed to be a form of bondage, but it turned out to be a gift, and all family history, it seems to me, must be a gift in a similar way (Lessard 1996: 4).

Suzannah Lessard

Suzannah Lessard is a great-granddaughter of the prominent architect of late nineteenth-century New York, Stanford White, who was shot to death in 1906 by the heir to an industrial fortune, Harry K. Thaw, jealous over the former's sexual affair with Evelyn Nesbit. There had been infusions of inherited wealth by marriage into her family, but it was the distinction of Stanford White and a certain aestheticism in architecture and other arts that defined a continuity in this family, along with secrets of danger and violence that were constantly evoked across the generations in the story of White and the uncanny reappearance of certain elements of it in the character and personalities of later descendants.

While much of my own research has dealt with families defined by and facing legacies of wealth cocooning them from the wider world, rather than by performative legacies of distinction in the arts, the military, the professions, or politics, the dynamics by which dynastic identity continues to survive from generation to generation in terms of the ironic reproduction of subjectivities is quite similar between families tied to fortunes and those tied more markedly to the distinctive actions and careers of forebears. Indeed, given the trend toward dynastic legacies of subjectivity decoupled from originating businesses and enterprises gobbled up by mega-corporations, the understanding of the subterranean but deeply affecting processes by which dynastic potential passes through and challenges subjectivities is even more important. Amid the voluminous genre of dynastic and upper-class memoirs, especially by women,[5] Lessard's is particularly worthy of note because in her elegant and rich narrative of family history it defines the hold of a past on the making of persons in famous families with such detail and an intensity that few other works achieve.

For my purposes, Lessard is especially important for identifying the sensual, aesthetic medium in which dynastic continuity takes hold in a particular family and impresses itself upon the individual as compelling. Her trope for this is architectural, which is quite appropriate given the role of her famous forebear in creating some of the most lavishly built environments of New York City. For Lessard, the key to dynastic memory and power over descendants is in the literal bodily effect that living and moving within White's architectural legacies generates. A look, a texture, a smell summons up past family experiences in the self. Her narrative telling of family history depends upon this recurrence of uncanny sensation.

In my own contacts with dynastic descendants, the same sensual and ambivalent reproduction of a compelling dynastic presence within themselves but outside their control had a more direct somatic parallel. Moments occur during middle age in which the sense of autonomous identity and subjectivity - just when it should be at its peak - among descendants of famous families is shaken by their catching themselves repeating characteristic behaviours and bodily features of either or both their parents, deceased or living, or through either of them, of a more distant important forebear. This uncanny doubling of the self - a kind of haunting of the self - through the sensation of being invested with the habits of a dynastic figure from whom descendants had thought they had distanced themselves, at least psychologically, is as close as we get in this culture to the sacred power of ancestor worship.

The stimulus for this sensation is often the contemplation of one's body - a profound alignment with (not just likeness to) a forebear in which one joltingly recognizes that one is repeating features of face or form, gestures, or the physical condition of a parent. This recognition might come from something as common as the act of looking in a mirror or in the casual comment of a friend or spouse about an aspect of one's appearance that one had not before noticed. Somatic alignments often lead to sustained reflections on other similarities, those having to do with character, mental habits, orientation to relationships, money, or sexuality; and finally, they threaten to challenge what had been one's unreflected-upon sense of autonomous selfhood. In many families, a person who is jolted by the uncanny can build upon recall of a diffuse discourse about the distinctive look, character, qualities, flaws, or eccentricties within the X or Y family. Suddenly, the adult father or mother he or she knew as a child becomes part of that person as an adult in a way that years of separation, growing up, and the pursuit of autonomous life never would have prepared the individual to experience.

There is of course nothing exclusive about this phenomenon. It is reported widely by many middle-class Americans whom I know - it is a common complaint of middle-age. But disturbing as such moments may be, for most people they do not come to much, or they inspire vaguely underplayed, persistent, ambivalent feelings as people go about their lives.

For others, these uncanny sensations of a merging of the bodily and essential self with those of parents do become the cause or central thematic experience of therapy. But for the special context of interest in this chapter - the contemporary conditions of descendant families situated within complex dynastic organizations of administered wealth, cultural patronage, and political influence - the hyperdevelopment of this common middle-class experience of the uncanny is a key to understanding the continuing hold of collective family authority over adult descendants who are at least three generations from the founder, who are openly suspicious of or even hostile to all attempts to exert parental authority in the name of the family, and who are powerlessly held to clanship by the entanglements of sharing complexly administered patrimony by the bearing of a public 'magic' surname.

Early in my research I understood how important was the construction of dynastic motivation and discipline within particular families through external agents such as lawyers, servants, and writers (including scholars and journalists) of wealthy family, sagas, each external agent acting for his or her own professional and personal interest. In such an external context, the dynastic family, as object, let us say, for constructed financial operation, bestseller, personal fantasy, or the like, nonetheless had powerful shaping and constraining effects on the ability of actual living family members to construct their own subjectivities - to know themselves - among themselves. In fact, I had come to see, in many cases, the family itself by the third generation as (or becoming) similar to a subsidiary of dynastic operations administering a range of legacies in the realms of business, philanthropy, and politics.

Still, when I considered interpersonal relations within the most mythically dynastic or apparently clannish families, there seemed to be more salient dynastic authority and collective identity than could be simply accounted for either by the institutional structures of tied-up patrimony and the external agents interested in it for their own reasons or by psychological dynamics alone. Furthermore, by the end of the 1960s, upper-class institutional supports (for example, prep. schools, Ivy League universities, private clubs) for reinforcing parental/ancestral authority within old-wealth families had weakened sufficiently to disappoint family leaders who would be patriarchs and matriarchs to their children. The immense personal power of the older generation of such families continued to be exercised in their public worlds, where the mystique of dynasty is actually quite strong. But it could no longer in any symmetrical way be exercised in their private worlds, that is, as affecting the younger generation. Thus, while the dynastic authority that is residual may not be mobilizable by leaders through straightforward rite, ritual, or rhetorical persuasion (as in tribal societies and modern corporations), it still is powerful for descendants within the very processes by which they both seek and assert their own autonomous subjectivities (or fail to do so). It is in the struggle of aging descendants in families of fame, property, and power to come to terms with their upper-class collective and middle-class autonomous selves where the experience of the uncanny reinvestment of the parent at the core of one's sense of selfhood takes on special significance. That experience becomes the resource by which the otherwise weakened manifestation of ancestral authority in families of dynastic wealth gathers renewed power.

Post-1960s American mainstream culture propels descendants more intensely than ever before to establish for themselves unique biographical narratives. At the same time, as trust beneficiaries, descendants are constantly being pulled into the administration of patrimony, and that pull is reinforced by their noted uncanny recognition of the bodily and behavioural repetition in their daily activities and practices of imposing figures from the past. These, indeed, have been themes recurrent in the autobiographical fragments that I elicited in conversations with members of dynastic families in Texas and, on occasion, elsewhere. Of course, these concerns weigh differently on family leaders, on males, and on females, but they are nonetheless a common preoccupation running through the commentaries of adult children, as siblings and cousins, anticipating the final stages of generational transition.

These sentiments remind me of the 'anxiety of influence' among poets that Harold Bloom (1973) described in his meditation on 'the melancholy of the creative mind's desperate insistence on priority', or, to use an epigraph he let stand for his argument: 'It Was a Great Marvel That They Were In the Father Without Knowing Him.' Bloom went on to describe several strategies by which poets have resolved this anxiety of influence by distancing themselves from their forebears. Yet in their mature work, at the end of a long process of achieving originality, they have found themselves uncannily repeating past masters, just as dynastic descendants perceive themselves to fail ultimately to establish unique selves even though they 'see through' any overt or obvious attempts by parents, or their servants, to exert the authority of a collective dynastic tradition. In Bloom's work is embedded a more general conception of the dynamics of tradition that I find very suggestive. However, what he takes as an *essentially* psychological (in his case, orthodox Freudian) dynamic, I want to understand as an equally cultural one: what makes a collective tradition without compelling social forms efficacious for descendants is precisely the conflation of tradition with the most powerful cultural construct in middle-class American culture - infinitely pliable, but self-determining, subjectivity. The power of tradition in this sense has the quality of the sacred evoked in Durkheim's sociology, or of charisma in that of Weber, in that ironic, suspicious descendants who oppose family attempts to exert authority nonetheless experience the *embodied* mystery of themselves becoming intimately more a part of an identity about which they 'know better'.

Here, it is worth contrasting briefly the American dynastic descendant with the members of small-scale, tribal societies of classic anthropological interest. For example, in his account of a Melanesian people situated on islands off the north-east coast of Papua New Guinea, Michael Young (1983) was concerned with how 'big men' - leaders of achieved standing in a society that to Western eyes would superficially appear highly individualistic - self-consciously enact in their lived (and often plotted) biographies the past lives of ancestors or legendary figures. This is very much an intended rather than an unwitting repetition of one's forebears' identities in one's own biography, and there is a considerable cultural aesthetic of performance embedded in the big men's own self-references as well as in the evaluations of their followers. The merging of notable past lives with one's own present celebrated life occurs with a certain seamlessness because the biographies - marked by historical events - are couched in mythical time. But it is important to be clear that individuals in Kalauna, or in any apparently exotic society that anthropologists have described, are not selfless or lacking in self-consciousness. However, public expressive ritual is powerful in its ability to affect experience; mythical narratives are shared; a coherent cosmology is at least understood; and there is nothing ironic or parodic about the self repeating in the present the timeless lives of ancestors or forebears.

The contrast between this construction of the self and that of dynastic descendants in Euro-American societies is striking. The trend in recent anthropology has been to downplay such 'us and them' contrasts as have a tendency to exoticize its primary subject-matter. Nevertheless, the differences between the cultural ideologies of autonomous selfhood manifested in discourses about experience and the body of two very specific cases are significant. Both were clearly marked social elites: the Texas lineages researched by me (or other such American families researched by others) and the Melanesians of Kalauna in the ethnography of Young. Among the Kempners or the Rockefellers or the Binghams, the descendant self should be and is willed to be a unique, autonomous self, with the constant possibility of change, modification, and improvement. Recognition of the repetition of parental/ancestral identities is received with a fearful irony that is absent from the character of similar recognitions in Kalauna or other such societies, where it is presumed that present experiences can reproduce past experiences of personhood, not just coincidentally or mysteriously, but in an embodied, willed, and cosmologically rationalized way. As noted, this uncanny awareness of irony, of the unique self's not being so unique after all, is a common perception among middle-class people, the mystery of which is a key impetus for the theories and practices of various psychotherapies. In families of inherited wealth, this perception is hyperdeveloped in order to lend sacred efficacy to the authority of an organization for the administration of wealth and the persons to which that wealth attaches.

Depending upon how a descendant is situated in a dynastic structure, this irony can play out in diverse ways - it can be emotionally disturbing, it can be humorous, it can be embarrassing to a desired social presentation of self (compare for example, Peggy Guggenheim becoming more like her uncles after years of rebellion; the contemporary leader of a Texas family plainly aware of his parodic role in terms of his father and grand-father). In societies where the self develops this ironic character in rela-tion to forebears (intimately associated, I believe, with the historic making of middle classes from the nineteenth century to the present), collective identities (family, ethnic, regional) become transmitted and formed by the processes that synonymously shape personal identities and, particular-ly, become transmitted and formed in terms of the cultural discourses available for constituting the latter. The power of this personal process, unlike that of any public or overt forms by which cultural values might be expressed and transmitted, is in its felt mystery, its uncanniness.

I want to distance the condensation of collective representations into personal ones from primarily psychological accounts of the process. This is not to deny the value of psychological analyses or concepts for explain-ing the uncanny repetition of parental identity - these are not only the scholarly and scientific way for doing so in American culture but are also the folk, commonsensical way, especially for the middle classes. However, it is precisely the cross-cultural perspective sketched above that suggests that psychological terms are neither the only nor sufficient ones with which to describe the ironic self, perhaps natural to us but indeed strange to a Melanesian still marginally situated in relation to global cultural and economic conditionings.

In any case, much in psychological explanations for the uncanny repe-tition must be taken on belief. In the many accounts of notable families that are written by descendants around such narratives of the profound visitations of past generations upon the present one, the process is noted, but details are left obscure or assigned to a general Freudianism. Psychological explanations assume close, powerful interactions between parent and child in which identities are shaped: much of the learning that occurs is unconscious - this is what makes it compelling and mysterious to descendant consciousness. I would argue rather that the power of the psy-chological effect upon the person is in the discourse of descendants them-selves that forms around the story of a struggle by a willed autonomous self to escape given, official family models of character, inculcated by a diffuse, redundant discourse that evaluates the worth of children through their likenesses to and differences from exemplary forebears. The fact of dis-turbed awareness of repetition is clear; the psychological process by which it is shaped is not. Dynastic folk beliefs rely on innateness, on eugenic explanations for the repetition of identities, although this mode is ideo-logically unmentionable in mass liberal culture. Indeed, it is this family eugenic discourse that descendants seeking their own unique selves rebel against; but years of hearing oneself evaluated in terms of forebears by authoritative voices in the family have already prepared the ground for a powerful effect once the uncanny arises. It draws the descendant willy-nilly into the fold of ancestral/dynastic authority.

Resonances of Famous Family Identity in Private and Public

Within dynastic families, descendants' understanding of the repetition of identities is most often in psychological terms, and in the most disturbing cases, descendants seek psychotherapy. But accounts of psychological dynamics aside, descendants receive a cultural conditioning in their family's discourse about its own special types of persons, distinctive through breeding - what I call its discourse about character - that is historically constructed exclusively for family members and is itself folk-psychological in rhetoric. This discourse, how it arises, and how it impinges upon biographies of descendants constitute a kind of tradition-based therapy. The mystery of tradition, condensed in a dynasty's discourse about character, is far more powerful and encompassing than the enlightening power of psychological explanations developed in conventional therapeutic settings. The descendant, the ward of a fortune, continues to find his or her own developing autonomy tied back again and again to the family's discourse about character. That happens because the descendant uncannily feels the truth of resemblances that were redundantly attributed to him or her during a youth spent among servants and in proximity to parents.

So, aside from whatever psychological (that is, unconscious) processes about cross-generational transmissions of personality can be identified, there is also a quite self-conscious and reflexive discourse that occurs among dynasts. This is a shared, disciplining discourse about a family's collective standard of personhood, expressed in broadly psychological, behavioural, and somatic terms. It is through this discourse, diffusely evident in the turns of phrase, stories, and repeated conversations of the family, that the sort of tradition that might otherwise be transmitted by collective representations, rites, and patriarchal commands is compellingly received by late twentieth century culturally middle-class persons caught in the family organizations of upper-class culture of an earlier period.

Before I say more about the controlling discourse concerning character and its fate in recent American history, I must first note how it is constituted as data, that is, by what medium it occurs and is located in the ethnographic research process. This is the exchange of autobiographical fragments, which is the predominant form fieldwork dialogues take, not only among dynasts, but also among most Americans for whom the self and personal recall are the narrative frame for relating matters in which ethnographers might be interested.

Autobiography is not just a literary genre that appeared in the West toward the end of the eighteenth century; it is also a willed act of the self. In a fragmented, protracted form, it punctuates the conversations and dialogues of everyday life at all levels of a society like the United States, with its pervasive self-conscious ideology of autonomous individualism and its accompanying habit of self-reference in framing casual language use. Life histories elicited from members of tribal societies, which have become a subgenre of ethnographic writing (like *Nisa* by Marjorie Shostak [1981], or *Tuhami* by Vincent Crapanzano [1980]), are usually more structured and prompted by the ethnographer than motivated by his or her subject.

19

On the contrary, life history, personal experience rooted in one's past, is the veritable frame for in-depth ethnographic interviews on all sorts of research topics concerning American middle (and upper) classes.

Little prompting or cajoling is necessary. In my discussions with family members held together by dynastic organizations of patrimony, it was indeed in the context of marked autobiographical fragments about family relationships that the experience of the uncanny recognition of profound likeness to parents and other forebears was repeatedly expressed. It is at this point of recognition, especially in a context where much more than just family pride rests on the continued identification by descendants with lineal dynastic authority, that there is a potential for a powerful critique of the limits of American autonomous individualism. Not being detached professional cultural critics or journalistic muckrakers, descendants struggling to contend with dynastic 'familiars' within themselves are not inclined to develop from their own experience generalized sociological insight about class in America. The potential for broader cultural critique, thus, dissipates in personal battles for self-autonomy among middle-aged descendants within dynastic families.

The dynastic family is one of the very few settings in American society, perhaps the only one, where the cultural production of the person and that of the group are equally and powerfully matched, entwined, and simultaneously in competition. It is certainly the only setting in which there is a complex effort to give a priority to the reality of collectivity over the unique, autonomous selves of its members. More than any other American setting, the dynastic family setting makes the culturally normalized construction of autonomous selves, corresponding to the autobiographical acts one elicits in fieldwork conversations, intractably problematic - in this case, for dynastic descendants - and establishes the potential for the sophisticated critique of American individualism embedded in dynasts' often frustrating attempts to relate their own autobiographies. Autobiography in the dynastic context is thus a contestation of dominant American cultural emphases on the definition of the unique self above all else and simultaneously of dynastic family tradition, communicated as moral narratives and judgements about particular views of the self, expressed as notions of distinctive character that the family *breeds*. This cultural critique embedded in descendant autobiographical narratives never resolves itself in detached argument but endlessly explores the conflict that it expresses, the conflict between the model of character that powerfully invades descendant self-identity and the equally powerful cultural injunction to be a unique self.

In taking another look at my firsthand data, with the critical dimension of autobiographical narrative in mind, I found an interesting disparity between responses to my questions specifically about collective family history and those to my questions about personal history or biography. Here, I refer to narrative responses by either dominant males or other males who might conceivably wield or resist authority in dynasties. Women, in-laws, 'black sheep', and youthful rebels are often the second-class citizens in dynasties to whom the authoritative narratives about character apply in complex ways. They generate the most marked and explicit critical discourse within dynasties; but here I am more interested in the critiques that arise subversively and subtly among those who are empowered and who are the central objects of dynastic culture - the men who are the primary and managing heirs to the resources of a dynasty.

When I asked about family history, I received a narrative response that told the family's experience in mostly familiar terms - like any American family. Origins in a founder, and then the history of autonomous selves who happen to be kin or else a response that developed the family's distinctive difference by an emblematic association of the family with some other cultural model (for example, 'we are like a tribe or a clan', as in one dynasty saga novel I came across that was based on a real-life family that caricatured themselves in this way). There was always a winking, humorous tone to the latter kind of response - there may have been a kernel of seriousness in these responses, but just as overt ritual as tradition is received transparently by dynasts, and even by their promoters, so are embellished stories or frameworks of distinction. At this explicit level of family narrative, at least as it is expressed to an outsider, there is no distinctive invested narrative that earnestly asserts identity. This undoubtedly has something to do with the illegitimacy of such explicit self-glorification among upper classes in mass liberal societies, except as self-parody.

Responses to questions about personal history that generated sustained autobiographical narrative were much more interesting and intense. In those accounts, the ironic recognition of the ancestor within one's self arose repeatedly. It is the controlling discourse about character that frames and gives specific substance to such elicited autobiography. This discourse is dynastic exclusivity gone 'underground' as a historical adaptation to the problems of status expression for upper classes living in mass liberal societies. This discourse of exclusivity no longer exists in the pure form of patriarchal command, but rather in the always contested, insidious, and collective part of a descendant's self, experienced as the uncanny, embodied return of the parent or forebear. This resisted, but received, experience of family character once again invading the autonomous self is what most powerfully communicates and accommodates traditional authority over descendants amid the triumph of middle-class, therapeutic models of the self. It is much more effective in creating dynastic identity among descendants than the anaemic and parodic but more overt and collective family discourse that empowered males tell with a wink. At its own level, this embedded narrative about character and its repetition in the unique lives of descendants is a kind of upper-class critical discourse against dominant liberal ideology concerning the malleability and autonomy of individuals.

In reading published autobiographies/family memoirs by members of dynastic families, I am impressed with how problematic the self becomes as it ambiguously competes with the family itself as the central object of such works. The mystery in autobiographical narratives, especially for those self-consciously trying to differentiate themselves from the collectivity, is the ironic and growing awareness that, in creating an autonomous self-identity, one inevitably makes use of the dominant official family discourse about its distinctive character, and thus ends by reproducing in whole or part what the act of autobiography itself mightily struggles to contest. The novelty and potential for broader cultural critique in these narratives lie in the dramatic forms created to constitute the ideal autonomous self, and in the failure to do so definitively.

The most salient sociological observation about the predicament of upper classes in the modern era of mass liberal societies is that they lack legitimate opportunities to assert and glorify in public their superior distinctiveness. This predicament is usually understood cynically by liberal sociologists. That is, upper classes have become sophisticated in public relations when they are visible - but mainly they try to remain invisible - and in private, they are not frustrated or stifled at all; rather, in their little worlds they indulge in bias, prejudice, and self-glorification. There is a certain truth to this, as there is for the private lives of all middle-class people. However, I prefer to see such public-status-display frustration as a real predicament in the internal conditions of families that cultivate ideologies about their own distinctiveness.

Appropriate to a culture of extreme diversity in which the possibility for self-improvement became the central theme, clannish, family-oriented American upper classes, particularly of the North-east, reorganized themselves during the early nineteenth century around private, non-profit educational and charitable institutions, which they founded, and around an ideology focused, not on overtly collective identity, but on the shaping of virtuous and morally appropriate character (see Hall 1982). The upper classes thus adapted the broader cultural emphasis on the individual to their own image, and through the cultural institutions that they founded character-building along certain lines was emphasized. Upper-class notions of character were something for middle classes to aspire to. Within the confines of very private families of wealth and power, oriented to their unique distinctiveness, normative discourses about character - in effect, a dynastic mode for developing and regulating biographies - became an effective way to transmit collective tradition to their members, while otherwise participating in a public culture in which the value of autonomous personhood was so pervasive.

Through the nineteenth and well into the twentieth century, the once conspicuously cultivated public collective mystique of notable families - with few exceptions - came to be recultivated in powerful private familial narratives about character, especially for dominant males in such families. For any dynastic family, these narratives still constitute a residual discourse that both resists and accommodates the modern liberal discourse that makes self-aggrandized elitism a matter of very bad taste. The family construct gave way to individualism, and, as we have seen, reappeared in the heavily moral intonations concerning character that permeate dynastic family narratives about the person - what it is to be (look like) a Rockefeller, a Kempner, or a Guggenheim, and so on. Such upper-class discourses about character, which once had considerable power in shaping descendant commitment, have withered in more recent times, and the most effective embodiments of collective tradition in the person became the stories about eccentricity or psychological dysfunction that are common knowledge within contemporary dynastic families.

Thus, while the focus on character served well as a morally concerned and prescriptive discourse about individualism well into the twentieth century, one hears such discourse rarely today, and when one does, it has a musty, anachronistic quality. Through the writing of cultural critics like Philip Rieff (1969), T. J. Jackson Lears (1982), and Christopher Lasch (1979), it has been persuasively argued that the triumph of the therapeutic vision of the self is the leading trend that American individualism has taken in the second half of the twentieth century.

What in particular has happened to authoritative traditional discourse in dynastic families that had found an effective vehicle in controlling narratives about the character of their members as individuals - frankly, I'm not certain. Such families no longer have so coherent a means to transmit authority now that descendants hear the discourse about character with the kind of suspicion with which dynastic ritual and patriarchal style have long been received. However, despite the decline of positive character discourse, I have been impressed by the continuing power and subtlety of an associated discourse about eccentricity or psychological dysfunction, which, in effect, had always been present as a mystique or at least as an ambivalent variant on character discourse. Eccentricities, especially, defined both family strengths and weaknesses - but from the point of view of the central tendency of positive character. Now that such a central tendency has grown transparent, eccentricity comes to the fore as a very effective form through which a dynastic family accommodates to a more dominant cultural discourse, that of the therapeutic self, but also continues to express a distinctive and superior status for itself.[6]

Finally, it is worth pointing out some of the specifically sociological dynamics that make dynastic discourses about character and their recent transformations so compelling. While diffused in the interpersonal relations among members of a dynastic family, character discourse is also subject to manipulation by the bureaucratic side of dynastic production, including advisers, experts of various sorts, and the family leader who bridges the parallel bureaucratic and familial spheres of dynastic organization. This management control centre attempts to crystallize character discourse into an ideology in the classic political sense. Dynastic commands are thus often made by appeal to sentiments about values of personhood that have deep resonances in the terms and categories by which descendants are capable of referencing themselves. But the power of the diffuse character discourse from which an ideology is drawn in order to support a leader's authority usually exceeds this effort to harness it. The leadership cannot finally control it, since its real power is in the talk and self-perceptions of adult descendants who find themselves ironically linked to lineage in the late twentieth century. It is not the force of patriarchal authority, however much it tries to idealize the family collective sense of distinctive character, but the felt irony itself in the creation of personal identities among descendants by which submission to dynastic identification primarily succeeds. As noted, the resistance to authorized family sentiments about character is enacted by women, rebels, and middle-aged adults outside the dynastic directorate, in the diffuse talk of their own experiences, including the always problematic attempt to establish their autobiographies free of family memoir.

With respect to the sociological aspects that directly affect the tradition - carrying potential of the discourse about character as it is manifested in descendant social relations, inside and outside the family, I wish to make two observations. First, when descendants have participated in psychotherapeutic sessions to establish their independence from the hold of family/parental authority, such therapy in its full social context has more often than not thrown the descendants back to the power of the family's own enduring mythic 'therapy', which consists of the infusion of character discourse in acts and moments of self-evaluation among descendants. Descendants may come to understand the uncanny repetition of forebears in themselves in therapeutic terms; but rarely does this understanding produce a fundamental break with family psychic dependency. In the long term, it is most often another stage in the management of collective wealth's continuing hold over a family's relationships.

Within the official, diffuse discourse about distinctive character, innateness, or likeness transmitted biologically - that is, a deterministic eugenics - is a powerful explanation of the uncanny repetition of parental personhood, and one that sustains and rationalizes the sense of mystery about this phenomenon. In the larger liberal society, eugenic arguments as they relate to behaviour, skills, attitudes, or other dimensions of the self are highly controversial; but in the character-forming discourse of many middle-class families, on which their self-esteem depends, such determinism is implicit. And in the discourse of dynastic families, who are redundantly reminded of their own importance, it is even more powerfully evoked and developed. There is often a smooth shift from the observation of somatic likenesses transmitted by inheritance to the similar inheritance of character, the 'right stuff', and so forth. As middle-aged descendants uncannily recognize the physical features of a forebear in themselves, they fear and often confirm that this is only the most apparent edge of ancestral investment of themselves. The dynastic uncanny also brings with it behavioural and mental determinations that such descendants might have thought they had modified or escaped by separation and self-development in an independent environment.

Second, I would argue that the uncanny on which much of the residual authority of and attachment to dynasty among descendants now hinges does not derive only from the alternative to the biological determinism in which descendants often believe - that of therapeutic doctrines of unconscious process rooted in early experiences with parents and others. Rather, the sociolinguistic process of authoritative character discourse working its way into the biography of a descendant, affecting his or her self-perception, and eventually being articulated in reflexive attempts at autobiography deserves equal attention. Here, the theoretical work of ethnomethodologists is helpful: their conceptions of the embedded linguistic practices by which subjects produce common sense and the appearance of 'natural' knowledge or truth about themselves and their bounded (and constructed) social worlds. The 'documentary method of interpretation' (Garfinkel 1967) provides a model for thinking about the way family character discourse is seamlessly diffused into the specific self-defining discourse of particular descendants. The method offers a conceptualization, registered in close attention to language use, of how the words of others about others are made into one's own words about oneself - that is, how the ancestor on occasion uncannily merges with one's autonomous self-perception, the recognition of which fact simultaneously attaches one to and detaches one from dynastic authority. This is one way of accounting for the compulsion and inescapability of the anxiety over of influence among dynastic descendants, whereby, to extend Bloom's epigraph, 'It Was a Great Marvel That They Were In the Father Without Knowing Him', and a greater marvel that they cleave the more closely to him when they did become aware of it.

Conclusion

The generic upper- and upper-middle class investment in human capital by elite American families of established and aspirant standing is assured by the funnelling of descendants into certain preparatory schools, universities, professions, social circles and locations of residence and leisure activity - along with the continuing ability of families to afford them. For a long time now, class institutions, or at least class-accented institutions, have taken over from families the primary responsibility of socializing their members from adolescence on. The fate, character, and composition of an upper and upper-middle class in the United States very much depends on changes in these institutions as to their accommodation of new participants and ideas. So much for the sociology of elites.

What remains are certain subterranean processes and patterns that remain very much within families and their traditions. These seem out of touch with and marginal to the great apparent shifts occurring in contemporary (postmodern?) society of the information revolution and various globalisms only if the story of these families is told in the same old ways. The preceding discussion of the dynastic uncanny is my effort to tell that which remains strong, pervasive, flexible, and dynastic in the cultural production of US elites, despite the great changes in US leadership institutions and ideologies over the past decades, which have diminished either overt class claims to a motivation of dynastic succession or the actual ability to bring such succession about even when family leaders have the bad taste openly to promote such a motivation. As I will argue in a moment, the present example of the family of George Bush is much more typical of how dynastic identity operates than that of the Kennedys, the ur-mythic case of the conventional narrative of the dynastic saga.

The medium in which the effective dynastic uncanny in many families plays itself out is often far from the usual paths of power - marriage choice, investment, profession - but lies instead in the terrain of the intimate, the soft - of what was thought in the last century to be the 'feminine'. This is the terrain of culture, identity, sensibility, the contours of which vary considerably from notable family to notable family. This is the terrain of inter vivos transactions in symbolic capital - the kind of capital that is not tied up in complex rules and schemes of cross-generational inheritance, that does not depend on the exercise of the 'dead hand'. The development of selves, subjectivities, character, eccentricities is something that the living in the dominant generation can watch among descendants, reflect upon, and, if not control, actively influence. This is where the irony of the return of the father or the mother is played out through the giving of personal possessions and tastes. It is the gift of culture itself, whose mystifications often provide the key contexts that lend power and authority to the dynastic uncanny - make it stick and endure - deep within the inevitable attempts of individuals in elite families at self-knowledge.

While this private, intimate side of the dynastic uncanny has been emphasized in this chapter, it is also worth emphasizing in conclusion the importance of the exposure of the dynastic uncanny in public arenas, as newsworthy stories of the doings of persons with famous names and identities. Here a name or identity re-emerges outside its original context of family self-regard, albeit with some of its original associations developed and elaborated in the popular imagination. Often this re-emergence depends on strong resemblances - physical and attributed - of a person to a predecessor of the same name. In the American political arena, an instance would be the case of the current rising political capital of George Bush's son in Texas, where the dynastic association is circumstantial, inevitable, and uncanny, in contrast to the mythic story of the Kennedys, where the political ambitions of the family were the font of its internal desire. My interest is in the former case, which I consider far more typical; the Kennedy case sustains the popular narrative, making the uncanniness of the return of the Bush family more normal, in conformity with a mythic saga that it does not quite fit.

One of my founding claims has been that the resonance of family name and identity is perhaps the most durable and valuable resource, even decoupled from tangible elements of organized family wealth and power as these dissolve over two or three generations. When the dynastic impulse and aura find their value not in aristocratic tradition, but in the relatively rapid circulation of elites in a democratic society, then the conditions for the survival of dynastic identity are very much determined by the ecology of institutions and power arenas in which a notable family has gone through its relatively short dynastic cycle in America. What is surprising is the power of the name and identity themselves - how they can revive family aspirations in ways and locations unexpected. They are a sort of wild card, where the appropriation of the name by a corporation or cultural institution to enhance a product or its own identity, or where an instance of an heir of a declining fortune's making good in a new arena of enterprise, and by so doing regenerating the dynastic legend of a family that has faded, shows just how much that identity is a part of American middle-class desire: one of its options, and one with considerable mystique.

Writing in a 1992 epilogue to *Lives in Trust* (1992), Peter Hall and I marvelled at the power of the mantle of dynastic wealth to cloak in prestige and respectability the new plutocratic concentrations of wealth in the Reagan years. We wanted to emphasize precisely the key value of the dynastic identity in giving moral stature to money. The portability of the symbolic capital of dynastic identity was marked in the politics of that era by the ascendancy of the Bush presidency. As we remarked (1992, p. 353):

> Except in a few cases, dynastic continuity has been a very short-run process even within the historic cohort (families whose dynastic origins occurred roughly a century ago) with which we have been concerned. Yet it has been a powerful ideal, fantasy, and value for professional, managerial, and middle-class people who have failed to live up to their promise. On the home front at least, nothing has diminished the tendency to value dynasty as a kind of moral domestication of wealth. Indeed, if anything, the emergence of the new plutocracy and its analogue, the meritocratic oligarchy - both amazed by their success and yearning for authenticity - has strengthened the myth. So Bush follows Reagan.

But of course, then Bush was soon gone, replaced by Clinton. Maybe we had overinterpreted in this example the powerful appeal of the dynastic patrician legacy embedded in self-made striving American middle classes, even when it had been entwined within the biography of Bush the New Englander proving himself in the Texas oil industry. Yet, writing now in 1998, we are witnessing the ascendant political career of George W. Bush, the former president's namesake and governor of Texas. The younger Bush is aspirant to the Republican nomination for president in the next election. Whatever the outcome, it is interesting to observe his rise, in its complete identification with his father's.

The return of Bush to power through the son was perhaps partly planned by the family; but it seems more opportunistic and a construction by the media and the public. The presidential aspiration depends on the legacy of dynastic subjectivity that serves this ambition - for the moment a complete resemblance between father and son that is frequently commented upon in newspapers and at political events. What must be appreciated here is the integral role of popular democratic narrative in the invention of a story of dynastic continuity. The dynastic impulse here is not so much with the family as with the people. If Bush succeeds, the identification with his father will have been key. And unlike the case of the Kennedys, the public construction of this continuity has a surprised inflection, as if the reappearance of Bush in his son at the highest level of politics was uncanny rather than natural. Still, the association is politically powerful, perhaps enough so eventually to make tangible dynastic continuity a solid and literal fact of the American presidency in the story of the Bush family - something that the fervently dynastic Kennedys never achieved. This is the kind of surprise that the floating dynastic signifier in American elite life holds for those who study it. So Bush follows Clinton?

Notes

1. The situation of Americans of 'good family' could be profitably contrasted with the 'good families' of Barcelona (McDonogh 1982), for example, one of the most detailed studies of a European dynastic elite byan anthropologist. There is a strong situated class determinant to this designation in Europe that depends even for bourgeois families on an aristocratic example. In the United States, this development only occurred historically in a few cities (Boston, New York, Philadelphia, and the South in general before the Civil War) and barely survives today. Being of 'good family' depends much more on the ironic mystique of the survival of dynastic identities both in terms of and against the tendencies of an American democratic ethos.
2. The psychocultural processes analysed here are apparent even in tribal societies, as in Meyer Fortes's classic on the Tallensi, *Oedipus and Job* (1938), although it is tinged with a deeply European bias and colouring by the very figures he employs.
3. Examples of the appropriation of a dynastic identity by corporations without dynastic motivations or structures themselves are the rise of the Getty Trust as a major philanthropic organization in the arts, following the death of J. Paul Getty, and the acquisition of the name of Praeger Books by a conglomerate, so that the founder of this company, Frederick Praeger, had no further right to use his own name in a later venture. The Getty Trust, in which I was a resident scholar during the late 1980s (see Marcus 1990), gained much in establishing itself from the aura of the mythic wealth associated with J. Paul Getty, more than the actual family ever did. The identification as J. Paul's primary heir was very important to the Trust in its early phases - interestingly, as an asset in the United States, but a hindrance in Europe, where the name did not have as much respect and held a different set of associations, demonstrating the difference concerning the social origins of the idea of dynasty between the United States and Europe.

The Praeger case is just a routine example of how businesses with dynastic structures exist at the behest of a particular ecology of institutions. When conditions of business or these institutions change, so too do the chances for the persistence of dynastic organization and leadership in particular sectors. One finds dynastic identity moving uncannily toward its patron institutions, which swallow family businesses while keeping their identities, at least for a while.

4. Large portions of this section appeared as a previously unpublished chapter of Marcus and Hall 1992.

5. For example, see my chapter (Marcus 1992) on the memoir of Sallie Bingham accounting for the break-up of the Binghams, the newspaper family of Louisville. Joan Branfman's study of the experience of inherited wealth (1987), written as a doctoral dissertation and thus archly formal in its use of social science rhetoric, is nonetheless an excellent source and analysis of this material, both from original interviews and the memoir genre.

6. For an elaborated argument about the role of eccentricity in American notable families, see Marcus 1995.

2

'How Did I Become a Leader in My Family Firm?' Assets for Succession in Contemporary Lisbon Financial Elites

Antónia Pedroso de Lima

In this chapter I shall discuss the processes by means of which family members become successors to top executive places in large Portuguese familial enterprises.[1] Succession has been a central topic in anthropological reflection about the continued existence of social groups through time. As Jack Goody stated in the introduction to *The Succession to High Office*, 'With groups of any significance, some provision is made either for their continuity or for their replacement. ... Unless they are simply to disappear from the social scene, all organisations ... must have some arrangement for the transition of corporate property and for succession of key personnel' (J. Goody 1966: 1). Thus Goody argues that, in order to guarantee their reproduction, social groups (corporate by definition) invest particular persons with a special kind of authority and of power and, consequently, that this urge for reproduction is a defining characteristic of society.

However, we should not presume the existence of these arrangements for succession of key personnel. They are produced only when the people involved identify themselves with some supra-personal identity in such a way that they feel the need to guarantee the existence through time of the social system in which they act. Therefore, what we need to know is how, in specific historical circumstances and with the existing power relations, certain people claim to be the most powerful leaders in the group, the ones that will promote its continuity. On the other hand, we need to analyse how those who will be invested with authority over the management of the collective resources are chosen. The actual existence of a succession project must be rooted in a collective vision of the future: a family project based on a shared past and on the will for a shared future. What seems of interest here is this urge for continuation: how and why people produce mechanisms that make continuity possible. Thus, the strategic conduct of those who want to be (and can be) potential successors - the processes by which they produce themselves as successors - are central to this debate. In this way, rather than talking about reproduction, we must analyse social continuity as a *constitution process*,[2] because every continuation is the product of the conscious action of social subjects, of men and women moved by their will, feelings and ambitions.

When we look at the processes of succession to leadership positions of large family companies, we can see that they are not single events that occur when an old leader retires and passes on the torch to a new leader. They are complex processes that are driven through time, in different domains of action, depending on the continuity of some elements that exist in the present. Rather than analysing succession as part of a reproduction process, we must look at the processes of differentiation between descendants. We must centre our attention not only on the strategies developed by the leading generation for passing on assets and different kinds of powerful knowledge to members of the next generation, but also in the personal investments the latter make, or not, to continue the family firm in the future. The question I want to discuss is, therefore, a complex one which involve the following items:

1. how family members transform themselves into heirs;
2. how potential heirs are heirs to different roles; and
3. how heirs to the same roles create distinctions between themselves in order to become more likely candidates.

The analysis of the dynamics of succession processes in these large-scale family firms can, thus, provide a central dimension for understanding the strategies that lie behind the transmission of leadership roles, financial assets and personal power among the Portuguese financial elite.

For this purpose I will focus the discussion on fieldwork I have been carrying out in Lisbon among eight high-status families who own large familial companies, in existence for at least three generations that belong to the list of the 100 most important Portuguese enterprises.[3] The continuity of the family firm is an openly stated aim of these wealthy families, and, as I will try to show, is what ensures the formation and perpetuation of elite dynastic families in Portugal.

Any study of the processes of choosing a family successor to management positions in family firms implies the study of the enterprise's developmental process as an integral part of the socio-economic national context in which they take place. This is particularly relevant in Portugal, where the political transition from a dictatorial regime to a democratic one, which occurred in 1974, introduced a great deal of change in the national economic, political and social order. These changes had deep implications for the developmental processes of the enterprises and their associated dynastic families, which constituted (and, once again, constitute today) the core of the Portuguese entrepreneurial elite.

Partners and Relatives

The large-enterprise-owning families I have been working with constitute a central element of Lisbon's social and financial elite. Although they do form an identifiable social group, they are not a neatly defined community.[4] They share interests, ideals, a way of life, attitudes, forms of behaviour, and ways of being, acting and dressing, and they form a close web of relations, into which it would be very difficult for an outsider to enter.[5] In fact, the primary context of production of these characteristics is the area of domestic relations. It is mostly there that the codes, values and attitudes specific to this social-cultural-economic group are learned, making it possible for children to succeed their parents in their social practices, their social relations and their jobs. The familial universe is, therefore, a very important context of analysis of this social group. It is worthy of note that these Lisbon elite families are organized in an explicitly 'conservative way', based on family values, such as patriarchal authority, seniority, birth order, gender belonging and a profound adherence to Catholicism.

The conservative character of these values seems to derive from the fact that they are based on the ideological model of the *Estado Novo* (The New State - the dictatorial regime of Salazar 1926-74), a political regime that members of these families supported and in which they occupied important public positions. Salazar, former leader of the Centre Catholic Party (Partido do *Centro Católico*), was a conservative, Catholic dictator who held that 'God, Nation, Family, Work and Authority' were the most important national values. In the areas of family life, youth education and culture in general, Salazar tried to mould civil society to his nationalist, corporativist and Christian conception of the 'world and man'. The social and economic policies of the *Estado Novo* were oriented by 'traditional' principles of Christian doctrine and morals, and were supported by the Catholic Church. Familial ties were of central importance for the maintenance of the social order during that period. Salazar maintained that the family was a metaphor for the Nation, which he saw as one large family. Just as men were the heads of their families, Salazar was the head of the Portuguese Nation. And, just as within the family children and wives must respect and obey the husband/father, the head of the family, the children of the Nation must also respect and obey Salazar (cf. Almeida 1991).

The revolution of 1974 opened the way on the development of democratic processes, not only in politics but at all levels of social life: domestic life, gender relations, choice of religion and educational principles. An expansion of civic and political freedoms and individual rights as well as the legalization of divorce[6] and economic development have had profound effects on the Portuguese family and familial relations. As a result, the *Estado Novo's* conservative family values are now clearly on the wane among most other Portuguese social groups. However, for the elite financial families I have been working with the preservation of these conservative values, constitutes a primary factor for the maintenance through time of wider family ties that, in turn, are a central element of the continuity of the large family firm.

There is a high rate of inter-marriage among elements of the families who constitute this financial elite. This endogamy makes it possible to maintain the social group as a unified and closed one. By systematically marrying inside the same group of families, previously existing ties of solidarity are strengthened, both on a social level and on a financial one. By way of the sacred commitment of marriage, matrimonial alliances between families are created that also enhance their economic relations. Later on, the birth of children will further strengthen these unions, legitimizing family fusion.

People from all the families I interviewed stressed the idea that the family-owned enterprise is felt to be a collective project, although each family member has different expectations of it and attributes to it different meanings and personal investment. That is why not all of them want to be actively and directly involved in the family firm. Some of them decided from the beginning that this was not a reasonable option for them, and they have assumed other roles in the family's life. Nevertheless, almost every family member is integrated in the collective project of the family firm, in one way or another, personally investing a great deal of effort in what is their primary source both of social prestige and of economic income.

The importance that individuals attribute to the collective economic project varies depending on whether they own shares in the enterprise or not. For the ones who are shareholders, the continuation of the business is central for the maintenance of their income, and of course, for their social status. But even for the ones who do not own shares, the success of the company is vital. The fact that their social identity is associated with the family (by means of the family name they carry) grants them considerable social prestige. Therefore, the association of the firm to the family is of central importance for these people. Thus, even though family and enterprise do not have the same importance and meaning to every family member involved, most of them invest something in their continuity and development, as they can safely expect to receive some dividends in return.

On the whole, one can argue that the formal organization of these large and complex legal and economic enterprises is consciously built according to the best organizational models available, and by the most competent managerial professionals. However, they are also constructed over a web of familial relations that unite shareholders, who also share a strong and conscious investment in their common familial relations. As a result, they live together, work together and socialize together. This daily familism creates an intense feeling, which is crystallized in the sense of sharing something in common: a family name, a history, ancestors, family houses, titles of nobility, enterprises and a common aim - to perpetuate all of this. The family enterprises constitute, therefore, a central part of the shared possessions that symbolize the family and guarantee the continuity of its unity. Business becomes, in this way, a central component of familial identity, and increases the dynastic sense of the family group. As these large family groups continue through time they legitimize their dynastic sense.[7] The fact that the enterprise is family-owned is therefore what guarantees the continuation of both the large family universe and the enterprise.[8]

Thus, in this social group, familial values - the ways of being and living in the family - are crucial elements in defining the ways by which the economic group works and continues. The reverse, however, is equally true. Familial relations are not only kinship relations. They are built over a web of economic interests, and they bind together people with opposed interests in the enterprise. The processes of choosing a successor to the leadership positions in the firm is central for the accomplishment of the objectives of continuation of both contexts in which they live. Through these processes, family and enterprise become not two things but one: they form business dynasties - what George Marcus called 'family-enterprise formations' (Marcus and Hall 1992: 15).

The Family Company and the Formation of Dynastic Families

In his book written with Peter Hall *Lives in Trust* (Marcus and Hall 1992: chapters 1-3), George Marcus showed how in Galveston, Texas the dynastic sense of the families he studied was promoted by their collectively shared fortune. 'There is no compelling reason for descendants to maintain other than casual relations, but for the fact their reified shared wealth intrudes constantly into their mutual relations and individual lives' (cf. Marcus and Hall 1992: 56). In Portugal what promotes that dynastic sense in these old wealthy entrepreneurial families is the family enterprise itself and the family urge to continue in time.

Let me demonstrate my point by introducing a particular case.

The Espírito Santo Group belongs to the family with the same name. It is the second largest Portuguese economic group, and its national and international activity is extremely influential and diversified: five banks (two in Portugal, one in Luxemburg, one in Brazil and one in Florida), two insurance companies (in Portugal and Brazil), telecommunications, real estate, agriculture and cattle-raising. Their first bank was founded at the end of the last century by José Maria Espírito Santo e Silva, who started life in Lisbon as a poor but daring middle-man of the Spanish lottery. In only two decades he made a considerable fortune, acquired important social relations and gained considerable respectability. He fathered five children and, through their successful business activities, father and sons built a formidable international web of business and friendship relations, forming the second most important portuguese economic group prior to 1974, with an enormous international sphere of influence. In 1974, the Democratic Revolution and the process of nationalizing banks and insurance companies forced a majority of the members of this family to flee to Brazil, England and Switzerland. Abroad, they established a new and soon powerful financial group, with international associate partners, but still maintaining the family majority. Their excellent relations and prestige in the international world of finance were central to this new beginning, as their financial rebirth required considerable financial credit and powerful associate partners.

In the mid-1980s, a slow return to Portugal was started. And as the privatization processes began, they bought back their old enterprises. By the mid-1990s, they had fully regained their top place in Portuguese economic life. Now in its sixth generation, what is called the 'Espírito Santo family' is a large and extended universe of people, divided into five large branches, and composed of 450 people. Although most of them can reconstruct their complex and extended genealogical relations by heart, they do not maintain a regular base of contact, nor do they maintain strong personal relations between the diverse branches. The Group's annual general assembly at Lausanne, Switzerland, is an ideal occasion for all the family members who own company shares to meet each other. The family also meet at institutional events held by the Group's enterprises and at funerals. Family rituals like Christmas, Easter, weddings or anniversaries are celebrated within the individual branches stemming from each of the founder's five children.

For the Espírito Santo family it is their common familial project - the financial group - that creates the conditions that maintain active relations within their very large kinship universe.

As a family grows into its fourth, fifth and sixth generations, its several branches form a very large group of people, some of whom are so distant that, if it were not for the fact that they share a link to the family enterprise (which they do not want to lose) they would, most likely, not know each other. Their family economic group acquires the role of a most valued symbolic patrimony. Being such an important part of the family group identity, the enterprise becomes the *raison d'être* of the family, since it engenders a sentiment of the family as a group of shared substance. Therefore, shared kinship is not what sustains active kinship relations in this dynastic family. The Espírito Santo family case demonstrates that the existence and continuity of the enterprise is the primary reason for maintaining effective kinship relations. Furthermore, I believe that this is true for most of Lisbon's elite entrepreneurial families. Within this group the main reason for the formation of these dynastic families is the fact that relatives are business associates, and not that they share a family fortune, or the family's constitutional cultural values - such as blood, sentiments or a shared past. In other words, working together in bringing about the development of the family firm is what actually unites them, and preserves them as an identifiable social unity. In fact, the many cases of extremely wealthy families who have shared a fortune and proceeded to consume it, show us that the mere existence of a fortune is not what produces effective binding family ties. What keeps family members together is therefore the fact that the large family firm is a collective project, and the consequent need that they work together in order to ensure its maintenance.

The rather special basis on which familial relations are built in this social group provides them with different kinds of kinship relations to those that characterize other urban Portuguese social contexts. The existence of these large familial firms over several generations creates, therefore, a particular situation in the large family universe. This could explain why, within this social context, it is common to find a deep density and relatively cohesive relations uniting people from the various branches, something that is otherwise quite unusual in Portugal today. Nevertheless, George Marcus noted the same occurrence among American dynastic families, and argued that these families 'have achieved durability as descent groups in a bureaucratized society by assimilating, rather than resisting, characteristics of formal organization which are usually assumed to be antithetical to kin-based groups' (Marcus and Hall 1992: 15). Thus it is possible that we are witnessing here a phenomenon with wider socio-geographical implications associated to these large family-enterprise formations. In this way we could say that, whenever an economic project owned and ruled by one family manages to reproduce itself with considerable success over decades, in both the economic and the social domain, it promotes the maintenance of rather close ties between members of the large family universe, and opens the way to the existence of large dynastic families in Western industrialized societies.[9]

The Importance of Bearing the Family Name

The relative cohesion of the diverse branches of the large Espírito Santo family is cyclically shaken during moments of succession to leading positions in their companies.

> The founder's three sons succeeded him as president of the Bank, in birth order. When the last of them died it was not clear who should succeed. The eldest son of the founder's first-born son was considered to be prone to conflict, and although he was the vice-president (and thus, according to the Bank's statutes the legal successor to the presidency), no one wanted him to assume the presidency. At that time, the group's senior member was CR, husband of a daughter of the founder's second son, who had exchanged his military career for a second distinguished career in his father-in-law's enterprises. But as he did not have the family name he could not succeed: 'you know, people have trust in our bank, in our family. For someone outside the family to assume a bank's leading position, even as old and important a partner as CR, would separate the image of the bank from the trust given to our family, it would betray our clients' confidence' (J.M.ESS). So, the eldest son of the deceased president, MR, who had the skills and the family name, was chosen. In this succession situation, between two very skilled men, blood spoke louder than business seniority. MR was a very consensual person, who had been thoroughly well trained by his father to become the president of the bank and the patriarch of the family. This is the argument as presented by the family. I found out, however, that in this succession crisis, the branch to which CR was linked was not at the time sufficiently strong and powerful to compete for the role of president, as it was formed by Espírito Santo women and their husbands. This fact was felt to be such a disqualification that, in his will, RES - the C's father-in-law - gave all his bank shares to his grandchildren, granting to his daughters only usufruct until such a time as his grandchildren became of age.

As we can see, in the context of family business, being a good profession-al is not enough to succeed to the presidency of the firm. To occupy that position the fact of carrying the family name, the name of the firm,[10] is of central symbolic importance. It gives expression to the notion that family members must occupy top leadership positions. In the words of JVG (pres-ident of the major Portuguese construction company) 'the owner's foot is the earth's manure.'[11] On another level, this example makes it clear that the family name is as much an important commodity as the family house or enterprise shares.

Business Men and Family Managers: Gender Bias among the Portuguese Financial Elite

If temporality is, as I have argued, a central issue to understanding this elite family context, so descendants are central elements to its continuity. We have seen that a credible successor must carry the family name. As in Portugal the transmission of family names favours agnatic continuity, only men can guarantee the continuity of family name and family nobility titles.[12] No daughter and no son-in-law, as good as they may be, are able to do this. So the continuation of the family depends on the existence of male descendants in every generation. This is a most important point, as it reveals the effectiveness of the symbolic power of the family name and, as a consequence, attributes a totally different status to boys than to girls. This became very clear to me in two fieldwork situations. The first was when a member of the administration board of an important Portuguese bank was making a list, at my request, of his brothers and sisters. He always referred to his sisters by the family name of their husbands, as if they were no longer part of his family. The second one occurred during a conversa-tion about family name transmission with MMB (great-granddaughter of the BES founder). With her family genealogical chart in her hand she said 'you see, it is very clear, blood passes through men'. Although equally loved, boys are generally more desired than girls, because they are the only ones who move the family through time. Therefore, boys have a sym-bolic value of central instrumental importance, as they can guarantee that the family, symbolized by its name, will survive across the generations by means of legitimate heirs.

The cultural values explicit in these gender distinctions are also neatly perceived in the different ways men and women participate in the family enterprises they both own. In this social context, business is clearly men's business. It is only in today's generation that we can find some women shareholders working in their family firms. Normally, however, they occu-py positions of lesser responsibility.

A 55-year-old lady once told me that when she was young she wanted to have a college degree, but her parents strongly maintained their ideas about what a girl in her position should do. She should prepare herself to be a good wife, with enough cultural knowledge to be an interesting and educated hostess for her future husband's social needs. So, after leaving the Convent of the Sacred

Heart in Brighton, where she attended high school, she went to Florence for two years to study art history, in a college where she met a great number of girls of her age, belonging to the European social and financial elite, who are still today some of her best friends.

This lady, however, is an exception. Most of the women of these families do not evince any desire to acquire professional training, or to hold a job in their family's enterprise. As they are socialized in patriarchal and male-centred family values they are the first ones to defend the importance of their exclusively familial role. As Sylvia Yanagisako noted 'this does not mean assuming that women have no desires, but rather assuming that their desires are shaped by dominant ideological representations of gen-der' (Yanagisako 1991: 334). Portuguese elite women are not supposed to work at the same level as men do. Their work is to keep their family healthy, both their own nuclear family and their universe of near kin. In fact, it is through women that family relations are kept alive in these large dynastic families. They are the ones who maintain up-to-date information about their relatives of every branch of the extended family by means of the intense and frequent uxorilateral relations that unite mothers and daughters and sisters and grandmothers. In this way, they create rather solid familial ties, and become the ones through whom men relate to each other. In this social group, a highly prestigious lady is one who has raised a perfect family, who is educated, charming and a good hostess. To be a lady, women must adhere to the cultural symbols that define a 'proper woman' in this context and not the ones that are used to value men.

Here again we can witness the influence of the Estado Novo ideology in the behaviour, values and attitudes of this social group. The expectations placed on feminine activities were so important to Salazar that, in his attempts to impose his doctrinal project to levels of Portuguese social life, he invested, in a most obvious way, in the 'education of women' through the creation of formal institutions, like the *Obra das Mães para a Educação Nacional* (Association of Mothers for National Education) and the *Mocidade Portuguesa Feminina* (Portuguese Youth Female Branch). The objectives of these institutions were 'to stimulate in young Portuguese women a culture of spirituality and devotion to social service in the love of God, the Nation and the Family' (quoted in Rosas 1996: 609) They sought to educate the 'new Portuguese woman, as a good Catholic, a future pro-lific mother and an obedient spouse' (ibid.). The woman-mother's mission during Salazar's regime was to dedicate herself to her family home and 'to be its guardian'.

It is in accordance with these ideals that the women of these elite com-pany-owning families are expected to co-operate in family business on a different level from that expected of men. They must take care of their family homes, the visible and public image of their collective prestige, where they maintain social contacts with the most prestigious families of the financial world. Women are also expected to carry out the fundamental activities of organizing the social events associated with their husbands' and brothers' business arrangements. Through these activities we can see how women carry out activities central to their family enterprise formations. Their invisibility is, therefore, only apparent.

As we can see, in this social context, sons are seen as successors to the business and daughters as family maintainers. This distinction is very obvious from childhood. In my interviews, a common item of male conversation was to talk about the visits they made when they were young boys with their fathers to the enterprises or alternatively about the work in unskilled jobs that they carried out during their holidays in one of the family companies. A parallel event occurs with women, who talk about being young and helping their mothers or grandmothers to organize important tea or dinner parties, learning which china to use on which occasion, which tablecloth is more appropriate or where to seat people at the table.

Since they are expected to perform different roles in their family's destinies and their family's enterprises boys and girls are treated differently. And yet, Portuguese inheritance law makes them equal beneficiaries of their fathers' fortunes. This legal disposition dictates an absolutely egalitarian distribution of family wealth among descendants, whatever their gender or birth order. However, people can always create a space for familial strategies of sibling differentiation. This can be done through a great variety of *inter vivos* transmissions of assets and of non-material capital. Therefore, if the leaders of the family firm want to make sure that only boys will be able to succeed to managerial roles, they must invest other dimensions in them than simply patrimonial transmission.

As work at the enterprise is the first step to eventually obtaining a leadership position, excluding daughters from the possibility of getting the kind of knowledge needed to work there is the most effective way of guaranteeing that they will not be potential successors to the leadership in the firm. So socializing young girls in the cultural values that associate men with business and women with family is therefore of central importance, as it guarantees that women accept their own exclusion from any active participation in their firms, and that they will reproduce it as they become mothers. Being a good professional would not be the right characteristic for a proper lady in this social context. I found out during interviews that these ladies almost became offended if I asked them if they had ever wanted to work in their family enterprises. Work is something that these women do not need to and do not want to do. So, family and gender cultural values associated with practices of knowledge transmission are the most effective methods for the formation of male successors in large family firms and for excluding women as potential successors.

But in these families, and in these enterprises, not even all men are equal. Only one among them will be chosen to be the leader of the economic group. It is by blood that one belongs to the family. And it is by blood that one acquires the right to accede to top positions, both in the family and at the enterprise. After that, however, other factors assume importance, as only a few that share the family substance will make it to top leadership positions.

Among Portuguese elite families there is an overall tendency for the eldest son to succeed his father in the presidency. The fact that Portuguese law has not allowed primogeniture since the application of the Napoleonic code through the Civil Code of 1867 creates an evident focus of tension in the family. However, this does not mean that efforts to adapt this ideal have not been made since the application of the civil code of 1867. In order to bring the family ideals of roles and property transmission into line with the current law, complex family strategies have been developed. How to prepare the eldest son to reach the leading positions in the firm, if by law he is equal to the others? There are many different strategies to bring about this ideal of primogeniture. The effectiveness of each one depends essentially on the existing family alliances and on the respect, trust and professional training each person manages to acquire.

This process of creating differences among equals is what most interests me. In fact, this is not a simple process of transmitting shares, positions, and fortunes to a particular person of the next generation. It is a complex one, where the leading figures are the members of the 'emerging generation',[13] who are preparing themselves to accede to important positions at the enterprise, against their peers. We are not dealing with a univocal transmission process, where continuity is a reproduction of the past. In fact we are dealing with a *constituting process* in which the new conjuncture is built by some members of this emerging generation, who articulate in their actions and strategies, references and values from the past (inherited goods, relations and values) in the context of the new needs and values of the present. The ones who achieve this with the approval and trust of the family will become the successful successors in the family.

Professional Formation and Relational Capital: The Major Legacies in the Successful Formation of Successors

The maintenance of the familial control over the enterprise is a central issue for the 'controlling generation'. This process involves a clear tension. On the one hand, it is of central symbolic importance that a member of the family succeeds to leadership positions in the firm. But, on the other hand, hegemonic ideas about who should fulfil these jobs in this social context are based on economic rationality and the belief that the only legitimate way to occupy those positions is by means of professional competence. In this context, the ideals of economic rationality and meritocracy, and not filial descent, must be followed. So, we find ourselves in a domain where the economic rationality that symbolizes the public legitimacy of prestige, status and wealth collides with the familial ideal of a filial passing on of the torch. The values and ideals of the family have had to adjust to the hegemonic ideals of the market society, which demand outstanding professional formation. Again, this is clearly seen in the Espírito Santo's family example.

In August 1995, however, an important new choice of president for the bank was required. This time the presidency was conferred on CR, who had previously been passed over. What had changed? By 1995, when MR died, the long period of living abroad had changed the balance of forces within the family. Two other factors, however, are of primary importance. In the first place, the new democratic social order installed in Portugal after the 1974 revolution, and, secondly, the fact that the Espírito Santo Group was now no longer exclusively familial. Thus, in 1995, in spite of his not bearing the family's name, the presidency was given to the only living member of the older generation - R - as a symbolic act to ensure the continuity of the old family project and by 1995, the CR's branch had acquired sufficient power to recapture the presidency of the group. They had invested great efforts in the professionalization of their members (now the fourth generation of the family) and have clearly proved their excellent management and leadership qualities with their central contribution to the processes of rebuilding the economic group abroad and recapturing the family's old business in Portugal. Now the CR is the president of the Group and his eldest nephew in his family branch is the executive president of the Group as well as the President of the Bank.

As this professional context is ruled by competence, enterprise leaders have to support strict principles of equal opportunities and meritocracy to fulfil their companies' board needs. In fact, at this high level of national and international economic relations, family members are very conscious that the stakes to be lost by poor decisions are substantial, and they know that their economic and social future depends on good choices. In fact, if they are to guarantee economic growth, credibility and trust from the public investors in their firms, leaders must ensure that they have the best managers in the key executive positions. Young members who want to enter into the business must train themselves in such a way that they can win an open process of selection for the most qualified posts. It is through their own personal investment that they can turn into good professionals or relative failures, and be chosen to occupy leading positions in their family firms. Of course, this is also a result of the great investment made by these families in the formal education of their children. But, if the children had failed to undertake the necessary effort, all of this would have been in vain. Successors must produce themselves, because professional training and managerial experience make all the difference between close male kinsmen.[14] Consequently, relatives who enter the family business must be competent professionals.

To assume leadership roles in the family enterprise, kinsmen must be seen to fulfil meritocratic criteria. This is the reason why these families make a great investment in their male descendants' academic education, in order to provide them with the most unimpeachable professional qualifications. On this basis, even in a situation of public competition, they can always be the professionals who are best prepared to occupy the central decision-making positions in their family enterprises.[15] Therefore, to qualify for a leadership position in their own company, family members must be able to demonstrate publicly that they have the requisite knowledge and ability and an interest in contributing to the company's development. In this environment, family members who reach the top executive positions in the firm truly have to be seen to earn their positions. In any case, we should not think that these are mere strategies of manipulating competencies, as the two things are interconnected in a complex way. We are in the presence of a new conceptual framework of kin meritocracy that legitimizes economic rationality and egalitarianism and the dynastic ideal of these families, and adjusts the legal requirements to family values and ideals.

It is their significant financial capital that allows them to have access to the best schools in the world, where they can guarantee the best cultural and professional capital for their children. The children from these families, usually, go to the same schools and, as they grow up together and become colleagues and friends, they will continue to reinforce and extend the web of their parents' economic and social relations.[16] But we must not forget that these young members of the Lisbon financial elite have access to a kind of knowledge that is not publicly learned in business schools, but that is learned inside the family and in the informal social relations within their social environment. This is what makes them different from other good professionals. The relational capital of their families and the privileged social environment in which they live are exclusive assets of this financial elite group, and cannot be bought or learned by others. Restricting access to these social and relational capitals to themselves, they guarantee their members' access to high managerial positions and, thus, informally, impede the entrance of outsiders.

The fact that, theoretically, these are open schools creates the illusion that the whole system is based on meritocracy. Meritocracy in this professional and social context is, therefore, forged as a result of the economic power of these families, their powerful social relations and their high social prestige. Through this process they reproduce inequality in the larger social system. In this way, they succeed in informally closing their frontiers in a formally opened social system, and in recruiting their own people under strict principles of equal opportunities. According to Abner Cohen, these processes constitute two of the most important characteristics of elite groups (Cohen 1981: 220).[17]

A superlative professional performance that is also well embedded in the family's relational capital and in the assemblage of family knowledge is what distinguishes the various family heirs one from another, enabling one or two of them to become top executive leaders in the family firm. Simultaneously, this particular investment in professional training and the transmission of informal knowledge made by their seniors are the most important legacies that these families leave to their future generations, guaranteeing that these families owning firms maintain themselves as an elite social group. What we can see here is that we are not in fact dealing with a purely economic form of the power of capital. We are dealing with a complex and composite capital in which the economic, relational, social and political family capitals form a *continuum* and are inseparable.

Top professional training is of particular importance in Portugal, where it is not common to find large family firms under the control of the type of professional administrators that George Marcus called 'fiduciaries'. According to Marcus, these fiduciaries are central figures in north American family-enterprise formations, where they have a 'central role in the perpetuation of both fortunes and families as corporate organizations' (Marcus and Hall 1992: 54). In Portugal, although there are a great number of very competent professionals who work in these large enterprises who do not have any kind of kinship relation to the enterprise owners, we do not find many of them occupying top management positions - such as presidencies (cf. Marcus and Hall 1992).

The reasons for the fact that outside fiduciaries are not common at present in Portuguese dynastic family-enterprise formations is probably to be found in the recent political history of our country. As a result of the Democratic Revolution, in 1974, the financial sector was nationalized, and so were other sectors of public interest. These processes took away the control these families had over their own businesses, which were then in their third or fourth generation. At the same time, the privileged social conditions in which these elite families lived before the revolution collapsed. It is worth noting that, before 1974, a small number of economic enterprises dominated Portuguese economic life, and these were, precisely, family-based economic groups. Between 1968 and 1973 the Portuguese monopolist nucleus was composed of seven large financial groups in which fourteen families predominated. In this way they controlled Portuguese economic, financial and industrial life. These families had an enormous social prestige, privileges, and a significant, yet indirect, involvement in national politics (cf. Rosas 1992 and Braga da Cruz 1992). The Salazarist concept of the family as the metaphor for, and the foundation of, the Nation constituted the conceptual basis for the legitimization of the fact that the most important Portuguese economic groups were family-owned.

The social and political conditions of the period following the democratic revolution forced most of the members of these families to leave the country (mostly to Brazil, United Kingdom and Switzerland), leaving behind them most of their material goods and investments. Abroad, they restarted their economic activities and, most of them, have quickly rebuilt their economic empires. Meanwhile, both political conditions and economic policy have changed in Portugal. After the period of socialist tendencies following 1974, the 1980s were characterized by a pro-European policy orientation that favoured privatization, and was initiated by the Social Democratic Party (PSD - a right-wing party, which included several important members of the previous dictatorial regime). Taking advantage of a period of economic and social stability, the Portuguese elite groups found the way opened to reconstituting themselves. At the end of the

1980s, when the social democratic government began the privatization processes, these families returned to Portugal to buy their old enterprises. Since then, we have witnessed the rapid growth of their enterprises, showing the great dynamism demonstrated by the new leading generation, the fifth generation in most of these cases. They have rebought their former enterprises and rebuilt their economic empires, and are now again the core of the Lisbon financial elite. The new political situation of the 1980s was particularly favourable to their return, and they took full advantage of it.

The internal processes of development of the companies owned by Portuguese families, quite as much as their owners' family cycles, were drastically shaken by the 1974 revolution. Because the family lost the control it had over enterprises, the family members were forced to start again their economic lives. For that purpose, they relied on two fundamental things: their family ties and their excellent social and business relations in an international context. They lost a great deal of their advantages, but they did not lose their most valuable assets: their social prestige and their place in the world's financial elite. This fact brings us back to a previous question. The power of this social group derives from the fact that the capital that provides them with their prestige is not exclusively economic. It is a complex compound of economic capital, relational capital and political capital. It is the fact that they have reacquired powerful positions in these artificially separated domains that shows us that even when defeated they maintain their hold on the conditions for their recovery.[18]

As we can see, in order to recapture their role in financial business, the members of these families could not rely on any sort of fiduciary. They had to do it on their own. After they accomplished their objectives - rebuilding their economic empires and recovering their leading economic positions in Portugal - they were so proud of it that they wanted to show to the world that they were still the rulers of their enterprises. For this reason, they could not consider handing over the command of their firms to a fiduciary. This may be a symbolic act, but it is also a demonstration of their professional success. Their professional skills and experience, allied with their social position, have turned out to be a most powerful combination. In this way, they have regained the ruling and executive places they once claimed by right as their own.

The Portuguese case clearly goes against the most well-known theory in the area of family firms studies, which states that familial firms collapse in the third generation.[19] The principal portuguese family-based economic formations of Portugal are now in their fourth and fifth generation, and there is no evidence either of collapse or of the introduction of fiduciaries to executive places. This seems to be a consequence of the inflection given to the economic and social order by the democratic revolution. The new social and political order that the country has experienced since 1974 has created very special conditions for the third, fourth and fifth generations in management positions. Individuals of these generations arrived at the top positions of their family firms in the late 1980s with an unusual dynamism and strength. Far from being able to rely on formerly acquired glory, they have had to prove their abilities in order to return to Portugal and to rebuy their enterprises and regain their position as rulers of the Portuguese financial elite. And, since they want to keep their ruling positions, they have had to provide the next generation with the same patrimony as they have had. This has turned out to be the most powerful weapon to legitimize management succession in Portuguese family-owned businesses.

To sum up, we can argue that the high professional positions of the members of Lisbon's financial elite are legitimised and empowered by a specific type of inherited capital which, in fact, is an articulation of several distinct types of capital. Each of these represents a most effective differentiating element:

1. they possess a highly valued material patrimony that passes from generation to generation, to which each one of them adds his or her own personal investment, further enlarging it;
2. attending prestigious international schools confers legitimacy on their academic training;
3. the entrepreneurial tradition of the family adds value to their professional experience;
4. personal and familial relational capital constitutes a precious good, just as transmissible as any other material good. Its effectiveness is evident in the example of the Espírito Santo family's having recovered their entrepreneurial patrimony. Furthermore, this is a capital that needs to be constantly fed by continuing social activities and contacts; and
5. each generation's group of friends - the sons and daughters of their parents' friends, school colleagues and relatives - forms a solid base for the constitution of the social group and for the network of close relations that will support them in their professional future and from which they will choose their spouses.

Concluding Remarks: Articulating Familial Motivations with a Globalized Economy

Throughout this chapter I have argued that large family enterprises that want to continue to be run by family members have to introduce criteria of economic competence in the selection of family successors if they are to continue to hold their top positions in the national and international economic contexts. This specific kind of enterprise is permanently challenged in its objective of continuation through time. Thus they have to coordinate their family motivation - the desire for direct succession - with the rational and objective logic of economics. We cannot, therefore, discuss succession as a fact of filial descent in this social context. The tools of traditional Portuguese family succession - such as male primogeniture and entailment - cannot be applied any longer, as there are legal constraints that enforce equal treatment of descendants, and because of the requirement of professional competence. This means that there are no natural successors to leadership positions. Family successors have to fight their way to the top by means of personal professional merit, which is, nevertheless, mostly a result of their parents' conscious investment in their formal education. Patrimonial transmission from parent to child must be seen as being composed by: the family name, professional preparation and relational capital. Through this process, these people guarantee their future not only as a firm, but also as a family.

We have seen how these processes of production of successors contribute to making Lisbon's financial elite a closed social group. As they continue to marry among themselves, they close even more their invisible frontiers, which contributes to the continuation of the privileged conditions for future generations. Privilege is passed from generation to generation. They have, thus, created a new process of succession, based on modern economic and meritocratic rationality, that substitutes itself for the traditional succession process. In this complex process we can see that there are, in fact, two perspectives: that of the declining generation, which is trying to produce successors on its own terms, and that of the emerging generation, which is constructing its own future by reproducing inherited capital in the face of new values and new economic requirements. Rather than merely reproducing its family firm in the terms dictated by the declining generation, the emerging generation creates its own means to construct the future of its enterprises.

Finally, I would also like to draw your attention to the fact that, in the social domain of the international financial elite, the world economy is based on face-to-face relations. In fact, the family-based economic groups that form a significant part of the Lisbon financial elite have a significant influence on Portuguese national life and, consequently, have a significant voice in international economic and Portuguese political relations. As part of the principal national enterprises and with their influential national and international web of personal relations, these people have an informal control over some sectors of public life. This being so, their personal relations have large-scale implications.

The study of personal relations can, therefore, acquire importance as a means to understanding global phenomena. Anthropology, focusing as it does these micro provides important insight into an area usually dominated by a macro-economic perspective.

Notes

1. I am grateful to João de Pina Cabral, Manuel Pedroso de Lima and Susana de Matos Viegas for comments on a first draft of this chapter as a conference paper. The discussion of this paper in the workshop Succession and Leadership in Elite Contexts, especially the comments made by the discussant, Sylvia Yanagisako, provided a stimulating basis for some reformulation.
2. I would like to thank Christina Toren for the introduction of this concept in the discussion, and for calling my attention to the advantages of an upwards perspective in the discussion of succession processes. In fact, the concept of succession implies a top - down process of transmission. But as there are two generations involved in this process, we must analyse the question from both sides.(Toren 1999)
3. This field research, 'Large families, Large enterprises', began in 1995 and has been co-ordinated by João de Pina Cabral with the financial support of Junta Nacional de Investigação Científica e Tecnológica, project number PCSH/C/ANT/851/95. In the course of fieldwork I interviewed various members of each family, trying to grasp as many points of view concerning both family and business as I could. For each of the eight families, I interviewed the presidents of the firms, the executive leaders, the family patriarchs, small shareholders, family members who do not own shares, women, young people beginning their professional lives in and out of the family business, and young people in the process of choosing a profession. This diversified universe of people allowed me access to a number of different experiences of living in that particular social context. Moreover, this allowed me to understand how different family members attribute different meanings to and make different investments in both the enterprise and the family. Collating information gathered from people living in the centre of the familial enterprise and on the margins allowed me to create a better picture of the social group as a whole.
4. For more on the discussion of elites as a specific social group see Nadel (1990). In this article the author discusses how a group of people who share the same social status are transformed into an elite: 'Elites ... must have some degree of corporateness, group character, and exclusiveness. There must be barriers to admission, ... they must form a more or less self conscious unit within the society, with its particular entailments, duties and rules of conduct in general' (ibid.: 33). He argues that for that to happen, people sharing an elites status need a minimum of corporateness to identify themselves as a group, and that it would be difficult for an outsider to be included in the group as a member.
5. This 'exclusiveness' and the 'difficulties in admission of new members' are important characteristics of elite groups as have been pointed out

by many authors who have discussed the subject (cf. Cohen 1981; Bottomore 1965; McDonough 1988; Mills 1956; Nadel 1990).

6. Before that legal divorce had been forbidden since the constitutional revision of 1933.

7. I use the concept of dynastic families following George Marcus's definition: 'A distinctive feature of the stronger families is a dynastic tradition or ideology that seems to have an emotional and cognitive hold on descendants' (Marcus and Hall 1992: 86-7) In this way a family dynasty is 'as much a family, as a fortune, as a class desire. ... It is a formal organization of an extended family, a corporate' (ibid.: 7).

8. I do not want to use the concept of 'extended family' because it connotes a unity of residence. 'The resident familial group alone is in question, not the kinship network, nor any "familial" relations between distinct households' (Laslett and Wall 1978: ix). The large elite family is a group of conjugal families and their descendants. Each one of these has a separate, independent and autonomous residence. The strength of the familial relations that unite them leads to the formation of a some what cohesive group of relatives. What we are witnessing with these large families is a deep density of relations between genealogically distant relatives, which is otherwise quite unusual in Portuguese society. By 'large family universe' I mean the universe of relatives of the diverse branches that derive from the founding couple. This was determined by the founder of the firm, whose importance in extremely well noted by Marcus: 'the entrepreneur created three things as an integrated part of his life history: a business organization, a family and a personal wealth. Family/Business formations developed in cases where the entrepreneur transmitted all three creations in a similar integrated way to members of the second generation'(1992: 21).

9. A similar conclusion led Marcus to characterize these rich dynastic families as 'an admittedly tribe like phenomenon' (ibid.: 4). Although it is of great interest to find this kind of occurrence at the top of the social hierarchy in Western bureaucratic societies, I believe we should avoid the introduction of these kinds of theoretically connoted concepts. Rather than being based on the filial descent criteria that have traditionally characterized tribes, these dynastic formations develop through complex succession processes based on the strategic manipulation of economic, political, and familial criteria. For this reason, even if these dynastic families do look like tribes, which they are not, we should not treat them like tribes. Nonetheless, anthropological reflections on descent theory have shown, since the 1960s, that not even tribes in segmentary societies follow a criterion of lineal descent. For more on this discussion see the chapters by   B r e m p o n g , Lentz and Toren in this volume.

10. It is interesting to note that most of the family businesses in Portugal are named after the family names of their founders.

11. 'O pé do dono é o adubo da terra.'
12. It should be stressed that, although there is an agnatic tendency in the family name's transmission, Portuguese law is not restrictive in this regard. This fact opens the way to a number of different legal combinations in Portuguese family names. João Pina-Cabral has argued that, in this flexible legal context, the choice of which family name people give to their children when they are born, or choose to use in their daily life (these are not necessarily the same) depends mostly on the social prestige attributed to the family name of their father or of their mother (cf. Pina-Cabral 1991: 174-6). MMB (grand grand daughter of the BES founder is an excellent example. She did not have the family name Espírito Santo, only her father's family name. At 37 years old she decided to apply officially for the inclusion of Espírito Santo (her mother's family name). After eight months of bureaucratic procedures she succeeded. This legal flexibility, and the consequent frequent use of the mother's family name has been the basis for some authors' classifying the Portuguese system of name transmission as matrilineal (cf. Bouquet 1993).
13. Cf. Lisón-Tolosana (1983) and Pina-Cabral and Lourenço (1993) for the use of the concepts 'emerging generation', 'controlling generation' and 'declining generation' to classify the relative position each age group occupies in the power structure of the larger society.
14. The MG family company is a good example of the consequences of not investing in the professional formation of the next generation. The family firm was founded in 1917, by a dynamic farmer and tradesman of the small city of Tomar. By 1930 the society had achieved great local importance, and by the 1960s it had launched in Portugal three industrial enterprises that became leaders in the national and international market in their respective areas of activity: red ceramics; transformation of oleaginous plants; and wood agglomerates. The administration board of the family society has always been constituted exclusively by family members. At the time of the death of the founder, the Presidency was assumed by his eldest son. As the result of the latter's sudden death, his own elder son took over the command of the group of enterprises. Later, a brother-in-law succeeded him, and later still, his nephew. Currently, the central firm of this group has been confiscated by the bank that was its major creditor. Many observers have attributed this economic failure to an excess of family spirit that dictated that only family members could assume roles of command within the family businesses. This ideal was so strongly rooted that it was not given up even in moments when it clearly led to the breakdown both of the firm and of family relations.
15. However, it should be noted that, in most cases, the children of these families do succeed to their parents' posts. This is, first of all, a result of the efforts of the new generation, who want to be involved and to participate in the family's project. Of course, it is also the result of the

great investment made by these families in the formal education of their children. But if the children had failed to undertake the necessary effort, all of this would have been in vain.

16. In her book *A Family Business?: The Making of an International Business Elite* (1989) Jane Marceau demonstrates how an international business elite is built and reproduced through the careful choice of which school to send young boys and girls to undertake their graduate education. She analyses the careers of 2,000 INSEAD (Fontainbleau, France) graduates from 1959 through to 1979. This study explores how the sons of the traditional bourgeoisie of Europe emerge as a self-conscious international business elite, and demonstrates the role of INSEAD in this process.

17. In his study of the Creole elite in Sierra Leone, Abner Cohen has brilliantly shown how it is through informal relations of kinship and amity that this elite group closes its frontiers and thus reproduces its privileged social condition. He also gives an excellent example of how they create a formal meritocratic system overlying an informal system of recruiting their own people.

18. The example of the Espírito Santo family again illustrates this point very well. It was through the direct influence of Valéry Giscard D'Estaing, then President of France, and of Robert McNamara, then President of the World Bank, that, in 1975, the revolutionary government of Portugal released the 6 top members of the Espírito Santo family from prison. These 6 members were released in August 1975 and escaped from Portugal to Spain. There, in Madrid, they met for the first business meeting of the new phase. They decided to re-enter business using all the money they had at that time (20,000 dollars) to open the Compagnie Financière Espírito Santo, in Luxemburg. In this way, they created a headquarters for their new business ventures. In 1975, at the first meeting of the Portuguese government with the World Bank, to negotiate an important loan, McNamara invited MR to sit at his right hand, as his private guest, to show the new Portuguese democratic government publicly whose side he was on.

19. For more on this item see the works of McDonogh 1988, Marcus and Hall 1992, and Gersick et al. 1997.

3

Patriarchal Desire: Law and Sentiments of Succession in Italian Capitalist Families

Sylvia Yanagisako

This chapter explores the relationship between law and sentiment in the dynamics of succession among wealthy, industrial capitalist families in northern Italy. Through the analysis of managerial succession and inheritance among family firms in the Italian silk industry, I demonstrate that law and sentiment operate in more complex ways than has been configured in anthropological models of kinship. Prevailing models of kinship succession represent law as the basis of the structural continuity of corporate kin groups, and sentiment as a destabilizing force that undermines it. I argue, in contrast, that the productive power of law incites desires and mobilizes sentiments that operate as forces both for and against corporate continuity.

In his study of dynastic, capitalist families in the US, Marcus has proposed a historical model of American family/business formations that emphasizes how legal rules and instruments become an integral dimension of family relationships themselves, even as they are being used to adapt family-owned concentrations of capital to the socio-economic environment. His model is based on family/business formations founded by entrepreneurs in commerce and industry during the late-nineteenth-century era of economic expansion in the United States, particularly those on which he has conducted research in Galveston, Texas.

In charting the role of law in these kinship formations, Marcus writes:

> It is important to know at the outset that the role of law in these formations has in no way replaced or negated the flexible normative content of middle-class kinship which characterizes American family life. Rather, law overlays, and to a degree complicates kin relations by giving a more formal organization to the extended family than that of most middle-class families. As will be seen from the Galveston case, formations are set on a structured course by their internal administration of patrimonial capital and businesses, but final outcomes of this process still depend very much upon the long-term emotional atmosphere of a dynastic family. Popular interest in formations has focused on their 'human drama' aspect to the exclusion of their legal dimension. I argue that without

consideration of this dimension, their distinctive nature as groups in modern societies cannot be fully understood (Marcus 1992: 16).

While Marcus's model is fashioned from research on family formations in the US that have endured from the late nineteenth century to the present as both extended family and business organizations, he has proposed that

> the basic model [of this chapter] also applies with some adjustments to contemporaneous formations in European societies (particularly Great Britain and Ireland) ... In the broadest terms, what I am describing is a major structural manifestation of the interrelationships between law, wealth-holding, and elite family organization over the past century in Western capitalist societies (Marcus 1992: 29).

In this chapter, I adjust Marcus's model to fit the processes of succession in industrial-capitalist families in northern Italy. In the course of making these adjustments, I reformulate his model to go beyond the idea that law 'overlays' and 'complicates kin relations by giving a more formal organization to the extended family'. I suggest instead that law is itself a crucial force that shapes the 'emotional atmosphere' of capitalist families and, conversely, that emotions operate as social forces that set families on a structured course. In attending to the emotionally-constitutive power of law[1] and the structuring power of emotion, I challenge a convention of anthropological studies of kinship in which emotions are viewed as prior to law and yet incapable of producing either structural continuity or structural transformation. I trace this convention to a critical juncture in the history of kinship studies in anthropology - namely, the ascendance of British descent theory and Radcliffe-Brown's theory of structural functionalism.

Northern Italian Industrial-Capitalist Families

The Northern Italian industrial-capitalist families on which this discussion is based constitute the wealthiest fraction of the capitalist families who own and manage firms in the silk manufacturing industry of Como, Italy.[2] From its pre-industrial beginnings to the present, the silk industry of Como has been characterized by a decentralized structure of production. As in the early development of the northern European textile industry (E. Goody 1982), in the nineteenth century merchants functioned as the industry's entrepreneurs by taking on both supply and marketing functions. Rather than grouping the weavers together in factories, the merchants bought the thread and had it woven by artisans who owned their own looms. Even after the industrial transformation of the industry, production has continued to be highly decentralized. Today, there are few vertically-integrated firms in the industry, and the vast majority of firms operate in only one phase of the production process. The twisting of the silk thread, its preparation for weaving, the dyeing, weaving and printing of the fabric, the preparation of screens for printing, and the packaging and marketing of fabric all take place in different firms. The industry is also characterized by the overwhelming predominance of local ownership by Como families. In 1985, out of the approximately 400 firms in the industry, there was only one joint-stock company that had been started by investors outside of Como, and there was no multinational ownership.[3]

The industry is often cited as a prime example of the flexible specialization that has led to the success of decentralized networks of small firms since the early 1970s. Whether these industrial networks are touted as heralding a new era of industrialism that will lead to the demise of Fordist mass production (Piore and Sabel 1984), as a new phase of disorganized capitalism (Lash and Urry 1988), or as a new regime of capital accumulation (Harvey 1989), most theorists agree that they have enhanced capitalists' ability to respond flexibly to global market conditions.[4]

At the top of the industrial network are the highly capitalized, vertically-integrated firms that employ the services of smaller, less-capitalized subcontracting firms. The discussion of succession in this chapter is limited to those families in my study that fall within the 'upper bourgeois' fraction of Como's industrial-capitalist class, although other fractions show similar dynamics.[5]

Succession and Patriarchal Desire[6]

In the official origins narratives of firms the ideal founder is one who has the generative power to create his own firm, his own family, and his own destiny.[7] Fathering a family and fathering a business are mutually interdependent projects of creation in the cosmology of kinship and business, family and capitalism, which are conveyed in firms' origin stories. To head a family is to provide for it, including providing the productive means of the independence of the family and the means to reproduce that independence in the next generation.

All men who head family firms and who have sons want to be succeeded by them.[8] Indeed, many men say that the only reason they have worked hard to build a successful firm is so that they can hand it on to their son or sons. In contrast, men without children say they are inclined to sell their firms when they retire. Moreover, they express strong reservations about the prevalent practice of filial succession in the industry, claiming that it often leads to disaster and to undermining the productive capacity of firms and the industry as a whole.

Fathers' desires to pass their firms on to their sons are best understood in relation to a dense system of meanings about the male self, its actualization through men's projects, its relation to the projects of other men, and its perpetuation through the lives of sons. 'Independence' is a key symbol in this ideology of masculinity, and a close examination of its configuration of meanings reveals a complex and contradictory set of desires among men.

Independence is something fathers want both for themselves and for their sons. In the realm of work, being independent means being your own boss, being an employer rather than an employee (which in Italian is to be literally a *dipendente*). In the realm of the family, being independent means being the head of your own family. Fathers want to give their sons the means of production, which are the means of their economic independence as well as their means of becoming the heads of their own families. As one successor son put it, 'My father always said to us [his sons]: "I will not leave you money, but the means to make a living."'

Endowing a son with the means to be independent of other men enables him to attain an ideal of male adulthood. To do so requires accumulating sufficient capital to reinvest in the firm so that it can survive competition with other firms. In other words, succession necessitates accumulation. To endow two or more sons with the means of their independence requires even greater accumulation, because the firm must have sufficient capital to expand or diversify.

Rooted as it is in an ideal of male parity and a disdain for any man who is subordinate to the authority of another man and who is constrained to work for another man's project, this desire to give one's sons the means of independence entails an internal contradiction. For what seems attainable in an abstract model of male parity is not so when it comes to relationships on the ground - or, rather, in families. Instead, it turns out, one man's independence results in another man's dependence. To retain his position as head of an enduring family a man must have a family to head. Once his children grow up, his daughters are lost to him through marriage, for married women are viewed as falling under the authority of their husbands, not their fathers. Fathers are also in danger of losing their authority over their sons, not through marriage but through the sons' employment. A son who works for someone else not only comes under the authority of another man (his *padrone*), but also has the financial means to be independent of his father. In giving his sons the means to be independent of employers, a father prolongs his headship of the family - often, until his death. Such a father has the good fortune of having both ensured his headship of an enduring family that includes his sons and, at the same time, provided for their independence from other men. Such a father, it could be said, has mediated the contradiction embodied in a male ideal of independence that entails the dependence of other men.

Whence comes this goal of endowing a son with the means of producing his independence? One line of reasoning points to the economic roots of lineal succession. Along these lines, Goody (J. Goody 1976) has contended that in both European and Asian kinship systems the need to provide 'security' lies behind lineal succession, which functions to preserve the status of offspring in a society with differentiated strata based on property-holding. He contrasts these systems with African systems, where devolution in an individual man's personal line is unnecessary because of hoe-farming and its associated productive resources.

Unless we are satisfied with an explanation that attributes contemporary capitalist desires for lineal succession to dispositions formed in a pre-capitalist past, Goody's explanation would appear inadequate for our purposes. Moreover, his reductionist model lumps all Asian and European societies together into a single structural-functional formation based on plough agriculture. Such a sweeping hypothesis does not enable us to differentiate Italian capitalist desires for filial succession from, for example, Japanese capitalist desires for lineal succession. Yet the latter do not appear to be spurred on by the desires for independence articulated by the Como bourgeoisie (Kondo 1990; Hamabata 1990).

The search for an answer that moves beyond a utilitarian, functionalist theory of culture might well begin with an investigation of the historical process in which these desires were formed. In the following section of this chapter, I suggest that it is in the forces that impede the fulfilment of patriarchal desire for succession that we can find clues as to incitement.

Impediments as Incitements of Patriarchal Desire

Several impediments stand in the way of the fulfilment of the patriarchal desire for male filial succession. The first is reproductive outcomes. The failure to produce a son can transform patriarchal desire into patriarchal denial, as was evidenced in the reservations about filial succession expressed by men without children. Those who have no sons, but who have daughters, respond in more subtle and complex ways to queries about their desires for succession. They also draw on a wider array of alternative strategies of succession. In the past, a common one was to marry a daughter to an enterprising young man with strong managerial or technical skills who could function as an interim successor, and then groom one's grandson as the eventual successor. As we shall see, this strategy is complicated these days by daughters' interest in succeeding to management leadership themselves. Another was to install a nephew as the interim successor, again with the plan of eventually replacing him with a grandson.

A second and more formidable obstacle to the fulfilment of patriarchal desire for male filial succession is Italian inheritance law. With the imposition of the Napoleonic code on Northern Italy in 1808, equal division of the patrimony among all children irrespective of gender became the law, if not the practice, in the region. When Napoleon's empire collapsed in 1815, Austria once again took over Venice and Lombardy. Their inheritance codes struck a compromise between the egalitarian principles of the Enlightenment and the values of a conservative, ruling aristocracy. After the unification of Italy, the Civil Code promulgated in 1865 was modelled upon the Napoleonic code, which had a strong Jacobin thrust, attacking the concentration of aristocratic wealth. This Civil Code governed Italian inheritance until it was revised by the *Nuovo Diritto di Famiglia* in 1975.[9]

Italian Inheritance Law

Italian inheritance law recognizes three basic types of inheritance rights: legitimate (legitim), testamentary, and legal. Legitimate inheritance has absolute priority over the others - it represents 'overriding duty' (Davis 1973: 175). What proportion of the estate is reserved for the heirs, who the heirs are, and the proportions they receive are complexly codified.[10] If there are legitimate descendants, then ascendants are excluded. If there are illegitimate descendants, then they inherit with the legitimate descendants or (if there are none) with the ascendant. The proportion of the estate that must be legitimately inherited varies between one-third and two-thirds. It is, for instance, one-third if the heir is a single illegitimate descendant. It is one-half if there is a single legitimate descendant. It is two-thirds with two or more legitimate descendants, and it is divided in equal shares among these descendants regardless of gender.

Until 1975, spouses were in the fourth category of priority under legitimate inheritance. This meant, for instance (see Davis 1973, Table 20), that if there were two legitimate children (which means two-thirds of the property is legitimately inherited) then they split $5/12$ of the total and the spouse received $3/12$. The legitim inheritance of spouses, however, was limited only to usufruct (ibid.: 176), not to full ownership. Usufruct, in Italian law, entailed the right to an income and to administer the property. Dowry, officially recognized under the Civil Code, was returned to the wife or to the giver of the dowry or their heirs upon the death of the husband (Davis 1973: 173).[11]

By means of this precise calculation of the division of patrimonial property, the Italian state has legislated a national, standardized model of the family as a property-owning collectivity, specifying the precise proportion of shares to which particular family members are entitled. This makes capitalist families - and, indeed, all families in Italy with any substantial property - more like each other than those in the United States where individuals and married couples have great leeway in deciding how to distribute their property. While legal instruments such as trusts and holding companies may be tailored for particular families, in both countries they are severely constrained in their ability to concentrate capital. The standardization of property distribution sets up a standard emotional structure in Italian property-owning families, which, in turn, generates standard human dramas of succession.

The legally constituted family - interpellated and buttressed by the state - is both affirmed as a property-owning corporate group and weakened in its ability to reproduce itself. As a deliberate attempt to break up concentrations of wealth and political power in aristocratic, landowning families, equal division of the patrimony undermines a father's attempt to concentrate the patrimony under the control of a chosen successor. Italian inheritance law thus favours the interests and sentiments of daughters and non-successor sons rather than that of fathers and successor sons.

The persistence of patriarchal desire for male filial succession despite nearly two centuries of state-decreed equal inheritance among siblings could be chalked up as yet another example of the strength of 'custom' over 'law'. But, this stock explanation obscures the ways in which patriarchal desire for filial succession has been incited by the same emancipatory ideology that led to the inheritance laws impeding its fulfilment. The bourgeois goal of independence from a pre-capitalist hierarchy, I suggest, incited both the law of equal inheritance and the desire to concentrate control of the patrimony in the hands of successor sons. As I have shown, a father's attempt to reproduce the family's independence in the next generation requires endowing his son with the means of their independence from the authority of other men. As Marx and Engels argued (1976: 434), from the standpoint of the bourgeoisie, liberation through economic competition was the only way of providing individuals with a new career freed from the old feudal fetters. This desire for freedom from a pre-capitalist hierarchy generates the internal contradiction I have already noted - namely that for a son to have the means to attain full adult male bourgeois status - to be truly independent - he must be dependent on his father's property.[12]

For fathers who grew up before the Italian economic miracle of the 1950s and 1960s, independence drew its meaning from an agrarian model of society in which the struggle of families to free themselves from the paternalism of landowners made sense of the paternalism within their own families. More recently, a concept of personal independence more familiar to North Americans has encroached upon the old one, peppering the speech of Como entrepreneurs and their children with such English phrases as 'self-made man'. The American version of the bourgeois liberal celebration of the independence of individuals has brought new significance to the contradiction already lurking in the older commitment to emancipation from subordination to authority outside the family. For younger men coming of age since the 1960s, independence has increasingly signified a self-actualization that requires emancipation from authority within the family.

Daughters and Patriarchal Desire

Bourgeois gender ideology rendered female independence an oxymoron. Daughters who were destined to be subordinate to their husbands were automatically disqualified from being the agents of the family's continued independence. Consequently, until recently, bourgeois hopes for reproducing the family's independence rested with sons. In the face of laws of equal inheritance, male succession depended on strategies for liquidating daughters' rights to the patrimony without depleting it beyond what was needed to maintain its capital-regenerating capacity. Daughters' claims had to be met without destroying sons' means of production and independence.[13] In the past, the threat that daughters' jural rights to inheritance posed to male succession was met by a variety of customary practices among propertied families in Northern Italy. Among the Como bourgeoisie, fathers gave daughters their share of the inheritance in the form of a dowry or other pre-mortem settlements. Once having invested in their daughters' education - whether in elite German or Swiss 'finishing schools' or, more recently, in Italian universities, where they commonly majored in foreign languages - fathers often invested capital in their daughters' husbands' firms. Over time, these shares were transferred to the daughter and her children.

It is highly unlikely that the dowries and other pre-mortem payments and investments that daughters of propertied families received came close to equalling the portion of the patrimony that was their legal due. Daughters did not have the resources, however, to enforce their claims. For one thing, their bourgeois husbands shared an interest in male inheritance and female dowry, and were unlikely to challenge a practice from which they benefited. For another, daughters themselves had some stake in the undivided strength of their natal patrimony, for fathers and brothers were their only refuge from a failed marriage. The continuity or expansion of her family's capitalist enterprises, moreover, was both a source of symbolic capital and a potential source of the means of financial independence of her own sons.

Mothers, on the other hand, shared their sons' interest in keeping the patrimony intact by virtue of the fact that the legitim inheritance guaranteed them by law as widows was limited to usufruct, not actual ownership. Dependent as they were upon sons to manage the business and provide them with a stipend, widows could not be strong advocates of their daughters' inheritance rights. Even today, widows who were raised in capitalist families emphasize the importance of an undivided patrimony and the perpetuation of their husbands' and fathers' projects.

The Transformation of Patriarchal Desire

Just as the emergence of bourgeois ideologies of independence incited both egalitarian laws of inheritance and the patriarchal desire for male filial succession, so have more recent political and cultural movements generated new laws and new sentiments that are shaping the 'emotional atmosphere' of Italian capitalist families and transforming patriarchal desire. Marcus notes that in the United States case, 'As the organizational core of a formation, the [legal] surrogate is challenged externally by long-term political and economic trends which have tended to constrain the inheritance of great wealth and to diminish generally the directing role of family interests in modern business organization' (1992: 17).

The burden of inheritance taxes and other legal impediments to the accumulation and transmission of wealth have been constraints to which family formations have had continually to adapt in the United States as well as in Italy. At the national level, political battles over tax law, inheritance law and family law have played out conflicting visions of the relations among property, class, kinship and gender. The outcomes of these battles in the form of new laws have called forth adjustments in the strategic practices of individuals and families among the bourgeoisie.

The 1975 Family Law in Italy is an excellent example of such processes. Advocated by the left and supported by feminist groups, the 1975 reform of the Civil Code both legalized divorce and strengthened women's property rights. In establishing spousal community property - considered a necessary protection in the event of divorce - the law granted widows actual property rights rather than merely rights of usufruct. As a consequence, a woman with two or more children is now entitled to at least one third of the patrimony if her husband dies intestate and at least one-fourth if he leaves a will disposing of that proportion of his property that he can freely assign to whomever he wishes. Falling within the community property of spouses are acquisitions made (even separately) during the marriage, the property assigned for the practice of an enterprise of one of the spouses founded after the marriage, and any increase in the value of the enterprise.

Wives' acquisition of community property and inheritance rights with the reform of family law in 1975 not only strengthened their position in relation to their husbands but in relation to their children, in particular their sons. Mother in the bourgeois family has become not merely than a moral and emotional force to be reckoned with, but an owner of capital who can bring considerable economic pressure to bear on her children. As a consequence, the new family law has reconfigured the emotional structure and dynamics of bourgeois families. As wives and mothers have acquired new power, they have awakened to new interests. These have emerged at the intersection of older gender ideologies about women's responsibilities in the family and new gender ideologies of equality.

The wives and mothers in Como capitalist families who came of age before the 1960s are, for the most part, conservative Christian Democrats steeped in bourgeois feminist commitments to *la famiglia unita*. As such, they are far from being advocates of *la liberazione delle donne;* nor do they pursue an Italian feminist vision of women's autonomy. What has changed is not their commitment to keeping the family together, but the kind of family they have in mind. The altered political-legal context of the family has led bourgeois mothers to advocate a new kind of collectivity - namely, the inclusive family of parents (or of a widow), their adult children and the latter's spouses and children. Even before they are widowed, wives look beyond their husbands' deaths to their futures in these new inclusive families. Whereas their husbands' goal of filial succession drives them to consolidate control over the patrimony, these wives' goal of keeping the family together drives them in turn to distribute the patrimony more or less equally among all children, thereby strengthening the continuity of the family as a unit of enduring solidarity.

Daughters in these families who came of age after the 1960s have a different vision of their rights and duties in the family - one that has been undeniably affected by the political-cultural movements that led to the 1975 reform of family law. Their sense of entitlement to both patrimonial wealth and managerial control has increased by the decade, and many of them under the age of forty hope to succeed their fathers or at least share management leadership with their brothers. Some already do. They are adamant that they will not be content to take on a marginal role in the firm. Nor are they willing to be bought off with investments in their husbands' firms or by being set up in allied, but much less capitalized, sectors of the industry such as wholesale or retail outlets.

Just as nineteenth-century bourgeois ideas of independence infused both law and sentiment in bourgeois families - simultaneously undermining and fuelling patriarchal desire for male filial succession - so new ideas of independence reflected in the 1975 family law and the sentiments of family members are reconfiguring patriarchal desire. Fathers with daughters who have entered the family business and who have shown a keen interest in management take a discursive middle path between the patriarchal desire for male filial succession and the rejection of it voiced by men without children. Whether they have only daughters or both sons and daughters who are potential successors, these fathers advocate a kin meritocracy in which all their children are eligible for, but not automatically guaranteed, management leadership of the family business. Which child will succeed to the headship of the family corporation will depend, they say, on which demonstrates the strongest management skills.

While fathers may well be rooting for their sons to surface to the top of this kin competition, the legal and cultural challenges to patriarchal control of succession have bolstered daughters' and wives' sense of their rights, necessitating an adjustment of patriarchal desire. Patriarchal desire is transforming from a desire for male succession to an increasingly gender-neutral desire for filial succession and family corporate continuity. At the same time, younger bourgeois women view autonomy as requiring rights to the family patrimony equal to those of their brothers. In other words, the desire for succession is being incited among women, who now feel like their brothers that they must be their own boss and endow their own children with the means of their independence. The cultural trajectory of patriarchal desire, increasingly uncoupled from ideas of masculinity, is now being charted by this emerging generation of successors.

Patriarchal Desire and Kinship Theory

In identifying the forces shaping dynastic families in Western industrial-capitalist society, Marcus contrasts his focus on legal and fiduciary arrangements with what he describes as the conventional focus of anthropological studies on lineages, descent groups, and 'the community of kin focused on reverence for ancestors in small-scale, tribal societies' (1992: 4). Anthropological common sense, he writes, has been to focus on the anthropological staples of 'the politics of kinship, family rituals, and reverence toward ancestors', whose role he views as less important in the reproduction of dynastic motivation and ideology.

> My interpretation goes against the conventional wisdom of anthropology: I suggest that lineages here and now are not what they appear to be from the vantage point of knowledge about places where and times when they were the dominant form of social organization. The fact that the dynamic processes that shape mature dynasties may not rest primarily within lineages of descendants requires a rethinking of anthropological categories in their repatriation (1992: 4).

Marcus is correct that the politics of kinship, family rituals, and reverence for ancestors have been 'anthropological staples'. At the same time, however, he overlooks the fact that the structural core of kinship theory has been, since the 1940s, precisely what he has focused upon: law and corporate continuity. For the past half-century, interpersonal relations and the symbolic realm of ritual have been deemed secondary to 'jural principles' in defining the structure and function of lineages and other kinship groups that have been viewed as crucial to the continuity of social order in non-state societies.

Continuity of the social order was a primary concern of Radcliffe-Brown and the other descent theorists who studied 'stateless' societies lacking formal legal institutions and coercive state sanctions. Radcliffe-Brown believed that any social system had to 'conform to certain conditions' to survive (1952: 43). One such law was the 'functional consistency amongst the constituent parts of the system'. Another was the necessity for continuity: 'We must appeal to another sociological law, the necessity not merely for stability, definiteness and consistency in the social structure, but also for continuity. To provide continuity of social structure is essentially a function of corporations' (Radcliffe-Brown 1952: 45-6).

By 'continuity' British descent theorists meant more than the stability of interpersonal relations throughout the course of an individual's life. In order to transcend the destabilizing effects of human mortality, social systems required the transgenerational continuity of aggregates of individuals organized into social groups. In the case of the classic descent-based corporate group, the lineage, this entailed 'perpetual structural existence in a stable and homogeneous society' that preserves the 'existing scheme of social relations as far as possible' (Fortes 1970: 79-80).

The extent to which kinship groups such as lineages play a part in the social, political or religious life of the tribe depends, according to Radcliffe-Brown, on the degree to which they are corporate groups.

> A group may be spoken as 'corporate' when it possesses any one of a certain number of characters: if its members, or its adult members, or a considerable proportion of them, come together occasionally to carry out some collective action - for example, the performance of rites; if it has a chief or council who are regarded as acting as the representatives of the group as a whole; if it

possesses or controls property which is collective, as when a clan or lineage is a land-owning group (Radcliffe-Brown 1950: 41).

Continuity, moreover, depended on shared understandings of rights and duties among persons.

> The sociological laws, i.e. the necessary conditions of existence of a society, that have been here suggested as underlying the customs of unilineal (patrilineal or matrilineal) succession are: 1. The need for a formulation of rights over persons and things sufficiently precise in their general recognition as to avoid as far as possible unresolved conflicts. 2. The need for continuity of the social structure as a system of relations between persons, such relations being defined in terms of rights and duties (Radcliffe-Brown 1952: 47).

In attempting to illuminate the social order of what they perceived to be societies most lacking in it, British social anthropologists fashioned a universalistic, jural model of society that granted structural primacy to those normative 'principles' and 'rules' that most closely resembled the state-enforced laws of Western European nations.

In the next generation of British descent theorists, Fortes argued that true corporate descent groups can exist only in more or less homogeneous societies - in particular those of central Africa. Yet his invocation of Maine's usage of 'corporation' in the analysis of testamentary succession and Weber's analysis of the 'corporate group' suggests that Africa served for Fortes as a 'simple society' upon which theories of European kinship and law could be mapped:

> The most important feature of unilinear descent groups in Africa ... is their corporate organization. When we speak of these groups as corporate units we do so in the sense given to the term 'corporation' long ago by Maine in his classical analysis of testamentary succession in early law (Maine 1861). We are reminded also of Max Weber's sociological analysis of the corporate group as a general type of social formation (Weber 1947), for in many important particulars the African descent groups conform to Weber's definition (Fortes 1970: 78-9).

> Where the lineage concept is highly developed, the lineage is thought to exist as a perpetual corporation as long as any of its members survive. This means, of course, not merely perpetual physical existence ensured by the replacement of departed members. It means perpetual structural existence, in a stable and homogeneous society; that is, the perpetual exercise of defined rights, duties, office and social tasks vested in the lineage as a corporate unit (Fortes 1970: 79-80).

Fortes's characterization of the central African lineage in these terms seems a clear example of the projection of a core legal structure of European capitalist society - the corporate firm - on to other societies.

The idea that the structural continuity of the social groups that constitute the foundation of a social structure is rooted in the system of rights and duties that is the functional equivalent of the formal laws of state society has continued to haunt anthropological kinship theory for most of this century. The legal institutions that Marcus contends are crucial in shaping dynastic families' 'distinctive nature as groups in modern societies' (1992: 16) are precisely those from which descent theorists derived their model of the jural domain in tribal society. Rather than rethinking anthropological categories, Marcus's model of the role of law repatriates a core analytic premise of descent theory: the primacy of law in the continuity of kinship corporations.

This assumption rests, in turn, on the more fundamental assumption that the 'jural principles' defining the rights and duties between kin in stateless societies can be differentiated from the diffuse moral commitments and emotional attachments between kin. That some kinship sentiments are themselves normatively prescribed was obvious even to the descent theorists who proposed this analytic distinction.[14] Kinship relations, after all, were viewed by them as structured not only by precise jural rules of rights and duties but by more diffuse moral norms such as 'prescriptive altruism'. Normative sentiments could not, however, be the basis of structural continuity.

The lack of confidence British descent theorists had in emotions as a force for a stability and continuity - indeed their distrust of sentiment - was exacerbated by their disciplinary battle against the 'psychologizing' of Bronislaw Malinowski, who was Radcliffe-Brown's strongest rival for theoretical hegemony in British social anthropology. As Radcliffe-Brown's brand of functionalism gained ascendance in British social anthropology after the Second World War, Malinowski's brand of functionalism became increasingly discredited. The critique of Malinowskian functionalism focused in good part on his ideas about the universal physiological and psychological needs of individuals, which Malinowski viewed as the fundamental requirements of all human societies. In elevating the focus of anthropological theory from the individual to society - itself viewed as a functioning organic system - Radcliffe-Brown and his followers eschewed Malinowski's concern with the organic needs of individuals. Any interest social anthropology might have had in the survival and reproduction of the human organism was displaced on to society through an organic metaphor. The continuity of the *social body* - construed as social structure - by means of its stable equilibrium rather than the continuity of human organisms became the proper object of theory in social anthropology.

The survival of the social structure, moreover, was viewed by Radcliffe-Brown and his successors as dependent on structures of law rather than structures of sentiment. Malinowski's fatal error was, for them, the attention he had paid to the latter rather than the former.

> In sum, what is inadequately stressed by Malinowski is that kinship relations have to be seen as a system, within the framework of the total social structure. Their *fundamental juridical nature* then emerges, as Rivers appreciated (Fortes 1957: 164, *my emphasis*).

Questions of right and duty are, however, secondary to emotion and sentiment in Malinowski's analysis of these [Trobriand] data (ibid.).

From the perspective of Radcliffe-Brown's model of society, Malinowski's attention to the power of sentiment, such as a father's affection for his son, rather than to structure-affirming law, constituted a *prima facie* case of psychological reductionism. Malinowski's belief in sentiments as motivating forces of social action was deemed as troubling as his theory of universal human instincts.

Malinowski had no sense for social organization ... Kinship is to him primarily a tissue of culturally conditioned emotional attitudes (Fortes 1970: 71).

As I have said, a psychological framework was essential to Malinowski's functionalism. Everything he wrote was riddled with psychological explanation partly because his functionalism meant seeing custom as motive, partly because its instrumental and utilitarian form led back to physiological needs, and the simplest way in which these can be visualized as emerging in action is as the driving forces behind instincts, sentiments and emotions (Fortes 1957: 170).

Rooted as it was in his theory of the universal physiological and psychological needs of individuals, Malinowski's focus on the psychological forces behind social institutions warranted this refutation. In purging 'psychology' from the study of kinship, however, Malinowski's critics threw sentiment out with it. Having concluded that 'kinship behaviour and not kinship sentiment is the study of the anthropologist' (Firth 1960: 576), they purged emotion from their theory of social action. As a consequence, they denied themselves the opportunity to analyse the interplay among sentiment, law and action. Instead, they lumped emotions with instincts, relegating them to the realm of universal human nature - ironically, just as Malinowski himself had done.

Subsequent contributions to kinship theory in anthropology have reaffirmed this distrust of emotion and sentiment. Despite his disagreement with British descent theorists as to whether descent or alliance lay at the core of kinship, Lévi-Strauss concurred with his British colleagues' distinction between 'moral norms' (the bonds in the restricted family, such as the value placed on conjugal faithfulness and parental attachment) and the legal rules governing broader kinship structures. 'Affect' was, for Lévi-Strauss (1963a, 1963b), something other than a product of cognitive processes, and he shared his British colleagues' view of it as an epiphenomenon of social structure rather than as a constitutive force.

Kinship theory in anthropology has taken several turns since the debate between descent theorists and alliance theorists and their respective total models of social structure.[15] Rule-based models of social structure have been supplanted by social interactionist (Barth 1966) and practice-oriented analyses (Bourdieu 1977). Feminist kinship theory (Reiter 1975; Strathern 1980, 1988, 1992; Yanagisako and Collier 1987; Yanagisako and

Delaney 1995) has undermined the assumption that all members of kin groups share the same commitments and goals, not to mention questioning whether they follow the 'rules' to the same degree. Yet, despite these challenges to rule-based models of kinship, law continues to be viewed as a more powerful structural force than sentiment.

The distrust of emotion as a productive force capable of shaping the course of kin groups or of reproducing the social order appears to stem from a dichotomous model of human social action that has deep roots in Western European cosmology. In the 1980s, M. Rosaldo characterized these oppositions of thought/feeling, cognition/affect, outer 'mask'/inner 'essence', 'custom'/personality as products of a 'bifurcating and Western cast of mind' (1984: 137), which she believed to be wedded to a Western cosmology of self and society. At the same time, she argued that the interpretative turn in anthropology (Geertz 1973) provided potent conceptual resources for challenging these dichotomies and rethinking our notions of selves, affects, and personalities (1984: 137). She pointed to developments in psychology (Ricouer 1970) and philosophy (Foucault 1972 and 1978) that enabled us to understand how human beings understandings of themselves do not emerge from an inner, pre-social world, but 'from experience in a world of meanings, images and social bonds, in which all persons are inevitably involved' (Rosaldo 1984: 139):

> ... instead of seeing feeling as a private (often animal, presocial) realm that is - ironically enough - most universal and at the same time most particular to the self, it will make sense to see emotions not as things opposed to thought but as cognitions implicating the immediate, carnal 'me' - as thought embodied (Rosaldo 1984: 138).

> ... recognition of the fact that thought is always culturally patterned and infused with feelings, which themselves reflect a culturally ordered past, suggests that just as thought does not exist in isolation from affective life, so affect is culturally ordered and does not exist apart from thought (1984: 137).

After a couple of decades in which cultural constructivist approaches have pervaded anthropological theory,[16] the idea that sentiments are no less culturally ordered and no more private than beliefs by now would seem a banal observation. Yet, Rosaldo's argument (1984: 147-50) that selves and feelings are more productively understood as the creation of particular sorts of polities and social relations does not seem to have been fully appreciated in many studies of kinship. Such an appreciation would open the door to the analysis of emotion, reclaiming it as a product of cultural processes as well as a process itself in the production, reproduction and transformation of social action. In such an analytic project, emotion would not stand outside law as a pre-jural, pre-political psychological force, but rather would be conceptualized as a constitutive force itself, incited by law and other social forces.

In this chapter I have attempted such an analysis. I have tried to show that in the case of capitalist-industrial families in northern Italy, law and sentiment operate in more complex ways than are configured in conventional anthropological analyses of succession. Law does not function simply as a force for the continuity of corporate kin groups. Nor is it accurate to characterize it as setting kinship formations on a 'structured course' whose final outcome is shaped by the 'emotional atmosphere' of the family (Marcus 1992). Rather, the productive power of law should be seen as inciting desires and strategies that work to skirt and subvert law, as well as ones that carry out its designs. Although Italian law provides legal instruments that can be used by bourgeois families to promote the concentration of capital, one of its major effects has been to undermine family corporate continuity. Conversely, while some family sentiments work to undermine family corporate continuity, others - such as the patriarchal desire for filial succession - operate as forces for corporate continuity. Our understanding of processes of succession, whether among the elite or other sectors of society, would benefit greatly from our jettisoning the bifurcated model of law/sentiment, thought/emotion, society/self that has impeded our understanding of the processes through which sentiment and law constitute each other as forces of cultural production.

Notes

1. See Coombe 1998 for a useful discussion of the constitutive power of law.
2. Since 1984, I have conducted fifteen months of research on family firms in the silk industry of Como, Italy, including ethnographic and historical research on forty of the approximately 400 firms in the industry. These forty firms constitute a stratified sample according to the dimensions of firm size (number of employees) and age (years since founding). I have interviewed the owner-managers of all these firms and, in a third of the cases, several of their family members and relatives. For each firm, a detailed history has been obtained on family and kinship relationships, gender division of labour in family and firm, managerial organization of firm, inheritance and succession, capitalization and capital accumulation. Finally, I have interviewed industry officials and union leaders and collected archival materials, including firm records, industry surveys, government censuses, and notarial documents on property transfers.
3. In 1985, the industry employed about 13,000 workers in the province of Como, thus constituting its leading manufacturing industry. Although the total number of firms and employees in the industry declined in the 1970s and 1980s, the size distribution of firms has been fairly stable since 1961, with 68 per cent of firms having fewer

than 10 workers, 18 per cent having 11-50 workers and only 14 per cent having 51 or more. Total sales figures continued to increase in the 1980s - in 1981 the industry sold goods worth 950 million dollars, 600 million of which came from export sales (Piore and Sabel 1984, quoting an industry report). Almost half the weaving firms are at least twenty years old, and 30 per cent are at least thirty years old.

4. Como's industrial structure bears some resemblance to what Ong has called 'the most important recent experiment in corporate production' - the 'flexible combination of mass assembly and subcontracting systems, of modern firms and home work as linked by units dominated by transnational capital' (1991: 283). It has strong similarities with Hong Kong's export-industrial economy, where most production takes place in subcontracting family firms (Salaff 1981). In the case of Como's silk industry, however, this flexible combination of mass assembly and subcontracting systems has existed since the beginnings of district's industrial manufacturing of textiles in the latter half of the nineteenth century. As in Japan, manufacturing in Italy has had a long-established pattern, where 'even under Fordism, small business sub-contracting acted as a buffer to protect large corporations from the cost of market fluctuations' (Harvey 1989: 152). According to Harvey, these subcontracting firms constitute the 'other end of the business scale' from the increased monopolization of certain industrial and financial sectors, in which flexible accumulation has brought about massive mergers and corporate diversifications (Harvey 1989: 158). Como family capitalism was reinvigorated by the mid-1970s world recession and the rising labour conflicts of the late sixties and early seventies, which underscored the advantages of decentralized, but co-ordinated, networks of small firms. While these Como firms are owned and managed by family members, this does not mean that they constitute an autonomous, regional production system that is isolated from translocal and even transnational flows of capital, technology, and labour. During its early history in the nineteenth century, the Como industry as a whole was tied to German and Swiss finance capital, German textile machinery firms, and French textile manufacturers - for whom it fulfilled many of the earlier stages of production, leaving the final, and most highly valued-added, phases to the French firms. With Italy's increasing industrial success, Como's firms have come to be tied in more with Italian finance capital; but the area is still integrally linked with transnational industrial and commercial networks.

5. I have divided Como's industrial-capitalist families into three fractions upper, middle, and lower - based on a combination of firm and family characteristics. Firm characteristics include annual gross income, number of employees, and location in the industry hierarchy (those who sell their own products, as opposed to subcontracting firms, which sell their productive services), and ownership of other firms.

Family characteristics include a number of indicators of social class and social class trajectory, including the class of the founder's father, founder's mother, and founder's spouse, and the education of the founder and his children. The nine families out of forty in my sample that fall in the 'upper bourgeoisie' own firms that have an annual gross income of between thirty million and five million dollars, with most of them clustering around ten million dollars. The numbers of the workers employed by their firms range from eight hundred and fifty to fifty. This wide range stems from the fact that some firms farm work out to subcontracting firms, as well as to outworkers who are not officially classified as employees of the firm. The number of the firm's registered employees, consequently, is not a useful indicator of a firm's annual earnings or capital assets. Neither is it a good indicator of the wealth of the family. More revealing of the character of this fraction is the fact that none of their main firms are subcontractors and six of the nine are vertically-integrated firms that include all the phases of production required to transform raw silk into finished fabric. Every one of these upper bourgeois families, moreover, owns all or a majority of the shares in at least two other firms. This not only means that these families control more capital assets than those included in a single firm, but that they also control firms that specialize in other phases of production and even firms in allied marketing and retailing sectors. The family characteristics of this fraction reveal even more about its social character. The class backgrounds of the founders of these firms are varied, with four of their fathers' having been themselves members of the upper bourgeoisie and four divided among the middle bourgeoisie and the petit bourgeoisie. Only one founder, whose father was a sharecropper, came from a non-bourgeois background. Six of the nine founders, however, had fathers who were already firm owners in the silk industry or an allied manufacturing sector.

6. My use of the term 'desire' rather than 'goal' or 'sentiment' is intentionally provocative. In doing so, I hope to blur the boundaries that have come to be taken for granted in much of cultural and social theory between goals conceptualized as embodied (e.g., sexual desire) and those that are construed as mental constructs and thus denied the energy associated with the body.

7. The official histories of family firms in the Italian silk manufacturing industry constitute narratives of origins not dissimilar to the stories of coming-into-being that have been the conventional object of analysis of anthropologists studying oral traditions in pre-literate societies. I use the term 'origin narratives' to draw attention to the mythic significance of these accounts of the beginnings of firms. I do not intend to imply, however, that these narratives are purely fanciful tales ungrounded in historical fact. Rather, I mean that these narratives constitute a discursive practice that can tell us a good deal about Italian bourgeois ideas of personhood, capitalist firm, family, and, suc-

cession.

8. Four of the forty firms in my sample are headed by women. One of these women took over the firm after the death of her husband, two co-founded the firm with their husbands, and one bought out and succeeded a non-relative founder. While these women heads of firms share some of the goals and sentiments of succession of their male counterparts, they also differ from them in ways that would require too lengthy a discussion to undertake here.

9. The 1865 Civic Code was revised under Mussolini in April 1942, when the Civil and Commercial Codes were combined, but inheritance provisions were not affected. Although the 1942 code did make some important changes in family law - among them redefining the family as asocial' rather than a 'natural' institution - many Fascist planners were disappointed that there was not a more sweeping revision (Horn 1994).

10. John Davis (1973: 174-86) gives a detailed description of the proportioning of inheritance claims.

11. Testamentary inheritance applies only to what is left after the legitim-distribution. The testator's will is restricted by a number of provisions, among them that the inheritor must be eighteen and mentally competent (Lessico Universale 1979: 199) and that illegitimate children may not, if there are legitimate children, receive more than would be their share if legal inheritance (see below) were followed (ibid.: 181). Legal inheritance takes effect when there is no will, and applies to the part not distributed by legitim. Again there is a complex set of rules governing the proportion received by various kin under different scenarios (summarized in Davis 1973: 181). In general, Davis notes (1973: 180), legal inheritance 'places much more emphasis on the nuclear family than does the law of legitim, which, by excluding siblings and other collateral kin, emphasizes the direct line of descent and ascent. Even in legal inheritance, however, priority is given to the descendants and then to ascendant over spouse and siblings.' If there are no surviving kin, the legal inheritance and the legitim go to the state (Mengoni 1961: 5).

12. A second contradiction generated by this desire for the intergenerational transmission of the means of independence is that it leads to the pursuit of capital accumulation, which in turn requires the appropriation of the labour of workers: in short, the independence of some families necessitates the subordination of others.

13. Fathers with more than one son obviously had to figure out how to endow them with the means of production without depleting the capital of the family firm. The ideal was to accumulate enough capital to diversify the family's holdings so that each son could have his own, adequately capitalized, firm. Short of that would be to expand the firm so that each son could head a department of the firm. A full discussion of these strategies cannot be undertaken here, and I have chosen

instead to focus on the challenges that daughters' inheritance rights pose for male succession.

14. Until feminist critiques called into question the universal, biological basis of gender, the mother-child relation and women's kin relations in general tended to be naturalized in kinship studies, while men's relations were characterized as socially constituted (Yanagisako 1979; Yanagisako and Collier 1987).

15. See Schneider (1965) for an excellent analysis of this debate and the theoretical premises informing it.

16. See also Abu-Lughod and Lutz (1990) for a similar argument against the psychological, universalist, and essentialist view of emotion.

Part II

Choice and Tradition

4

Elite Succession Among The Matrilineal Akan of Ghana[1]

Nana Arhin Brempong

Introduction: The Changing Basis of Legitimacy among the Akan

This chapter seeks to show that, within the framework of hereditary matrilineal succession to stools[2] among the Asante and other Akan peoples of central and south-western Ghana, there is a trend towards the selection of the highly educated, professionals, or successful businessmen as stool occupants in the traditional state or 'traditional area';[3] and that these successful competitors for stools belong to Ghana's educated or business 'elite', defined as 'functional, mainly occupational groups which have high status' (Bottomore 1964: 8). The presumed or actual members of the elite are identified in the Akan language as *mpanyimfo*, the elders, echoing the gerontocratic nature of traditional government, the members of which were generally men of mature age. The *mpanyimfo* are indicated by their lifestyles - the possession of cars, European clothing, the location of their houses and their types of house, which all point to their high positions in government, administration or business, and to their potential membership of the modern ruling group. It is argued that this trend is a concomitant of the colonialist and post-colonialist transformations in the economic, political, and socio-cultural systems of the peoples of Ghana, which have altered the roles of traditional office-holders to the extent that they are obliged to demonstrate qualifications similar to those of the players in national politics; and that the trend suggests incipient changes in the basis of legitimacy in stool occupancy.

The chapter proceeds as follows:
1. the first section describes the rules of succession in traditional Akan polities;
2. the second section the colonialist and post-colonialist transformations and their effects on aspects of traditional rule;
3. and finally, the third section the succession to Asante stools.

The ethnographic 'present' is used here to describe the rules of succession, though there has been considerable change in their operation, because informants usually present the old rules without regard to changes in their application by the various bodies of selectors of rulers in Akanland. I have avoided the term 'chief', usually found in the literature on African political systems, because I have long felt that it does not adequately convey the ideas associated with Akan traditional rulerships. In place of 'chief', I use the term 'power-/authority-holders', depending on whether or not there is delegated authority, or the terms the Akan themselves use for the various grades of power - or authority-holding. I shall use mainly material from Asante for illustrative purposes, since I know it best.

Hereditary Sucession and The Traditional Elite

It should help appreciation of the present-day trends in the application of the Akan rules of succession to outline what are said to be the traditional rules, and the character of the elite that they engendered.

The Akan consist of sub-groupings distinguished by their occupation of well-defined territories and distinctive though mutually intelligible dialects of the Fanti-Twi language. They predominate in five of the ten regions of Ghana as follows:

Group	Region
Asante and Brong	Brong-Ashanti
Asante	Ashanti
Akuapem, Akyom, Asante	Eastern
Agona, Assin, Denkyira, Fanti, Twifo	Central
Ahanta, Aowin, Nzema, Sefwi, Wassa	Western

Akan-speaking peoples are also to be found as temporary or permanent migrants (Dakubu 1988: 52-6) in the other regions, particularly in Greater Accra, the location of the national capital.

As far back as their memory goes, the Akan have always lived in centralized political systems, in polities or states that they call *aman* (sing. *oman*). The Akan state is usually an aggregation of towns/villages, and their dependent or satellite settlements, farms or hunting lodges, the embryos of villages and towns. The territory of a state is divided into districts (*amansin*, sing. *omansin*) occupied by capital towns (*Nhenkro*, sing. *ahenkro*) and their dependent settlements. The district may also be seen as a purely geographical area in which a number of states may be located.

Within a state, there is a hierarchy of three basic offices: headship of the state, *omanhene*; headship of a division of the state, *ohene*; and headship of a town/village, *odikro*. The rights of succession to these offices, or stools, are regarded as the corporate property of the matrilineal descendants of the real or presumed founders of the capital town of the state; or of the division; or of the town/village. These descendants are known as royals/aristocrats, *adehyee*, and thus qualified to compete for the offices when they become vacant on the death or destoolment, removal from the stool, of an incumbent.[4]

The headships of these royal offices are male and female dualities: the occupants of both must belong to the royal descent group and complement each other. But there is a difference in the manner of their appointment. A male ruler has absolute discretion in appointing his female counterpart, though he may engage in constructive consultations with his councillors. But a female ruler (*ohemma*) is permitted to name a successor to a vacant stool to the electors[5] only after due consultation with the elders or heads (*mpanyimfo*) of the segments of the royal lineage; and the electors have the right of acceptance or rejection of the nominations by the royal lineage.

In the past, the royal lineage was guided by two basic rules that tended to enhance lineage unity. They were the rules of seniority and alternate succession. Senior men in age were expected to precede the junior; and succession to office was circulated among the men and women of the major segments of the lineage. Thus the offices of the *ohene* and *ohemma* were expected to be occupied by men and women of different segments. It is obvious from newspaper accounts of succession disputes that these rules are not now strictly observed. Early in the 1950s Busia stated that lineage unity was under heavy siege (Busia 1951: 211-17).

The consultation process means that the Akan reject the rule of primogeniture, combining the hereditary with selective principles. It is conceded that the maternal relatives of the founder of the town and occupant of the first consecrated stool (*apunnua*)[6] of a polity collectively have exclusive rights of succession to the stool. But it is also agreed that the ruled, represented by the heads of the major subordinate units of the polity, have the right to consultation and choice among the eligible successors. Therefore the choice of an *ohene* is an outcome of consultations between the ruling house(s) and the ruled.

These elements of negotiation and joint exercise of rights in the elective process are the basis of flexibility in the process and its adaptability to changing circumstances.

Wilks has suggested that the founders of the early Akan states, both in the forest areas and also in the coastal hinterlands, were men of enterprise, *abrempon*, who used their acquired wealth to purchase labour for the clearing of the virgin forests and started the process of expansion. Attempts were apparently made to re-enact the tradition of the use of wealth for the acquisition of followers or retainers and hence of power in the 1920s and 1930s: Wilks reports an applicant for two Kumasi stools as stating that though he knew himself to be customarily unqualified for their occupancy, he felt himself qualified in his application on the grounds of his wealth, while the legitimate successors were poor (Wilks 1979: 10-11; 1993: 91-120). In 1935-1940 the Asante traditional rulers, organized in the Ashanti Confederacy Council under the headship of the Asantehene, increasingly protested during meetings at the rate at which non-royal persons were seeking headships of traditional states and their sub-divisions through the offer of considerations of various kinds to the kingmakers (Busia 1951: 211-17).[7]

In addition to their hereditary rights of succession to the stools, the matrilineal descendants of the founders of states also constituted the economic elite. They were heirs to the wealth of the original founders of the state: land, gold and labour in the form of slaves, war-captives, debtors and pawns. The wealth of the aristocrats facilitated a distinctive life-style for them, though the simple nature of material culture in the period before colonial rule meant that distinctions in life-style were discernible mainly in personal wear and adornments (Bowdich 1873).

The administrative system of the Akan states was patrimonial. It was an extension of the king's household or palace, and the personnel collectively known as *gyasefo*, the people at the fireside, were retainers recruited from a variety of sources: the children of slave wives, war-captives, purchased slaves, the children of debtors, pawns, and free dependants (Rattray 1929a: 116). In Asante, an early law accredited to the first Asantehene, Osei Tutu, 1685-1712/17, which accorded Asante citizenship to these servicemen and forbade public references to their origins, promoted voluntary immigration of people from the neighbouring areas into Asante, some of whom entered the king's service (*som*).

Rattray, Wilks, McCaskie and Yarak have shown the complexities of the palace organization, and also the sources of remuneration in a non-wage economy.[8] In sum, practically every aspect of the Asantehene's private and public life was the subject of ministration by a distinct group of attendants who had a head: for example, *adwarefohene*, head of the bathroom attendants; *anonomsahene*, head of the stewards; *daberehene*, head of the bedroom attendants; *nsumankwahene*, head of physicians (Rattray 1929a: 116). The heads and the servicemen (*nhenkoa*, servants of the King) were remunerated, as in all patrimonial systems, by means of their participation in the administrative system: land grants with settled bondsmen and the exercise of judicial authority over them, a source of 'income'; benefices from the state in the form of shares in war booty, and commissions on tribute, tax and levy collection; shares in judicial fees; extortions in the judicial process; and trading capital. These were sources of wealth that formed the basis of their status as a political and economic sub-elite. They were collectively known as *obinom*; individuals were known as obi, an important person.[9] They may be distinguished as authority-holders, permitted by the heads of state and its divisions to exercise authority.[10]

Headships of the units of the palace organization were the gift of the heads of the political units. But over time, the process of appointment became subject to consultation with the 'elders' of the position, though the King's will always prevailed: consultation did not mean a veto.

Colonial and Post-colonial Transformations in The System of Traditional Rule

Traditional rule and its system of succession in the period of sovereignty were subverted by aspects of colonial and post-colonial governments (Busia 1951: Chapters 8-9 and Arhin 1991: 27-47).

As is well known, after two centuries of trading on the Gold Coast and its hinterland, the British imposed their rule over those territories; the present Central, Eastern, Western, Greater Accra and Volta Regions, collectively known as the Gold Coast, in 1874; the present-day Ashanti and Brong Ahafo Regions in 1896; and the present Northern, Uppereast and Upperwest Regions, then known as the Northern Territories, in 1901 (Fuller 1920: 214; Melcalfe 1964: 524).

Colonial rule meant the abolition of the sovereignty of the traditional states and their subordination to the colonial authorities, represented by the District, Provincial and Chief Commissioners and the Governor. The colonial government assumed the right of recognition of existing or newly-appointed traditional rulers, which meant the right to accept or reject the choices of the kingmakers. In Kumasi and elsewhere in Asante, the colonial government imposed individuals as traditional rulers for services rendered during the Asante revolt of 1900-1901. In certain areas in the Northern Territories the colonial government substituted traditional rulers of the Akan type for ritual figures, such as custodians of the earth, who had previously been moral leaders, with powers of persuasion only in dispute settlement (Rattray 1927; Fortes 1940: 239-72).

In the Akan areas, the assumption by the colonial government of the right to make and unmake traditional rulers subverted the traditional system of government by consent. It is true that the right of consent or rejection was exercised by a gerontocratic body of elders. But the elders, heads of political sub-units, normally represented the peoples of those units, so that there was, as both Rattray and Busia have tried to show, an element of non-formalized democracy in the system of government: the democratic element was strengthened by the correlative rights of the electors to remove rulers from office (Busia 1951: 64; Arhin 1994: 148-58).

In addition to the formal attack on traditional rule as the erstwhile embodiment of the sovereignty of indigenous government, and the subversion of 'custom' as the sanction of the right to rule, there were other aspects of the colonial situation that encouraged attempts at usurpation of the rights to office by what may be described as 'new men'. These aspects were the introduction of formal education; the 'rise' of an economic sub-elite as a consequence of changes in the economy; Christian proselytization; and changes in the roles of traditional rulers, resulting from colonial and post-colonial legislation.

Formal education began first in the Fanti areas of Elmina, Cape Coast and Anomabo, where the European trading forts were situated. Although education was at first limited to basic reading, writing and arithmetic, it was later broadened in scope and intensity when the 'merchant-princes' or principal trading men sent their sons to be educated in the United Kingdom. A result of this intensified education, principally through the agency of the Christian Missions, was to produce a body of educated men. These at first sought to support traditional rulers in safeguarding their authority against the encroachments of creeping colonialism, in such organizations as the Fanti Confederacy Council 1870-71, and the Aborigines Right Protection Society (1894-1947), but later competed with them for the leadership of the people in the search, successively, for constitutional reform and independence from Great Britain.[11]

In Asante between 1896, when colonial rule was imposed on a supposedly dismantled Kingdom, and 1935, when the kingdom was restored as the Ashanti Confederacy Council, intensified education by the Christian Missions and the colonial government at the capital towns of the Asante traditional states produced bodies of educated men who organized the Asante Kotoko Society in 1916 (Fuller 1920: 214-29; Busia 1951: 102-64 and Tordoff 1965: 188-204). The Kotoko Society included the future Asantehene, Sir Osei Agyoman Prempeh II (1931-70), and had two aims: to persuade the colonial government to repatriate the exiled Asantehene, Prempeh I, from the Seychelles Islands, and also to guide the Asante rulers in 'modern' ways. As in the other Akan areas of the Gold Coast colony, the educated Asante were later split into adherents and opponents of traditional rule, grouped, respectively, in the United Gold Coast Convention (UGCC), founded in 1947, and the Convention Peoples' Party (CPP), in 1949.

Changes in the economy under colonial rule reinforced the effects of education in the emergence of new men, who, by virtue of their wealth, were potentially rival leaders to the traditional rulers. The major changes in the economy were the introduction of cash cropping, mainly cocoa and marginally kola and coffee production, and an increase in retail and wholesale trading undertaken as agents of the European mercantile firms (Fuller 1920: Busia 1951 and Tordoff 1965).While there had been trading in the days before colonial rule, the expansionist Asante state had sought to regulate the acquisition and display of wealth in order to protect the integrity of the political system. One of the principal means of doing this was the exaction of taxes and levies, including death duties.

In 1901 and 1933 the Asante Akonfofo, wholesale and retail traders whom I have elsewhere called a 'non-literate sub-elite', protested to the British authorities against the proposed re-imposition of death duties, alleging that the exaction of those duties had hindered socio-economic progress in the days before the British (Arhin 1986: 25-31).

The Asante Akonkofo were the 'new men' in Asante. Some of them had acted as the collaborationists of the British in the Yaa Asantewa War (1900) against the British, and been granted the occupancy of some major stools (Tordoff 1965: 132; Wilks 1979: 6-7). On the whole, they opted to operate within the framework of traditional rule, while, as may be seen in the deliberations of the Ashanti Confederacy Council, some of them sought to use their wealth to 'buy' stools and replace legitimate heirs (Busia 1951: 211-17). They interpreted legitimacy in terms of economic success - a throw-back to the origin of the Akan states, so Wilks suggested (1979: 6-7).

Christian proselytization, which started on the Gold Coast in the late eighteenth century and intensified in the second half of the nineteenth, spread to Ashanti in the wake of the establishment of British rule. In all the Akan areas, Christian converts not only professed themselves freed from the 'worship' of the deities of traditional religion, but also from those services to the traditional rulers that they thought were associated with the veneration of ancestral spirits, such as was expressed in the libations during the periodic *Adae* and *Odwira* festivals. The converts considered as 'pagan' the ancestral spirits, *nsamanfo*, held in the Akan system of belief as the principal custodians of the material and non-material welfare of the political community, whose living descendants were therefore entitled to rule.

The converts also believed drumming and dancing on state occasions to be hateful to the Christian God. They protested at the ban imposed by traditional councils on farming in certain farm areas and on days dedicated to the Earth or river deities, which amounted to a defiance of the authority of the traditional rulers by the converts. The protest and defiance added to the crisis of confidence in traditional authority created by the activities of the colonial ruler (Busia 1951: 191).

Between 1874 and 1951, when Africans first entered the government of the Gold Coast, Ashanti, the Northern Territories and Togoland, the British successively attempted first to weaken and then to strengthen traditional rule. Early legislation sought to make it clear that traditional rulers were subject to the will of the British Government through the Governors of the Gold Coast and their subordinates. Later legislation, particularly the 1927 Native Administration Ordinance, also enacted for Ashanti and the Northern Territories in 1935 and 1948, made the Councils of traditional rulers junior partners in colonial rule, as local government bodies and as units in the colonial court system.[12]

It was as local government bodies and courts that the traditional councils antagonized the 'young men' by their levies and what were perceived as judicial extortions. In 1949 the 'young men' left the UGCC, led by lawyers and businessmen who were closely allied with the traditional rulers, and joined the CPP, led by the literate lower middle class. The leaders of the CPP thought that the traditional rulers ought to have only ceremonial functions.[13] Accordingly, when they won and exercised effective political power in 1957-1966, they stripped the traditional councils of their local government and judicial functions, and also retained the colonial government's erstwhile right of recognition of traditional rulers. They set up regional houses of Chiefs and gave them the responsibility of re-examining customary laws in various parts of the country for the purposes of uniform codification, and of the settlement of disputes among the traditional rulers. But traditional rulers were deprived of their financial base when the new local government bodies were granted portions of land revenues, formerly the preserves of the traditional councils. The 1969 Constitution of the Republic of Ghana established a National House of Chiefs, as a national integrative device, but with the same functions as the Regional Houses of Chiefs.

Enactments by the colonial and post-colonial governments on traditional rule diminished the customary roles of the traditional rulers. They were no longer war leaders, law-makers or law-enforcers. The significance of their role as 'priest chiefs' was greatly reduced under the onslaught of Christianity and the exigencies of colonial rule that, as in Asante, discouraged the major festival of *Odwira* in the fear that it would rekindle what they thought were the dying embers of Asante nationalism. The traditional councils no longer regulated economic activity through the observance of the periodic festivals; and therefore traditional rulers, already impoverished through the workings of the political economy of colonialism, ceased to be economic leaders. It became clear in the course of the twentieth century that in order to cope with the demands of their mediatory position between the colonial authorities and the educated and economic sub-elites, Akan traditional rulers had to be educated: the most successful traditional rulers on the Gold Coast, such as Nana Sir Ofori Atta I, Omanhene of Akyem Aboakwa in the present Eastern Region (1916-43) and Nana Sir Tsibu Darku, Omanhene of Assin Attandasu in the Central Region (1930-1982), were educated and offered examples to the Asante rulers.

The mediatory role of traditional rulers in the context of the colonial and post-colonial government entailed the following sets of activities: leading the political community into 'modernity' while safeguarding the essentials of the customary value systems; liaising between the central government and the political community for the purpose of attracting community development, roads, schools, health posts, and market-places; and mobilizing the people for communal work or financial contributions for public projects. These roles required education, and Table 4.1 below showing summaries of the biographies of the principal Asante rulers indicates the Asante response to the challenge of the new leadership roles.

Modern Asante Rulers

The impoverishment of traditional rulers and the progressive minimization of their significance during the rule of Convention Peoples' Party apparently made traditional political office unattractive, so that one needs some explanation to account for the tendency of well-educated, professional men and apparently prosperous businessmen to contend for, and sometimes to pay heavily for, succession to stools, particularly in Asante.

Table 4.1: **Summary of the Qualifications and Careers of the Asantehene and Asante Amanhene**

Name	Position	Age	Level of Education	Profession	Other Employments	Date of Enstoolment
Jacob Matthew Poku (Nana Opoku ware II) Clan: Oyoko	Astantehene	78	Secondary School Inns of of Court (B.L)	Draughtman Surveypr Barrister at Law	Building Inspector Barrister at Law Minister of State	1970
S.O. Gyimah -Kessie (Nana Osei Bonsu II) Clan: Brctuo	Mampomg- hene	58	University	Barrister, Aministrator	Legal Practitioner Bank Official Assistant Clark of Parliament University Registrar	1996
K.Oduro -adiyea (Nana Oduro Numa- pau II) Clan: Aduana	Esumegya- hene	69	University Trained in Accounting in the City of London	Chartered Accountant Adinistrator	Board Secretary Chief Internal Auditor Bank of Ghana Chartered Accountant[a]	1975
Kwama Asuma -du Nana Asumadu Sakyi II Clan:Aduaua	Kumawuhe -ne	55	University	Planning	Planning Officer	1973
Edward Yaw Boakye (Nana Otuo Siriiboe II) Clan: Oyoko	Juabenhene	53	University	Electrical Engineer	Electrical Engineer Farmer Businesman Industrialist (Palm Oil manufacturer)[b]	1970
Anthony Kwasi Mensah (Nana Wiafe Akenten II) Clan: Asona	Offinsohene	54	Elementary School		Clerk, Storekeeper	1993

Name	Position	Age	Level of Education	Profession	Other Employments	Date of Enstoolment
Robert Anane (Nana Aboagye Agyei II) Clan:Asoma	Ejsuhene	66	University Diploma Professional Training in Law	Legal Practitioner	Social Welfare Worker, Legal Practitioner	1993
Samuel Kofi Asiedu (Nana Owusu Aduanin II) Clan: Aduana	Denyasehene	70	University Diploma	Pharmicist	Business owner of Pharmach shops	1987
S.K.B Asante (Nana Susubir-irbi Krobea Asante) Clan: Asokore /Ekuona	Asokorehene	65	University doctorate in Law	Law Lecturer Legal Practitioner Administrator	Law Lecturer Legal Practitioner International Public Servant	1995
Kwame Akuoko Sarpong (Nana Akuoko Sarpong Clan: Aduana	Agogohene	58	University	Legal Practitioner	Legal Practitioner Minister of State Presidential 'Staffer'	1976
E.F. Apianing (Nana tiefun Ampratwum II) Clan: Bretuo	Ofoasehene	61	Elementary School, Trade School, Farm Trg	Technician in Mechanical Engineering	Technician in the Civil Service Poultry Farmer	1993
Victor Effah-Appenteng) Clan: Aduana	Bompatahene	52	University	Administrator	Diplomat, Civil Servant	1976

Name	Position	Age	Level of Education	Profession	Other Employments	Date of Enstoolment
Emmanuel Kwaku Dei II (Nana Okofrobu Kwakye Dopoah II) Clan: Oyoko	Asankarehe-neo	82	Elementary		Forestry	1970
Osei Tutu- (Ohene-ba adusei Poku) Clan: not relevant[c]	Akyempim-hene	49	University Doctorate in Law	Public Service	Diplomat	1992

a. Nana Oduro Numapau is also an oil palm grower, and a former Deputy Chairman of the Electoral Commission of Ghana.
b. Nana Otuo Sereboe II is perhaps the most enterprising Asante Omanhene. He has been a block-maker; and he nurses oil-pam seedlings for sale to his people in order to encourage agricultural diversification among them. He recently won the National Award for small- scale industries.
c. The Akyempim stool is reserved to the sons of Asante Kings, and, since they belong to their mothers' clans, the stool cannot be said to be 'owned' by any particular clan.

Two possible explanations come to mind. Firstly, the Asante and the other Akan groups regard rights in the stool as the highest possible kind of property. Therefore fellow lineage members and members of political communities generally put a good deal of pressure on the highly educated and others to secure the ancestral property in the legitimate line against possible usurpers.

Secondly, while the democratization of local government and the courts and the introduction of partisan politics debarred traditional rulers from areas of 'partisan' politics and reduced their influence, *coups d'état* enhanced their political status. The military regimes that have ruled Ghana for twenty-three out of forty years of independence[14] (1957-1997) used the 'durbars' or meetings of traditional rulers and their peoples as forums for delivering messages to, and eliciting the support of, the people.

In the periods of prohibited 'party politics', traditional rulers replaced regional and local party bosses as agents of politicization and for securing legitimacy for the military or 'revolutionary' regimes. In effect, stool-holding became an alternative means of securing political influence for those unable or unwilling to engage in national party politics: such aspirants have had to match the prestige of the performers in national politics, such as members of parliament.

Table 4.1 shows the level of education and *savoir faire* and the variety of employment of the major stool occupants in the Ashanti Region. The present Ashanti Region covers roughly the area of the old Asante Union, which since 1699 has been under the headship of the Asantehene. Table 4.1 shows that stool occupants are becoming increasingly educated, and that, in the contest for stools, the highly educated invariably win; sometimes the winners have rather tenuous claims to the stools.[15] In 1943, only the then Asantehene and Esumegyahene were literate to the elementary school level. The table also shows that nearly all the major stool holders are successful professionals who also command considerable resources. The biographical data that form the basis of the table show that many of them are engaged in other businesses than stool-holding, now scarcely regarded as full-time occupation, so that they need not depend on 'stool revenues' for their upkeep. Indeed, modern stool electors or 'kingmakers' prefer affluent candidates who, even in clear cases of rightful claims, are expected to make heavy payments for various purposes.[16] The heaviest givers succeed in securing the stool. In sum, kingmakers exploit the keen competition for stools to make money for themselves while apparently preserving the framework of legitimacy. It is extremely doubtful that the possession of 'blue blood', without professional qualifications or wealth, is sufficient to enable one to obtain a major stool. And there is increasing evidence that where there is wealth a clan membership rather than the membership of a localized lineage may be accepted as a qualification for a major stool.

Having noticed the growing significance of education as a qualification for stool occupancy, it appeared to me that the members of the stool-owning lineages would respond to the growing trend by showing collective interest in giving maximum education to potential successors, so that stool or public revenues would be used for the purpose:[17] in the 1940s, the Ashanti Confederacy Council imposed levies throughout Ashanti for the purpose of raising funds for scholarships for secondary and university education for Ashanti students. But when asked about the education of their young royals, a senior member of the Asante royal family denied collective interest in the education of the younger generation; he stated that the education of children was the exclusive responsibility of the child's father or real, not classificatory, mother's brother. It became clear that, since, traditionally, competition for stool occupancy was between segments of the stool-owning localized lineage,[18] which, as stated above, led to what Goody calls 'circulating succession' between segments, members of such segments would not collectively but severally seek education for their young members. Detailed investigation would show that the most successful competitors for stools are those whose fathers or mothers' brothers gave them high education.

There is also evidence of growing segmentation within royal matrilineages in the area of corporate rights in property and stool revenues. In the more economically important cities and towns, including Kumasi, members of the royal lineages are given plots of building land. But the wealth accrued from stool revenues, such as from building plots, tends to be expended on members of the stool occupants' minimal segments or their own children. I have heard complaints in several state capitals about the increasing impoverishment of royals belonging to segments other than those of past or present stool occupants. This, in part, explains the present intense conflicts and drawn-out disputes over succession to stools in the Akan area. These conflicts are essentially over the actual and potential wealth incidental to stool occupancy.

It facilitates the trend towards what may be called the auctioning of the rights of stool occupancy that voting has nearly replaced consensus-seeking in the making of power-holders. In situations of dispute with the female ruler, representing the royal lineage, or among the kingmakers, the latter resolve the matter by majority decisions. The resolution of disputes by voting has usually been followed by litigation at the judicial committees of the Regional and National Houses of Chiefs and the Supreme Court. These are the bodies authorized by the 1969, 1979 and 1992 Constitutions of Ghana to resolve chieftaincy disputes.

Conclusion

It has been argued in this paper that the flexibility of Akan rules of succession has enabled present-day selectors of their rulers to adapt their selections to the demands of the changing roles of traditional rulers. The selection of the members of the modern Ghanaian elite as traditional rulers is, perhaps, a continuation of the original Akan tradition of choosing those the state drummer calls 'men among men' or *abrempong*, men of enterprise, as fit to rule. But, clearly, the basis of the right to rule is undergoing transformation from the membership of a royal family to the possession of elitist qualifications. It is quite probable that, in the not very distant future, royal lineages without members with elitist qualifications will lose their rights of succession to those with affluent and educated members pretending clanship ties with the legitimate heirs.

Notes

1. I am grateful to Nana Asante, Registrar of the Ashanti Regional House of Chiefs, for the biographical data used for the construction of the summary table on the careers of the present major Asante traditional rulers.
2. 'Stools' and 'skins' are the physical symbols of traditional political office in the forest and savannah areas of Ghana respectively. The king of Asante (Anglicized as Ashanti), Asantehene, is said to sit on the Golden Stool, *sika kokoo*, signifying his incomparable wealth.
3. An area within the jurisdiction of a traditional paramount ruler, *oman hene*, that is, one who does not owe customary allegiance to another traditional ruler, is known to the Constitution of Ghana as 'traditional area', meaning 'state'. Such an area is normally divided into divisions headed by *ahene*, usually translated as 'chiefs'. I have tried to avoid the word 'chief' because it does not convey adequately the indigenous ideas about rulers.
4. There is considerable literature on Akan political organization; the basic texts are: Sarbah 1897, 1906; Rattray 1927; Busia 1951. For an early account, see Bosman 1705.
5. The electors, known currently in Ghana as kingmakers, normally consist of the most important of his subordinates, abrempon (sing. obrempon), who compose his council.
6. Known as the 'blackened' stool, usually kept in the stool room or stool chapel, *nkonuafieso*, and 'fed' and 'served' drinks during the forty-day *Adae* ceremony: see Rattray 1927.
7. Busia 1951: 211-17; also Ashanti Confederacy Council (ACC) Minutes 14 June 1935, in particular the Adontinhene's contribution; and the Minutes of the ACC for 13 June 1935
8. Rattray 1929a and 1929b; Wilks 1975, 1989: 414-76; McCaskie 1995: 27, 37-73, 1980: 189-208; Yarak 1990: 279-87
9. Baffour Osei Akoto, a senior counsellor, *okyeame*, of the Asantehene, told me of this meaning of obi, othewise understood as 'somebody'.
10. On the remuneration of court officials, see Wilks 1989; McCaskie 1980.
11. See Sarbah 1897, 1906; Arhin 1992.
12. Arhin 1991: Busia summarized his findings on the weakened position of the traditional ruler as follows:

The more fundamental causes of destoolment have been indicated in this and previous chapters: the rivalry among royals; the confused state of custom in a society in transition from a subsistence to an exchange economy; lack of definiteness about the chief's functions: his loss of economic resources: the emergence of the educated commoner or the successful cocoa farmer: the presence of a superior authority. These and the other changes discussed have destroyed the correlation between the chief's political power, religious authoirty, economic privilege and military strength, with consequent decline in his prestige and authority.

13. See a review of the Report of the Watson Commission set up by the Government of the Gold Coast to enquire into disturbances in the Gold Coast Colony in Arhin 1991.
14. The periods of the military regimes in Ghana were: 1966-1969, 1972-1979, 1981-1992.
15. It is widely believed in Ashanti that two or three of the major Asante rulers have very weak claims to their stools.
16. I was told that in one town in the Kumasi traditional area, the contestants paid ¢1.2 ($500 in current value) ¢1.3 and ¢1.5 million respectively and that the candidate who paid ¢1.5 million won the stool; see Busia 1951: 112-16 on discussions by the Asante rulers on the matter.
17. Busia1951: 211 quotes the Asantehene Osei Agyeman Prempeh II as saying: 'It is a disgrace for any chief not to train his nephews who will succeed him in future. The practice of offering and accepting bribes in connection with the enstoolment and destoolment of chiefs is very bad and should be stopped.'
18. On the Asante lineage and its sub-divisions see Fortes 1950: 252-84.

5

'Tradition' Versus 'Politics': Succession Conflicts in a Chiefdom of North-western Ghana

Carola Lentz[1]

In large tracts of what is today north-western Ghana the institution of chieftaincy was introduced by the British colonial government. The 'stateless societies' of the north-west knew the office of the earth priest, the custodian of the shrine to the earthgod, which was ideally vested in the patrilineage of the first settler of the locale, and fulfilled religious as well as secular functions of conflict management. In some settlements individuals other than the earth priests also held positions of power - 'strong men' would be the translation closest to the indigenous terms. They played an important role in local politics, especially during the latter part of the nineteenth century, when Zaberma and Mande warlords like Babatu and Samori made their incursions into the region. Some of the local 'strong men' would belong to the same patrilineage as the earth priests, but many would not; they were rich farmers, outstanding warriors, petty freebooters or traders who commanded a big 'house' and had built up a large following which often included slaves. Whether the resources of the 'strong man' - and hence his position - could be transferred to the next generation of the same patrilineage or whether they were 'lost' (through, for instance, the matrilineal inheritance of the movable goods) is a question that needs further research. But there is no doubt that the position of the 'strong man', unlike that of the earth priest, was not an inheritable office. Likewise, the 'strong men' were not organized into any kind of centralized polity.

During the first decade of this century, the British appointed 'native chiefs' who were to assist them in the administration of their newly acquired protectorate of the Northern Territories of the Gold Coast, and set up a hierarchy of village headmen, sub-chiefs and, at the top echelon, headchiefs (later called paramount chiefs). In many cases, the first subchiefs and headchiefs were recruited among the local 'strong men', who then used their networks of relatives, friends and clients to establish the chain of command that the British expected. However, while some elements of 'strongmanship' continued in the new institution, the inheritability of the chiefly office and the fixity of the hierarchy, on which the British insisted, were a radical departure from pre-colonial patterns. The colonial officials themselves were more or less conscious of this. With respect to the pre-colonial states of the Northern Territories, they were convinced that succession to chiefly office was automatic and without conflict if only the proper 'traditional' rules were respected.[2] But in the case of the stateless societies, they were aware that there was no single 'tradition' on which succession to chiefly office could be modelled unambiguously. In the early years of colonial rule, the British left it more or less to the house of the deceased chief to present a suitable successor. Later, they experimented with different methods of selection, based on patrilineal succession combined with plebiscitary elements. But even these attempts at closer prescription left a wide margin for conflict and local decision-making.

In these often conflict-ridden incidences of succession during the colonial period the ruling families and their factions as well as the wider communities developed competing notions of chiefly 'tradition'. Today, the litigants in chieftaincy conflicts usually claim that they act in accordance with the authentic 'tradition', while their opponents' aspirations are merely backed up by 'politics', i.e. involvement in the domain of the state and party politics. Chieftaincy affairs, the general opinion holds, belong to the domain of 'tradition' and should steer clear of 'politics' - which, of course, in actual fact plays as important a role in present-day chieftaincy conflicts as in succession disputes during colonial times.

Given the record of colonial experimentation and, more generally, of a whole century of tumultuous change and radical transformation of the stateless societies of the north-west, the notion of 'tradition' seems to be the most unlikely one to be invoked. What exactly this notion means to different groups and why and how it is being manipulated by the various local actors as well as external arbiters are some of the questions that this chapter seeks to address. The dichotomy of 'tradition' versus 'politics', which informs all post-independence chieftaincy conflicts, seems intimately linked to the continued attempts of investing the colonially created office with some measure of local legitimacy of *longue durée*. This chapter will therefore look at the various registers of legitimacy brought into play in chiefly succession, such as local rules of inheritance, accustomed patterns of 'bigmanship' and the authority of the office of the earth priest. I will discuss the contested production of chiefly history, and more specifically, 'family legends' that are used to back up a certain candidate in succession disputes. Finally, I will investigate the tensions between out-group ('political') factors, which demand a universalistically legitimate candidate - emphasizing, since the 1950s, the candidate's education and his relations with the Ghanaian government - and in-group factors, which partly operate in favour of candidates who are not easily acceptable to the wider community.

The case of Nandom, a small paramount chiefdom, which I will use to illustrate these themes, is a particularly suitable example: in the course of the past nine decades, there were six instances of succession, four during the colonial period and two after independence, providing us with a wealth of information on the patterns of decision-making and criteria of legitimacy. The history of the Nandom 'skin', as the chiefly office is now usually called (in allusion to pre-colonial northern Ghanaian kingdoms, where chiefs sat on a lion's skin), is certainly extraordinarily conflict-ridden - which is precisely the reason why local and colonial decision-making has found its way into written documents and is remembered in great detail. At the same, the conflicts are by no means untypical, but merely bring out processes that also inform the neighbouring chiefdoms.

Succession to the Nandom Skin: An Overview and Methodological Remarks

Kyiir, the first Nandom Naa, whom the British appointed in 1903 and made headchief over twenty-nine villages in 1905,[3] must have been a strong man well versed in the world beyond his natal village. According to most of my interlocutors, Kyiir was a relatively wealthy farmer and headed a large house with numerous wives and many sons. He was a trader in cloth, which he bought from the Mossi region further north and sold to the villages around Nandom; and he also knew how to sew. Some informants had him travel as far as Bobo-Dioulasso, and held that, because he returned safely from such a far-away place, he was believed to command magical powers. Others insist that Kyiir was also a prominent local freebooter and acquired a good number of slaves. A British report noted, among other things, that Kyiir was a Muslim - an observation that, if true, would underline his exceptional position in the local society of 'unbelievers'. Much controversy surrounds the question why and how he was made the first chief of Nandom. Some are convinced that it was the Nandom earth priest (belonging to a different patriclan) who eventually bestowed the chiefly office on his friend Kyiir. Others maintain that the British, without any interference from the earth priest, merely recognized Kyiir's already powerful position.[4] There is little doubt, however, that Kyiir looked the part and spoke various languages, which may have contributed to his colonial appointment. A most important qualification was his wealth (and the able command over the wealth of his relatives): it allowed Kyiir to 'entertain visitors', namely the British officials and their following, and to pay the fines that were levied on the chief and his subjects for the virtually inevitable breaking of some colonial commands.

In the early years, then, the duties of a chief seem to have required substantial pre-existing material resources rather than having allowed one to accumulate wealth. It is not until the early 1920s that the chiefs were able to command their subjects to perform free labour not only on government roads and resthouses, but also on their own fields. Eventually, the most important qualifications of an influential (head)chief were no longer pre-colonially acquired wealth and a 'strong man' position, but versatility in the communication with the 'white man' and the ability to organize the village headmen and their subjects into an effective workforce.[5] From the 1930s onwards, the command of English and a certain degree of formal education played an ever more important role in the discharge of the duties of a paramount chief. Since the end of colonial rule, finally, many people expect the chief, among other things, to represent his local community successfully to the outside world and to attract development projects and other resources for the benefit of his subjects.

These changing qualifications reflect the changing roles of the paramount chief in the local society and the wider world. They informed the opinion of the colonial (and later Ghanaian) government and, partly, of the local community on chiefs and suitable candidates. They also influenced the decision-making in the chiefly family itself. But they were only one of the factors that guided the family's decision between a number of candidates who were regarded as eligible according to an altogether different criterion, namely descent. Embittered debates over who is eligible to chiefly office and who are the correct decision-makers have characterized much of the history of the Nandom skin. Before entering into details, let me start with an overview over the six instances of succession and some remarks on the methodology of research.

The archival documents consulted for this overview (Table 5.1) clearly reveal that succession to the Nandom skin has been contested since the 1930s; it may have been so even from the very beginning. Particularly the last three transitions, in 1940, 1958 and 1984-85, were rife with conflict. Violent clashes in Nandom - allegedly between the followers of Rear-Admiral rtd. Kevin Dzang and Dr Charles Imoro - had occurred only two years before I started research in the area, and tensions are still simmering. Evidently, this affected my research, not only with respect to the present situation, but also the history of chieftaincy. Many of my interlocutors were, in one way or another, entangled in the conflicts, and tended to present a picture of the past that best suited their interests. Of course, I attempted to interview members of the different factions as well as apparently less involved outsiders, and to learn as much as possible about my interlocutors' engagement in current affairs. But even when I was beginning to understand who revealed what to me and for which motives and what was silenced, it was not I myself who set the terms of research, but the local elite.

There is another effect of such a conflict-ridden situation, rife with gossip and histories, that I would like to mention: namely, that it seduces the observer into over-estimating the importance of the contested office. My main research topic was the local history of ethnic identities; but by virtue of my curiosity and detective instinct I was drawn into devoting much more attention to chieftaincy affairs than I had planned originally. From a more detached point of view, I believe that, although succession conflicts

Table 5.1: Successions to the Nandom Skin 1903-1985

Name	Years of Rule [a]	Patriclan; genealogical position	Matriclan	Contestants	Remarks
Kyiir	1903/5-1908[b]	Bekuone	Somda	–	
Danye	1908-1918/9	Bekuone; distantly classificatory 'son' of Kyiir[c]	Somda	–	'destooled' or 'resigned'[d]
Boro	1918-1930	Bekuone; hotly contested genealogical position: a) according to the District Commissioner, Boro is Kyiir's 'son' and a 'very capable man with a large following'[e]; b) according to his sons, Boro is the grandson of Danaa (one of Kyiir's elder brothers) c) according to others, Boro was a son of Kyiir's sister's daughter and adopted into the Danaa family	Somda	–	
Konkuu	1931-1940	Bekuone; direct son of Kyiir	Some	Gome, a brother of Boro	contest decided by vote of the earth priest, the sub-chiefs and the village headmen[f]
Imoro Puobe	1940-1958	Bekuone; grandson of Kyiir Imoro's father Kyiir Der is Konkuu's full brother	Kpoda	Yuori, a son of Boro	contest decided by vote of all Nandom compound heads, village headmen and chiefs and headchiefs of Lawra and Jirapa; Imoro won by 627 votes against 402 for Yuori[g]
Polkuu	1958-1984	Bekuone: grandson of Kyiir direct son of Kolor, but brought up by Kolor's full brother Konkuu	Hien	Yuori, a son of Boro	contest decided by a government appointed commission of enquiry
Dr Imoro Charles	1985–	Bekuone; direct son of Imoro Puobe	Some	Gbeckature, a son of Boro; Rearadm Kevin Dzang; Dr E.N. Delle, C.Y. Dery	contest decided by government gazetting; contestants insist that conflict is still pending in court

For notes from table please see over.

a. It was not always possible to ascertain the exact dates.
b. See National Archives of Ghana, Accra (NAG), ADM 56/1/412 for Kyiir's appointment as chief in 1903 and ADM 56/1/50 for his appointment as headchief of Nandom; his death is reported in ADM 56/1/434.
c. Interview with Dennis Tiwiir, a son of Danye; see the list of interviews in the references.
d. According to the Lawra District Record Book (NAG, ADM 65/1/11: 40) Danye resigned in 1919; according to some local informants, he was 'destooled' because of the misdeeds of his eldest son.
e. Lawra District Record Book; NAG, ADM 61/5/11: 360.
f. Lawra District Record Book; ibid.: 373.
g. District Commissioner (DC) Lawra-Tumu to Chief Commissioner Northern Territories (CCNT), 23 Dec. 1940; Regional Archives Tamale (RAT), NRG 8/2/73.

easily stir up the public imagination and although chieftaincy continues to be a vital link between local communities and the state, the institution isonly one among others that affect the north-westerners' daily lives. The Catholic Church, schools and various government agencies, as well as the many peasants' and labour migrants' associations, are just as important, not to mention the role of kin and friends. Hence the reader needs to bear in mind that this chapter focuses on just one aspect of local history and politics in the north-west.

As was to be expected, I was accused of being partisan - incidentally by each one of the parties to the 1984-85 conflict - and my first publication on the history of the Nandom skin (Lentz 1993) was harshly criticized as 'washing dirty linen in public'. But my apparently increasing knowledge of precisely the 'dirty linen' made many interlocutors volunteer additional information in order to 'correct' the 'wrong picture' that I allegedly held. Consulting the relevant archival sources helped to specify dates and other details as well as the role of the colonial officials; but the British reports left important gaps that only oral history could fill. There remain many instances in which it has not been (and probably never will be) possible to come up with any 'objective' account of the events that would go beyond mutually exclusive interested versions. Even if such 'objectivity' could be attained (and some versions can indeed be classified as non-factual), it is still of great interest to research into the politics of the historical imagination of the different actors.

It is, however, highly problematic to put into writing and publish what has so far largely been an 'oral' history of conflict. The few documents that exist and are accessible to the litigants, such as the colonial lists of chiefs, have become ammunition in the recent succession conflict. It is certainly no coincidence that the only copy of the proceedings of the 1958 commission of enquiry, which contains verbatim records of the oral testimonies of all witnesses on the history of the Nandom skin, is kept under lock and key by the incumbent Nandom Naa. He feels that it is one of his trumps, and told me in no uncertain terms that he would only disclose it in court. It was one of his contestants who allowed me to copy the summary of the proceedings (see below) - but he also expressed his fears that anything I wrote could be used in court. There is no doubt that wrote documents, including the anthropologist's reconstructions, have become a new source of power, especially when a case moves from the local and regional levels to the National House of Chiefs and the High Court in Accra, over which local actors have little control. I have no ready-made answer to the political and ethical questions this entails. I can only avoid presenting contentious details that are highly relevant to the local actors, but less central to the more general themes I wish to address. In what follows, I will emphasize what I see as the underlying structural dimensions of the conflicts of succession, which also allow one to compare Nandom with other cases of a colonially introduced chieftaincy.

Rules of Inheritance - Lines of Conflict

Although the new chiefs were backed up by the colonial powers, they needed to invest themselves with a modicum of legitimacy according to accustomed local standards if they were to exercise their office effectively. Fear of the coercive measures that the district commissioner could inflict upon those who opposed the new dignitaries was a necessary, but not a sufficient, basis of chiefly authority. One source of legitimacy was certainly the office of the earth priest. In many cases, the new chiefs were selected from the earth-priest families, and initially regarded as a sort of messenger of the custodian of the earth shrine. The other source of authority was, as was mentioned above, 'bigmanship'. There are few documents on the methods of selection of the first chiefs, but the records do witness to a process of trial-and-error during the first two decades of colonial rule. A number of chiefs - in colonial parlance 'wicked' or 'weak' ones, whose subjects repeatedly fled across the border to French territory and boycotted the colonial 'road labour' demands - were replaced by office-holders who seemed to command more respect. In some cases, these new office-holders came from a different patrilineage, and the fact that chieftaincy had first been bestowed on another house could give rise to embittered disputes in future successions (see Lentz 1998a: Chapters 3 and 5).

Nandom Naa Kyiir, as outlined above, did not belong to the earth-priestly lineage, and drew rather upon his pre-colonial 'bigmanship'. Apparently he had no great difficulties in bringing under his authority the twenty-nine villages that still today form the nucleus of the Nandom Traditional Area, as it is called since the 1970s; and by contrast with what occurred in neighbouring chiefdoms, only a few complaints of 'lack of control' were recorded. This would not have been possible had Kyiir not built up a leadership position before the arrival of the first colonial officials.[6]

Incidentally, Kyiir was the first headchief of the new Lawra District who died. His succession must have been the test case for the question whether the colonial regime had bestowed the chiefly office on an outstanding individual or on a corporate group, and if the latter was the case, how the boundaries of this group were to be defined. Clearly, the British left little doubt that they wanted the new office to be inheritable. For the local actors, however, this may not have been so obvious, particularly in cases like Kyiir's, where the chiefly office was not vested in the earth-priestly lineage. Unfortunately, we know little of the kind of debates that may have arisen after Kyiir's death. We do know, however, that the Nandom skin has always remained within the same patriclan (Bekuone), and that from the 1930s onward there have been (successful) attempts to narrow the group of eligible candidates down to an ever-smaller segment of Kyiir's patrilineal offspring.

At this juncture, I should explain briefly the rules of inheritance that are predominant among the Dagara of the Nandom area. Each person belongs to one of over forty exogamous patriclans that are inherited from one's father, and to one of the seven matriclans, which are inherited from one's mother. Marriage is virilocal, and in polygamous families the sons of the head of the house usually belong to the same patriclan, but different matriclans. The land, the house and the ancestral shrines are inherited patrilineally; movable goods, such as cattle, clothes, money, etc., matrilineally. Full brothers of the deceased were the preferential heirs, but if there was no patrilineal offspring with the 'correct' matriclan, wealth moved out of the house (see J. Goody 1956, 1962). There were a number of strategies to circumvent this, and particularly since the advent of the Catholic mission in the 1930s there has been a strong trend towards the patrilineal inheritance of movable goods. However, during the reign of the first three Nandom chiefs, the matriclan still played an important role for the inheritance of movable wealth.

If chieftaincy was to be inherited, was it to be treated like a movable good? Or was it similar to the succession to the headship of the house, which followed patrilineal lines? These questions were important because, as I explained above, the duties of a chief required some wealth, and a merely patrilineal heir of the deceased chief might not have inherited the movable wealth of his predecessor. From my evidence it appears that the matriclan was indeed taken into account in the first two successions to the Nandom skin. Kyiir, Danye and Boro belonged to the same matriclan (Somda). Danye, a respected Bekuone family head in a neighbouring village, was wealthy on his own account; he was made chief because Kyiir's sons were still too young to succeed their father. As the potential spoils of chieftaincy became more evident, however, Kyiir's sons seem to have developed an interest in bringing the office back into their house.

This is where Boro came into play. The only fact, however, on which all of my interlocutors agreed was that Boro had a strong personality and commanded some wealth - to which he is said to have greatly added during his term of office. The origin of Boro's wealth and his precise genealogical link with Kyiir are hotly contested. It is not altogether clear whether the disagreement dates back to Boro's times or whether it developed during later succession conflicts. Be that as it may, during the 1985 succession conflict members of the Boro house wrote petitions that assert, among other things, that Boro was a patrilineal 'grandson' of Kyiir, but from a different house - because Boro's father (Vana) was a son of one of Kyiir's elder brothers (Danaa). How did Boro become Nandom Naa? According to this version from the Boro house, 'old man' Danye suggested to the British that Boro should succeed him and that afterwards, in turn, Danye's son Kumbile should take over from Boro.[7] This version also claims that Kyiir was merely a head of family, not a chief, and that Boro was the first substantial Nandom Naa because he was the first to receive the colonial chiefs' medallion.[8]

In this account, considerations of matriclan and inheritance of wealth are not mentioned. The versions from members of Kyiir's house, on the other hand, attribute Boro's strong position - which was acknowledged by making him chief - not least to the fact that he was one of the heirs of Kyiir's wealth. They claim that Boro was an 'illegitimate' child of one of Kyiir's sisters or nieces and thus belonged to the same matriclan as Kyiir and, because children of unmarried women are adopted by their mother's paternal house, the Bekuone patriclan. Boro, as one interlocutor saw it, could lay claim to Kyiir's wealth on account of his unique position in the clan system, and was supported by Kyiir's sons (of different matriclans), who thus ensured that part of Kyiir's inheritance remained in the house. It was Boro's wealth, in addition to his leadership qualities, so the argument continues, that enabled him to replace Nandom Naa Danye. The Boro-house critics of these versions insist that if Boro had actually been an 'illegitimate' child, he would never have been eligible for the skin.

Whichever version one finds more plausible, after Boro's term of office considerations of matriclan seem to have decreased in importance. The conflicts now rather revolved around the competition between two patrilineally related houses, namely Kyiir's and Boro's, whatever the matriclans of the contestants. The competition made itself felt for the first time after Boro's death. However, there is consensus that when Gome, a brother of Boro, contested with Kyiir's son Konkuu in 1930, he did so single-handedly, while the rest of the Boro family had agreed that Konkuu - whom Boro himself allegedly nominated as his successor - should become the new Nandom Naa. The Boro family insist, on the other hand, that they only agreed to Konkuu on condition that afterwards the chiefly office would return to their house. But after Konkuu's death in 1940 Puobe Imoro, one of Konkuu's brothers' sons, challenged the candidate of the Boro family. The contest was fierce, and it is this succession that most of my informants regard as the beginning of 'outside interference' in the succession to the Nandom skin.

The Colonial Creation of 'Traditions of Customary Succession'

Nandom Naa Konkuu's death in April 1940 occurred a few years after the introduction of 'indirect rule' in the Northern Territories. In 1934, the colonial officials had amalgamated a number of the smaller chiefdoms and established confederate 'native authorities', which consisted of various previously independent headchiefs (now called divisional chiefs) and their sub-chiefs. The 'native authorities' were responsible for the collection of the head tax, the construction of roads and schools, and - important for our context - the codification of 'native laws and customs'. The chiefdom of Nandom became one of the four divisions of the Lawra Confederacy Native Authority, which was presided over by the senior headchief, first Nandom Naa Konkuu, and, after his death, Lawra Naa J. A. Karbo.

One of the first topics that the Lawra Confederacy chiefs discussed at length during their regular conferences was the question of succession to chiefly office. The assembled chiefs asserted that there were no long-standing 'native customs' with respect to chieftaincy, but agreed that it was necessary to create 'traditions of customary succession'.[9] The first attempt to fix such 'traditions' drew upon the locally dominant rules of inheritance, and decreed:

> Lobi. Sucession is matrilineal. If a man dies his eldest brother by the same mother will succeed, failing this his sister's son the sister being by the same mother. Failing both these the succession goes to the maternal uncles' family in the same way. ...
> Dagarti. Succession is patrilineal. If a man dies his eldest brother by the same father will succeed, followed by all the other brothers in order of seniority i.e. age. Failing this, the succession will go to the sons of the deceased and his brothers in order of these sons' seniority i.e. age.[10]

In addition, certain 'disabilities' were to make a candidate ineligible, namely 'blindness', 'leprosy' and, interestingly, 'unpopularity'.[11] Clearly, the rules were by no means unambiguous. Nandom, for instance, was regarded as 'mixed Lobi-Dagarti' and could have drawn on either 'custom'. None of the divisional chiefs who made the rules had acceded to his office in accordance with them. Lawra Naa Karbo, a 'Lobi', belonged to a different matriclan than his predecessor; Nandom Naa Konkuu, regarded as a 'Dagarti', was neither the direct brother nor the son of the late Naa Boro.

These first codified rules remained without practical consequences. When in 1938 the Jirapa Naa, one of the divisional chiefs of the Lawra Confederacy, died, the district commissioner began by examining whether the candidates were 'eligible by birth' and not 'too old, too young or too characterless', but then proceeded to introduce an additional criterion of legitimacy, namely the 'secret ballot'. One of the candidates insisted he had been nominated by the late Jirapa Naa himself, but the district commissioner brushed this aside. He would have liked to guide himself by 'native custom', explained the British official, 'but in this district where no chiefs existed before our arrival, there can be no question of consulting any custom, except our own. And it may be said that our own custom is to see that the man appointed is congenial to the other chiefs and people, trustworthy by government and as far as possible of unblemished character.'[12] In the eyes of the British, the 'secret ballot' - ten votes for each divisional chief, five for the Jirapa sub-chiefs, three for headmen, two for the Jirapa earth priest and finally one vote for each compound head of Jirapa 'town' - was the best method to ascertain the popularity of the future chief. The district commissioner was surprised, however, that the vote in Jirapa was not competitive and that the successful candidate won with only two dissenting votes.

The unanimity in Jirapa notwithstanding, the district commissioner insisted that the 'secret ballot' be codified as 'native law'. The discussions at the Native Authority conference that preceded the agreement on the new 'customs' of succession are an instructive example of the search for some measure of local legitimacy for the new chiefly office. The chiefs emphasized their relationship with the earth priest, and eventually suggested a mixture of criteria - the veto right of the earth priest, principles of patrilineal descent, and the colonially introduced 'secret ballot':

> The Lawra Na related, and the meeting agreed ... that chiefship was a modern innovation, and that very little custom attached to rules of succession. A very lengthy discussion then took place, in which the views of nearly every chief present were heard. The method of the secret ballot adopted in the appointment of the present Jirapa Naa was explained and discussed. It transpired that the first chiefs appointed on the European arrival were nominated to the first Commissioners by the Tingansobs [earth priests], and that in this action lay the only 'Custom' that could be said to pertain. It was agreed that in all future appointments the following principles and procedures should be carried out, and should be regarded as 'customary':

a. that a candidate for chiefship must be a member of the patrilineal family of a former chief;
b. that a candidature must be approved by the Tingansob of the area concerned;
c. that election of a candidate to the chiefship shall be by secret ballot ...[13]

The new rule of patrilineal descent of the candidate was both more exclusive and more flexible than the rules laid down in 1935. On the one hand, considerations of matrilineality were excluded; on the other hand, it was never defined who belonged to the 'patrilineal family of a former chief'. The vagueness may have been deliberate, because at the time of the chiefs' discussions the contest over late Nandom Naa Konkuu's succession was already in full swing. Boro's son Yuori and Kyiir's grandson Imoro had presented their claims, the earth priest gave his assurance that both candidates were eligible, and the district commissioner convoked a 'secret ballot' to which he invited the compound heads of the whole of the Nandom Division, in addition to the neighbouring divisional chiefs and the Nandom sub-chiefs. Imoro won with 627 against 402 votes - a result that convinced the British official that 'the election has not been previously "fixed"'.[14] Some of my interlocutors, however, insisted that Imoro won by a very narrow margin, and only because the votes of the neighbouring divisional chiefs, as a result of certain marriage relations, tipped the balance in his favour. Imoro's supporters, in turn, believed that he had won nearly unanimously. None of my informants estimated the number of votes anywhere near the above-mentioned result. All agreed, on the other hand, that the ballot was an imposition of the colonial government and went 'against custom'.

The Lawra Conferederacy chiefs had protested against the colonial introduction of a popular vote on the chiefly successor as early as 1954, and decided that 'balloting for chiefship' was undesirable if there were 'capable sons of the deceased chief'.[15] Balloting indeed no longer played a role in the Nandom succession conflict of 1958, but neither did the 1954 rule of filial succession: Yuori, who competed again, stood against Polkuu Paul, a patrilineal 'cousin' and not a son of Imoro. This time, the conflict was eventually decided - in favour of Polkuu - by a government-appointed commission of enquiry. Interestingly, Yuori's followers later insisted that there should have been the 'traditional' ballot.

By the late 1950s, then, the candidates could draw on a number of different 'traditions', created by the colonial officials, the chiefs' conferences and local precedents: patrilineal descent, nomination of the candidate by the deceased chief, agreement of the family elders on a suitable successor, consultation of the earth priest, and secret ballot. Moreover, succession conflicts became an arena in which the inner-family criteria of acceptability of a candidate competed with outgroup criteria such as the new chief's education and his political standing. In the next section, I will show how the different rules and criteria were brought into play and how party politics became an important factor in succession conflicts.

Education and Party Politics: The Succession Conflict of 1958

The succession conflict of 1958 created a deep rift between the competing factions that has continued to affect chieftaincy affairs in Nandom until the present day. When the tension rose after each party had installed their candidate as the new Nandom Naa, the government of the now-independent Ghana saw the necessity to appoint a committee of enquiry. The committee consisted of a member of the Ministry of Local Government in Accra, one northern and one southern chief, and was 'to inquire into the correct method in tradition of selecting a Nandom-Na and to report whether Konkou Polkuu Paul or Borrow Yuori is properly the occupant of the Nandom skin'.[16] The ten committee hearings developed into an arena of contest over the history of chieftaincy in Nandom. I will briefly outline some of the arguments and then explain the political context in which the conflict and the hearings took place.

Yuori explained to the committee that after Nandom Naa Imoro's funeral he had told the Nandom earth priest that he, Yuori, wanted to be the next chief. The earth priest, Yuori asserted, 'agreed to install him as chief'.[17] Polkuu, in turn, insisted that Imoro, on his deathbed, had nominated him as his successor. With the exception of the Boro section, Polkuu reported, he enjoyed the support of 'the Members of the Royal Family' and particularly those members who were 'entitled to elect a Chief'.[18]

When attempting to invest their claims with historical legitimacy, Polkuu, Yuori and their witnesses presented different accounts of the origins of chieftaincy. Yuori stated that the first Nandom Naa who the British appointed had not been Kyiir, but Daga, a member of the house of the earth priest, and that later Daga asked Kyiir to take over as chief because he, Daga, 'could not perform the double duties of a chief and a priest of the land-god'. In accordance with the Lawra Confederacy chiefs' conference discussions, Yuori claimed that traditionally the earth priest 'selects a chief and presents him to the People'.[19] Conversely, Polkuu asserted that Kyiir, 'a brave, rich and noble man', had even in pre-colonial times been 'virtually a chief of his people,' and that, owing to specific circumstances, only Kyiir's family was present when he was officially appointed chief by the British, not the earth priest. In consequence, the earth priest had 'no official duties to perform at the installation of chiefs at all'. Rather, it was by nomination through the dying chief and later approval by 'the Royal Family' that a new Nandom Naa was 'traditionally' selected.[20] Unsurprisingly, Polkuu and Yuori presented the past four accessions to the Nandom skin in a way that demonstrated how firmly the rule of succession that favoured their own claims was rooted in 'tradition'.

In the eyes of the committee, the incumbent earth priest failed to support Yuori's case when he stated that 'after the transfer of chieftaincy to Chiir by Dagar, the chiefs were nominated by the dying chief and approved of by his [the earth priest's] predecessors and himself'. The committee took this for evidence which supported Polkuu's claims and concluded that:

1. The Correct method in tradition of selecting a Nandom-Na is by Nomination by the dying or retiring chief.
2. The second traditional method which may be used in certain cases is selection by the Members of the Chief's Family and the approval of the People which is signified by general acclamation.
3. That Kunkuu Polkuu Paul has been made Chief by these two methods combined and therefore Kunkuu Polkuu Paul is properly the occupant of the Nandom Skin.[21]

The formulation here of the second 'method' in particular was ambiguous, because it could be interpreted as reintroducing the plebiscitary element once established by the colonial officials and later dismissed by the Lawra Confederacy chiefs. Consequently, when Yuori, supported by nineteen village headmen, petitioned against the committee's decision he no longer insisted on the earth priest's prerogatives but on the 'tradition' of the ballot. However, Yuori not only appealed to 'tradition'; he also drew on the secular radical-democratic (and partly anti-chief) discourse that was *en vogue* particularly in the circles of Kwame Nkrumah's CPP (Convention People's Party), the party that had led Ghana into independence:

> So long as there is rivalry there should be ballot ..., that there is no record in the pass [sic!] in our tradition and customs that empowers or obligates any Royal Family to elect a Naa for the people. Why? Because he is not going to rule only the Royal Family but all the people and therefore we the masses are at the liberty to give our wish which must be respected ... Sir, the tradition in all respect must be recognise [sic!] or honoured, as long as there are two claimants to the vacant 'skin' we must go on ballot to elect one; that we want every compound owner of the Nandom Division to cast a vote each, and that we shall accept whosoever is unanimously elected per the majority votes.[22]

The Governor-General dismissed the petition on the grounds that no right of appeal existed once government had accepted a committee of enquiry's findings, and gazetted the new chief.

It is not clear if the committee of enquiry actually had a popular ballot in mind when stating that the new chief needed 'general acclamation'. But by claiming that the family's candidate should be acceptable to 'the People', it certainly pointed to the complicated relationship between ingroup and outgroup factors of chiefly legitimacy. Tensions between these factors played an important part in the 1958 conflict. With respect to the support of a wider local constituency, namely the village headmen and chiefs of the Nandom Division, Polkuu and Yuori seem to have been on a par. But there were other extra-family criteria. By the 1950s, some measure of formal education had become an important prerequisite for the discharge of chiefly duties, particularly at the level of the paramount chiefs, not least because they continued to play a part in the increasingly literate local government institutions. Moreover, educated chiefs were more likely to become successful representatives of their communities in the wider political arena. In this respect, Polkuu had clear advantages over Yuori: while Yuori was basically an illiterate farmer, Polkuu was a trained teacher who, due to his education in the Northern Territories' capital Tamale, could benefit from close connections with many members of the regional political and chiefly elite. Even my interlocutors from Boro's house admitted that with regard to the 'changing times' of the 1950s and 1960s, Polkuu was the more suitable candidate. The Boro house, too, explained one of them, would have put up an educated candidate, had not Yuori insisted that his seniority prevailed over the aspirations of younger (but more highly educated) members of his family. However, members of the Boro family insist that Polkuu won the contest not only because of his better education, but also due to the 'manoeuvres of government' and 'through politics'.

'The time when politics came', as local informants refer to it, is the time of the 1950s and early 1960s, when party politics and local conflicts became deeply entangled. After the Second World War the colonial government had replaced the 'native authorities' by a dual system of State

Councils, which were to concern themselves exclusively with chieftaincy affairs, and District and Local Councils, which were responsible for all local administrative matters and whose members were one-third appointed by chiefs and two-thirds elected by general vote. In addition, the north was finally granted representation in the colony-wide Legislative Assembly. It was in this context that political parties such as the UGCC (United Gold Coast Convention), from which the CPP later broke away, started to proselytize also in the north, particularly among the small educated elite. Many northern chiefs, however, supported the oppositional NPP (Northern People's Party). Programmatically, the NPP was formed in order to safeguard northern interests in the new political union of the Gold Coast Colony, Asante and the Northern Territories, which in 1957 amalgamated into independent Ghana. In practical terms, however, it was mainly personal networks, created through chieftaincy and patriclan ties, to which the educated NPP activists - just like the CPP followers - appealed when canvassing for votes.[23]

Lawra Naa J. A. Karbo was among the founding fathers of the NPP in the Lawra District. His son Abeyifaa, then teacher at the Lawra middle school, won the Legislative Assembly seat of the Lawra-Nandom constituency in the elections of 1954 and 1956. In Nandom, the most active NPP member came from the Gaamuo house, a section of the earth-priest family - W. K. Dibaar, a teacher and a colleague as well as a friend of Abeyifaa Karbo. Dibaar never stood in elections, but won his extended family over to the NPP. Initially, Nandom Naa Imoro also supported the NPP. But owing to long-standing rivalries between the Nandom and Lawra chiefs, when Imoro 'became aware that the NPP candidate would be Abayifaa Karbo ...', he changed his mind, preferring to support a candidate from his own town regardless of party' (Ladouceur 1979: 120-1). In the 1954 elections Imoro supported a candidate not only from his own town, but his own family, namely Polkuu Paul, who stood as an independent candidate - but an 'independent CPP', as my informants explained. In 1956, Imoro came out openly in favour of the CPP candidate, and at the same time petitioned that the Nandom Division should secede from the Lawra Confederacy.

Soon afterwards, Imoro was told in no uncertain terms by the Lawra Confederacy State Council that he should consider himself 'removed ... from his office as a chief'.[24] It was a coalition of the NPP-supporting paramount chiefs of the Lawra Confederacy, the Nandom earth-priest family and a number of chiefs and earth priests from other villages of the Nandom Division who joined in the attempt to destool Imoro. Some of Imoro's local opponents had old grudges against him, such as, for instance, the Nandom earth-priest family, who had quarrelled with Imoro over land rights and the allocation of rents; others seem to have mainly taken offence at Imoro's change of mind from NPP to CPP and his attempt to secede from the Confederacy. But because of the constitutional separation between local and party politics on the one hand and chieftaincy affairs on the other, the party-political motivations of the destool-ment attempt were never voiced officially. Before the Lawra Government Agent - until mid-1958 still a British official - Imoro's critics claimed that Imoro had gone against 'the customary law of our land and the rules of our chieftaincy' and therefore had to be destooled by the very Lawra Confederacy chiefs who had voted him into office in 1940 (see Lentz 1998a: Chapter 13).[25]

Before any definitive decision was reached, Imoro died. The factions in the ensuing succession conflict continued the alliances of the destoolment attempt. Polkuu was backed up by the descendants of Kyiir and by the CPP supporters on the local as well as on the national level; Yuori counted on the Boro house and the Lawra Naa and his son Abayifaa, as well as local NPP followers, particularly from the Nandom earth-priest family. When discussing the details of these alignments with my interlocutors, however, partisan points of view made themselves felt. Some claimed that Yuori had initially supported the CPP and changed to the NPP only after his defeat in the chieftaincy conflict; others asserted that he had already had a hand in the destoolment attempt, and joined the NPP in order to further his own claims to office. Similarly, some stated that Imoro as well as Polkuu Paul had supported the CPP throughout, while others stressed aspects of 'political gamble' and pointed to the CPP government's tactics of backing those candidates in chieftaincy conflicts who would in return promote CPP interests. And, unsurprisingly, Polkuu's opponents claimed that he was supported by the commission of enquiry only because of his CPP affil-iation, while Polkuu himself emphasized his 'traditional' legitimation.

In any case, there is no doubt that from the mid-1950s onwards chief-taincy affairs and (party) politics became inextricably entangled, not only in Nandom, but in the whole of Ghana (see Robertson 1973; Staniland 1973; Arhin 1985: 112-14 and Wilks 1989, for some examples). While con-stitutionally chiefs are no longer accorded any official political role, polit-ical parties do use the influence of chiefs to canvass for votes, and military governments to secure a modicum of rural support and to explain gov-ernment politics to the people. Aspirants for chieftaincy, on the other hand, trade their support of a political party or the government of the day for the latter's assistance in securing the desired office. Nevertheless, Ghanaians insist on distinguishing between the sphere of 'politics' and the sphere of 'tradition', and while they acknowledge that in practical terms it is necessary to use 'politics' in order to become chief, the legitimacy of the chiefly incumbent is ultimately seen to rest on 'tradition'. In the final sec-tion, I want to explore these notions of 'politics' and 'tradition', using the example of the most recent succession conflict in Nandom.

'Tradition' Versus 'Politics': The Succession Conflict of 1985

Predictably, when the Nkrumah government was overthrown by a military coup in 1966, Yuori attempted to redress his defeat. He sent a petition to the Chieftaincy Secretariat in Accra that complained that only because they had been 'staunch supporters of the Kwame Nkrumah rigime [sic]' Polkuu Paul and his section 'unlawfully claimed also to be entitled to the Nandom skin'.[26] However, it seems that Yuori did not enjoy much support and that Nandom Naa Polkuu was popular enough to ride out the attack. It was only after Polkuu's death in 1984 that the old factions re-emerged with renewed vigour. This time, Yuori's junior brother Gbeckature, then working as regional stores inspector, put forward the claims of the Boro 'gate', as he now called it, and secured support from Gaamuo Le-ib, who claimed to be the legitimate earth priest of Nandom. As for Kyiir's house, matters were more complex. Nandom Naa Konkuu, Imoro and Polkuu had all come from a single section of the Kyiir family, who now maintained that only they were entitled to the Nandom skin.[27] Disagreement within this section, however, resulted in the presentation of two competing candidates: C. Y. Dery, a brother of the late chief Imoro, contested in the name of the house elders and on the principle of his own seniority; Imoro's son, Dr Charles Imoro, based his claim, in continuation of Polkuu's arguments in 1958, on an alleged will of his predecessor. In addition, Dr E. N. Delle and Rear-Admiral (rtd) Kevin Dzang, who come from other sections of the Kyiir family, put forward their claims and argued that the Imoro-Polkuu section had monopolized the chiefly office for far too long.

Shortly after the final funeral rites for the late Polkuu, and while family consultations were still going on, Dr Imoro's supporters organized his installation ceremony, which seemed to receive the tacit support of the Rawlings government. This provoked a flurry of petitions by Dzang and Gbeckature to the Upper Regional House of Chiefs and to the Chieftaincy Secretariat in Accra. When the petitions remained without response, Dzang seems to have wanted to create a fact of his own, and he also had himself installed as Nandom Naa. A few months later, however, the Rawlings government officially recognized Dr Imoro as the new Nandom Naa.[28] The defeated parties continued to write petitions and letters of complaint; but when they were finally due to be heard before the House of Chiefs in September 1992, the oncoming session was postponed, and eventually indefinitely adjourned. Shortly before the presidential elections of November 1992, a decree by the Rawlings government abated several pending chieftaincy suits, including that of the Nandom Naa, and declared the disputed office-holders chiefs for life. Rawlings's electoral victories in 1992 and 1996 and Dr Imoro's high political offices - he has been elected into the Council of State and was made vice-president of the National House of Chiefs - seem to have taken the wind out of his opponents' sails.[29] Nevertheless, a future change of government could give a fresh impetus to their aspirations. Moreover, the new constitution finally abolished the procedure of government 'gazetting' of chiefs, which the British had introduced, and leaves the settlement of chieftaincy disputes entirely in the hands of the houses of chiefs and their judicial committees.

Consequently, the contestants for the Nandom skin disagree whether the abatement decree of November 1992, proclaimed under a military regime, is still valid under the new democratic constitution.

It would take us too far to outline all the chiefly candidates' arguments in detail. They repeat the arguments of the 1958 dispute, but also bring new elements into play. Dr Delle's and Rear-Admiral (rtd) Dzang's argument, for instance, that not only a single section, but all sections of Kyiir's house have a right to the Nandom skin provoked a protracted debate on the question whether some of Kyiir's wives, namely Delle's and Dzang's grandmothers, had been 'slaves', and, if so, whether the descendants of 'slaves' were eligible as chiefs. Delle's and Dzang's claims forced the Boro house, on the other hand, to find additional arguments for its aspirations. On the basis of the Chieftaincy Act of 1971 and the models of chiefly succession that prevail in pre-colonial chiefdoms such as Dagbon or Gonja, Gbeckature Boro argued that only persons whose fathers had been chiefs were eligible - an argument that would exclude C. Y. Dery, Dzang and Delle from the list of contestants. Secondly, Gbeckature claimed that considerations of seniority should decide between the eligible candidates - which would exclude Dr Imoro. And thirdly, he insisted that the passage of the chiefly office from Boro to Konkuu in 1930 was meant to initiate a system of rotation between these two houses or 'gates'.

Just like the witnesses before the 1958 commission of enquiry, the petitions of the chiefly candidates foreground exclusively the 'traditionalist' arguments of 'customary succession'. The exact definition of this 'custom' is contested, and different family legends are constructed in order to give weight to the candidates' own arguments. But none of the parties questions that chieftaincy needs to be based on 'tradition'. Outside this official register, however, the 'political' aspects of the succession conflict are debated extensively. On the one hand, political considerations influence the evaluation of the suitability of a candidate. No one denies, for instance, that the potential political clout of the chief-to-be plays an important part in the considerations of whom the family sections should put forward as a candidate. Who will best be able to rule the Traditional Area and to represent Nandom in the wider world? One of the reasons why so many candidates presented their claims in 1985 and the contest became so fierce is precisely that for the first time in the history of the Nandom skin, there were several candidates with a higher level of education and a certain political experience who could be expected to link the local community successfully with state institutions. In addition to such universalistically framed arguments, particularistic expectations of tangible benefits from the new chief - and the better his position in the outside world, the more can be expected in return - also played a role (and all candidates complained that the others had 'bribed' the family elders).

On the other hand, all my interlocutors were keenly aware and highly critical of what they perceived as 'political interference' in Nandom chieftaincy affairs. In particular, the question why the Rawlings government backed Dr Imoro and not Rear-Admiral (rtd) Kevin Dzang, who had served as its Secretary for Defence in 1983-84, was the subject of much debate and speculation. During the elections of 1992 and 1996, Dr Imoro is said to have pulled his weight in supporting Rawlings's NDC (National Democratic Congress), while Dzang kept somewhat aloof from party politics and Gbeckature openly canvassed for the NPP (New Patriotic Party), the current reincarnation of the NPP-UP tradition.[30] Some commentators believed that in return for Dr Imoro's support for the NDC the parliamentarians of the area supported his candidature to the Council of State. The seat in the Council of State guarantees not only access to the corridors of power but also quite lucrative allowances, which, in turn, can be invested in generosity towards sub-chiefs and followers, splendid festivals and ostentatious hospitality, building up the chief's prestige.

Nobody in Ghana would deny that these observations bear witness to the general and in practical terms unavoidable interpenetration of chieftaincy affairs and 'politics'. On a normative level, however, all agree that crude material and secular political interests should have no influence in chieftaincy affairs, and that succession conflicts should be regulated exclusively by reference to 'tradition'. Even the most trenchant comments on the increasing corruption of chieftaincy by 'politics' do not suggest abolishing the institution altogether, but a return to an unspoiled, 'traditional' conduct of office. When in early 1996 the Rawlings government proposed an amendment of the constitution, intended to allow chiefs to participate actively in party politics, there was a public outcry that the move would be 'inimical to the prestige, honour and the very survival of the institution of chieftaincy'.[31] Chiefs, it was argued, must guarantee the unity of their respective communities, and should not dabble in party politics. Their status is regarded as guaranteed by 'tradition', not by the grace of the government of the day. A candidate to chiefly office would therefore certainly impute self-interested motives to his opponents, but present his own aspirations as a service and a sacrifice undertaken in the interest of the family, the local community and 'tradition'. At first sight all this might appear to be merely a transparent rhetorical trick. But the normative separation of 'tradition' and 'politics', which dates back to the colonial period, has become entrenched in popular concepts of legitimate power.

That the notion of 'tradition' now also influences chieftaincy debates in previously stateless societies, where chiefly 'traditions' are admittedly of recent date, shows how successfully the political organization of these societies was transformed by the colonial regime. In Nandom and the neighbouring chiefdoms, the notion of 'tradition' comes to stand for some measure of locally derived legitimacy for the new institution, even if the exact content of the 'tradition' is contested. By contrast, 'politics' stands for a potentially illegitimate external interference in local affairs. The appeal to 'tradition' serves as a backdrop for a critique of the abuses of power; 'tradition' speaks to the quest for continuity and stability in a local world that has experienced a century of tumultuous change through 'outside' interference. There is, then, a systematic denial of the 'external' origins of the chiefly office and the rules of succession, particularly by the 'royal family' itself. But other registers of discourse and patterns of legitimacy co-exist. Among ordinary villagers, for instance, and particularly when the language of debate changes from English to the vernacular, one can often find that chieftaincy is called the 'white man's chieftaincy' (*nasa naalu*, in Dagara), and thus distinguished from other forms of authority such as the earth-priestly office or the power of the family elders. Nevertheless, these villagers, too, agree that 'chieftaincy has come to stay', because it forms a vital link between the local community and the state that none of the other more 'autochthonous' forms of social organization could provide, and they too share the critique of 'political' opportunism in chieftaincy affairs.

Appendix 5.1: List of Interviews

Members of the chiefly family (Nandom):
Dr Daniel Delle, Trier, 30.7.1989
Dr Edmund N. Delle, Accra, 17.12.1992
Rear-Admiral (rtd) Kevin Dzang, Teshie-Nungua, 15.12.1992
Kyiir Fatchu and Gbellu Lee, Nandom-Pataal, 27.11.1989
Gbeckature Boro, Nandom-Pataal, 7.12.1992
Nandom Naa Dr Charles Imoro, Nandom-Pataal, 4.12.1989, 22.12.1993, 4.12.1994; 22, 23 and 27.12.1996
Dennis Tiewiir and Doria Doglier, Burutu-Danyegang, 9.12.1992

Members of the earth-priest family (Nandom):
W.K. Dibaar, Nandomkpee, 29.11.1994
Gaamuo Kog and Gaamuo Der Tubor, Nandomkpee, 28.11.1989
Gaamuo Mwinpuo Le-ib, Nandomkpee, 11.12.1989
Soglikuu Saakum and Kuur Der, Bilegang, 17.12.1994

Divisional chiefs, Nandom Traditional Area, and others:
Tantuo Naa Tampula Nituorna Beneo, Tantuo, 27.12.1996
Tuopari Naa Naabone Dery, Tuopari, 25.12.1996
Guo Naa Sugem Gyiele, Guo, 24.12.1996
Oscar Pagzu, Nandom-Segru, 13.12.1989
Ko Naa Gabriel Tangsege, Ko, 18.12.1994
Puffien Naa Benon Tangzu, Puffien, 30.12.1996
Tom Naa Severo Termaghre, Nandom-Pataal, 12.12.1989, 26.12.1996
Gegenkpe Naa Yabepone Babai Tuolong, Gegenkpe, 26.12.1996
Patrick Viiru, Nandom, 10.12.1992
Panyaan Naa Edward Dery Yirbekya, Panyaan, 23.12.1996
Kokoligu Naa Michael Zuwera, Kokoligu, 24.12.1996

Neighbouring paramount chiefs (and families):
Lambussie Kuoro K. Y. Baloro, Lambussie, 28.11.1989, 2.12.1994
Salifu Bawa Dy-Yakah, Tamale, 2.12.1992, 31.8.1993
Lawra Naa Abeyifaa Karbo, Lawra, 22.12.1989, 23.12.1994
Jirapa Naa Bapenyiri Yelpoe, Jirapa, 19.12.1994

Notes

1. The field research (various periods between 1988 and 1996) that went into this chapter was supported by the Deutsche Forschungsgemeinschaft. I also have to thank the Institute of African Studies at the University of Ghana, Legon - and particularly its then director Professor Nana Kwame Arhin - where I enjoyed the status of research affiliate during my fieldwork. With respect to the information used in the present article, it is the Nandom Naa Dr Charles P. Imoro, Rear-Admiral rtd. Kevin Dzang, Mr Gbeckature Boro, Dr Daniel Delle and other members of the chiefly family of Nandom, as well as Mr W. K. Dibaar and the late Soglikuu Saakum from the earth priest's house who above all deserve my heartiest thanks for their trust and openness. Cornelius Debpuur and Isidor Lobnibe were most helpful and informative field assistants. Last but not least, I would especially like to thank the organizers of the Lisbon conference, João de Pina-Cabral and Antónia Pedroso de Lima, and the participants for the stimulating discussion of the paper on which this chapter is based.
2. See Ferguson and Wilks 1970 on the inadequacy of this British conviction and the political problems it entailed.
3. In order not to make this chapter unnecessarily bulky, I omit a detailed discussion of British politics vis-à-vis the Nandom chieftaincy; for details and the respective archival references, see Lentz 1993, 1998a.
4. Further detail see below and Lentz 1993.
5. Until the introduction of a head tax in 1936, the colonial government prescribed 24 man-days per year 'road labour'. Since the early 1930s, the (local) government pays the chiefs a monthly salary for the discharge of their duties.
6. Some local historians (see, for instance, Der n.d.) therefore conclude that already pre-colonially Nandom was a 'unitary state' and Kyiir a sort of paramount chief with a well-established chain of command over subordinate village chiefs; however, village-level oral traditions of the non-existence of a paramount chief make this thesis very implausible. See Lentz 1998c on the debate over the pre-colonial political organization among Dagara intellectuals.
7. Tiewiir, the only surviving son of Nandom Naa Danye, also felt that in principle he and other descendants of Danye had a right to the skin, but said they would not enter into conflict over this claim; interview of 9 Dec. 1992.

8. See Trenchard Domegure Yuori, *History of Chieftaincy in Nandom, from 1918-1958*, unpublished manuscript, Bechem 1987: 32ff., and letter of T. D. Yuori to C. Lentz, January 1994. I was not able to trace all of the archival files perused by T. D. Yuori, but the British documents available to me leave no doubt that Kyiir was the first British-recognized chief of the Nandom division.
9. Lawra-Tumu District, Annual Report, 1938-39, RAT, NRG 8/3/78:31.
10. DC Lawra-Tumu to CCNT, 17 April 1935, RAT, NRG 8/2/52.
11. Ibid.
12. DC Lawra-Tumu to CCNT, 30 Aug. 1938, RAT, NRG 8/2/73.
13. Lawra Confederacy Native Administration, Minutes of Conference 10-12 Sep. 1940, RAT, NRG 8/5/17.
14. DC Lawra-Tumu to CCNT, 23 Dec. 1940, RAT, NRG 8/2/73.
15. Minutes of the Lawra Confederacy State Council, 25 June 1954, RAT, NRG 7/10/1.
16. Gazette Notice No. 866 in Ghana Gazette No. 38, 28th April 1958, RAT, NRG 7/2/2, Nandom Affairs.
17. Report of the Committee Appointed to Enquire into the Nandom Skin Dispute - Lawra Confederacy (1958): 7.
18. Ibid.: 5.
19. Ibid.: 6, 9. Incidentally, Yuori's explanation shows that the above-mentioned argument of Boro's descendants that Kyiir had never been a substantial chief is a recent one, probably constructed in the conflict of 1985.
20. Ibid.: 2-3,9. For more details see Lentz 1993.
21. Ibid.: 12
22. Petition to Government Agent Lawra, 25 Oct. 1958, RAT, NRG 7/2/2.
23. See Ladouceur 1979: 99-155 for details on northern politics and Lentz 1998a, Chaps. 11-14, for the history of party politics in the Lawra District.
24. Lawra Conf. State Council, 3 April 1957, RAT, NRG 7/4/5.
25. Ibid.
26. Borroh Yuori to Secretary Chieftaincy Secretariat, 26 Dec. 1966, RAT, NRG 7/2/2.
27. Konkuu, Imoro and Polkuu were all related to one of Kyiir's wives (who was mother to Konkuu and grandmother to Imoro and Polkuu).
28. Local Government Bulletin, No. 16, 28 June 1986.
29. See Lentz 1998 b for a portrait of Dr Imoro and the debates surrounding his legitimacy as Nandom Naa.
30. Dzang was appointed as ambassador to Japan, and some informants conjectured that this was Rawlings's move to both appease and distance the aggrieved contestant.
31. Ghanaian Chronicle, 16-19 May 1996; see Lentz 1998b for details on the recent debate on chieftaincy.

6

Making The Chief:
An Examination of Why Fijian Chiefs Have To Be Elected

Christina Toren

The question of why Fijian chiefs have to be elected arises in part out of the recent history of Fiji, where in 1987 a middle-ranking chief from the western side of the main island of Viti Levu, Dr Timoci Bavadra, was ousted in a series of bloodless military coups from the office of Prime Minister, to which he had been elected only a month before. Until this point Fiji, whose first general election had taken place in 1972, had apparently been governed successfully by a parliament based on the Westminster model bequeathed to their ex-colony by the British. What had gone wrong?

Explanations have centred on relations between ethnic Fijians and Indo-Fijians (the descendants of indentured labourers brought to the country by the British in the late nineteenth and early twentieth centuries), who at the time formed something more than half the population.[1] But it is not my intention to address here the politics of ethnicity (which have been ably discussed in depth by many others) or the restoration of democracy in the general election of 1992 on the basis of a revised constitution.[2] Rather, I want to show how it is that ethnic Fijians can be committed to the idea and practice of democracy and at the same time insist that only high-ranking Fijian chiefs are fitted to hold the highest offices of state. And further, I want to argue that there is neither contradiction nor paradox here, for this is another manifestation of an old Fijian idea in which the continuity of a properly constituted polity depends on equal and hierarchical relations being made to play against one another in such a way as to produce the peace and plenty that characterize a successful Fijian chiefdom.

Chiefship in the Old Days

I begin by considering how men born into a chiefly clan come to be accorded the status of paramount. The following remarks are extracted from a conversation I recorded in 1983 with Ratu Sefanaia Laua of the chiefly *yavusa* Nadawa in the chiefly village of Sawaieke on the island of

Gau, central Fiji, where I did fieldwork. We were discussing *na gauna makawa*, 'the old days', that is to say, the pre-colonial days, and their significance for contemporary chiefly statuses in Sawaieke country (*vanua* - here referring to a confederation of eight villages).

[The] priest [to the ancestor god/chief] was Tunitoga, if the chief wanted anything he told Tunitoga, it was up to him then to decide about it. There was his herald, Tunimata. The chiefly status then following was the *sauturaga*, Naraitena [whose prerogative it is to install a high chief]. If the [high] chief was absent then Narai could take over. Chiefs (Turaga), Raitena [designated owners - *itaukei* - of the country], Priests, Heralds, Warriors, then the sea people and the landspeople - *liga ni magiti*, hand of the feast... [W]hen there are seven statuses like that, you have a government (*matantitu*) ...

In the old days there was no country that did not fight. All the villages fought one another ... this was the old way of it: the chiefs usually sought to take a girl to marry in a village and thereby perhaps that village would be silent, because the girl was married there. Its pledge was the woman. Yes, you will see this in [the village of] Nukuloa, they have there a *yavusa* [group of clans connected by ritual ties and intermarriage] which is the fellow of *yavusa* Navure [in Sawaieke]. They were carried there that they might go as a war-fence. This is the proof of it; there is ... *mataqali* [clan] Sisiwa, *tokatoka* [sub-clan] Sisiwa. The family of the Retired Methodist Minister ... is living in Nukuloa because of this... The Minister is dead, but his lady is living. He was made Tui Nuku [installed chief of Nukuloa] when his strength was going.

CT: Why was no one else installed since as Tui Nuku?

RSL: It's up to the gentlemen in Nukuloa. You see here we have Takalaigau [title of the high chief of the eight villages of Sawaieke country, including Nukuloa]: he is still only called Takalaigau, but he has not yet drunk, the power has not yet been given to him. But that will then just be up to the *sauturaga* [to the commoner *yavusa* who install the high chief]. If they find that he is a good chief, that he cares for the country, they will not delay in making him drink. If his bearing seems to be bad then they will stand back that they might watch for a while. It's possible they might simply cancel [their initial selection] and take another chief.

CT: Is there someone in Nukuloa who can take the title Tui Nuku?

RSL: Yes there is, but the politics of the matter are such that they may consider it and say it's not a good idea. I understand that European leaders such as Prime Ministers of different governments are also installed like that.

CT: What about in Navukailagi - Na Ratu?

RSL: Yes, Navukailagi also, if it is correct according to the land that there is a good chief there, it is right that he should run their country.

CT: What do you think - will a chief be installed here as Takalaigau?

RSL: Yes, I believe so, since there is something that they all know - [the putative] Takalaigau and the land chiefs here. The late Takalaigau went around all the villages and strove to ensure that when someone was to be installed as paramount (*Tui*), this country should be of one voice. If not, each one would just go its own way. According to custom the status of one who has been installed [is such that] he is promised the people, the earth, the grass that he may be its overall leader. This [the current situation in Sawaieke] is called *sauvi* - marked out, standing in wait. Here Sawaieke is just marked out. [The installation] is being considered to see if it is right or not. It takes a long time but it is not my

task to go and tell [them] that it should be done ...
You have been here a long time in the land, [you] know that it is a life that
envelops with love. If a chief is good, everything will be his. Look, here is a good
proof of it: [suppose] one of these people falls ill, but his behaviour towards the
people of the country has not been always good, they will just see that he is lying
on his bed [but] they will not be concerned. This is one proof of it that I have
already seen here (cf. Appendix 1).

I have quoted from this conversation at length because it illustrates a
number of points. Firstly, it suggests that the various clans (*mataqali*, lit.
kinds) owe certain ritual obligations to each other.[3] Secondly, it shows that
Fijian chiefship is not a matter of predictable lineal succession from father
to son. Other high-status men, including the chiefs of commoner clans, in
particular those whose task it is to install a high chief, have a significant say
in who is to be made paramount. If they are unsure of a man's fitness for
office, they will delay his installation - for years if not for ever. This is an
indication of the relation of reciprocal obligation that obtains between a
high chief and his people - if a chief does not fulfil his obligations then the
people withhold their service. Thirdly, chiefs are considered necessary to
the continuing autonomy, prosperity and well-being of a country, and are
expected, especially in times of war, to provide protection. Fourthly, the
specific references to marriage as alliance alert us to the necessity of looking at the nature of the relations it implicates. Finally, Ratu Laua's assertion 'that it is a life that envelops with love' (*ni dua na bula e ologa ena
loloma*) implicates the idea that the fundamental conditions of social life
are given by kinship, which ideally encompasses all relations between people, including marriage, and which ordains, as it were, for any particular
kinship relation, the precise nature of the duties that are entailed by *veilomani*, 'caring for each other' or 'loving each other'. The Fijian term for
kin, *weka*, may be extended to include all ethnic Fijians, and kinship terms
are routinely used in both reference and address; with the exception of
the relation of competitive equality between cross-cousins, all kinship relations are hierarchical.[4] I discuss these matters further below. For the
moment I return to ethnographic sources.

In his unpublished *The Heart of Fiji*, which concerns the chiefdoms or,
as Fijians say, countries of Lomaiviti (i.e. central Fiji, of which Sawaieke
country, on the island of Gau, is a part), Hocart quotes from his translation of an article in *Na Mata* of 1906:

Matanitu, lit. Face of the Chief, or State [CT: 'powers that be']. In the old days
men used to seek their chiefs, they used to betrothe ladies from various lands
where there was a noble line to marry into their own land so that her children
might be noble and their land become a *matanitu* land thereafter. Some put at
their head a successful (*yaco*) man or strong man in battle and installed him as
their big lord or chief, because they wished to become a *matanitu*. Therefore
the leaders of the various clans met together and made over their villages to
him whom they had installed as their chief ... As regards *mata* the beginning of
the word, this refers to all the people of the land who are to be the *mata* or mes-

sengers of the great lord or chief (*tui*). The true spelling should be *mata-ni-tui...* (pp. 327-8 of manuscript).[5]

Moreover Hocart records many instances where the offices of high chief (*Roko Tui*, in his translation 'noble lord') and/or war chief (*Vunivalu*) are supposed to move between different clans. For example:

[On the island of Batiki] [t]he chief clan is divided into two; Upper Tora ni Bau and Lower Tora ni Bau, by reason of brothers being appointed to live some above and some below. The first chief remembered comes from the lower branch. He was followed by one of the upper branch, then three of the lower branch (ibid., p. 294).

[In Verata] [t]here are two houses from which the chief is chosen, Vunivalu and Sanokonoko. The *kava* goes from one to the other. If a man from one house is installed the other house 'carries the sovereign' (*cola sau*). The two together form the clan of Vunivalu. They say two chiefs cannot be appointed successively from the same clan, but in practice it happens. In order of clans Mataniwai was placed first. It was described as 'substance nobles' [*turaga lewena* (CT: 'substantial chiefs', 'chiefs of the blood')]. They used to hold the c h i e f t a i n s h i p while the clan of Vunivalu upheld the heraldship and the sovereignty to the *sau*; but this rule was weak so they gave the chieftainship to the clan of Vunivalu while they upheld the *sau* (ibid., pp. 400-1).

There are two chiefs in Rewa: the Noble Lord of Dreketi of the clan of Bi House, and the War Chief of Nukunitabua. They came together from Nakauvadra. They divide Rewa and all subject villages and carpenters between them, there is not a village in which they have not both got authority. They are the two cloths of the land ... There are four noble clans besides the two clans to which the chiefs belong ... Next comes a group of six clans called *sauturaga*. They decide who shall be Noble Lord of Dreketi and who War Chief; they instal the War Chief (ibid., pp. 431-2).

Hocart was well aware that historically Fijian chiefship was a matter of ritual precedence, rather than unalloyed hierarchy; nevertheless, he argues in *Kings and Councillors* that government evolves out of ritual organization in such a way that equality, or a balanced organization of functions, necessarily gives way eventually to centralization and 'a vertical hierarchy' (Hocart 1970: 37) and, in *The Northern States of Fiji*, that this process was well under way in the Fiji of his time (ibid. 1952: 58).[6]

As will become plain below, I take a different view. As I see it, today as in the past, the shifting of high offices between clans and the choosing of those men who are to fill them, are structural necessities, expressions of a polity in which instituted hierarchy and competitive equality have to be understood *as aspects of one another*. This radical opposition between hierarchy and equality is such that it constitutes a single idea of antithetical duality as fundamental to Fijian social life.[7] Thus the dualism so superbly described by Hocart in his various works, but which he saw as having given way to a 'vertical hierarchy', far from disappearing, continues to pervade daily life, and informs, for example, sexual relations, kinship, chiefship and ideas of the person.[8]

The argument of the present chapter addresses a point that I have not previously considered. It is that Fijian chiefship *has to be elective* in the sense of being seen to be conferred by the people on the chief, for only thus can it bring about the condition of 'peace and plenty' expressed in the term *sautu*, of which the base *sau* may be a cognate for *sau* meaning 'a high chief', and also 'the commandment or prohibition of such a chief' (see Capell 1973). If so, *sautu* may be rendered literally as 'established *sau*', which itself suggests that 'peace and plenty' is inevitably the condition of a country where a high chief takes precedence over all and everyone fulfils his or her material obligations to others; here the idea is not that a despot commands and a cowed people do his will, but rather that the willing attendance of the people on one who has been chosen from the appropriate chiefly clan by leaders of the appropriate landspeople clan and installed as paramount, in and of itself produces a genuine prosperity for all.

That Fijians themselves hold this view is suggested in the formulae of ritual speeches, of which the following are examples. They are extracts from speeches made at the mourning ceremonies for a dead chief; here a man of chiefly status is offering a whale's tooth to the people whose task it is to attend on the chiefly dead:

> I am touching, sirs, the string of the *tabua*, that our chiefs may be healthy, that our country be one of peace and plenty, a country of mutual love [or, that the *sau* be established in our country, that it may be a place of caring for one another]. The word is already heard. It is effective, it is true (cf. Appendix 2).

The tooth is accepted by a man of one of the commoner clans that compose the *yovusa* that attends on the funerals of members of the chiefly clans:

> I am untying, sirs, the string of the chiefly tooth, a tooth of gratitude, a tooth that is offered to the chiefs Raitena, and all the people of the houses that are gathered together. We accept that it is a good tooth. Well established are our chiefs, well established is everything in our country. If trouble befalls us, may God hear us, let our leader always be Christ. It is effective, it is true ... (cf. Appendix 3).

The idea that chiefship is a good thing, and that a well-regulated country is one where chiefs are well-established, is generally held; indeed I have, over the years, had only one informant who seemed to think that chiefship should be abolished and the country run on purely democratic lines.[9]

Turaga is the Fijian term for 'chiefs'; it can equally well be translated differently according to context, e.g. as 'gentlemen', or as 'married men'. Thus 'the chiefs Raitena' referred to above are elderly and/or high-status men of the landspeople's *yovusa* Raitena - the men who lead that *yovusa*;

they are commoners, not of chiefly birth. Hocart (1913) makes an argument to the effect that 'the word *turanga* [sic] ... leads us back to gerontocracy; it is properly the title of the old men who sit in informal council over feasts and ceremonies'. Be that as it may, the broader application of *turaga* to all married men is also suggestive - for it is through marriage and parenthood that a man becomes eventually the head of his own household and 'a chief in his own house' - if not elsewhere.[10]

Given that I have already analysed different aspects of marriage as process in a variety of contexts and in some detail, I simply point out here that the hierarchical relation between husband and wife requires a transformation on marriage of the equality of relation that obtains between cross-cousins (by definition, *all* marriages are between cross-cousins), and that over time the relation between husband and wife, while it remains axiomatically hierarchical, in effect transforms yet again into one between equals. In a lifetime in which *all* one's relationships prescribe either hierarchy or competitive equality, only marriage makes it clear that each form contains the possibility of the other. But what is crucial for my argument here is that marriage effectively removes from any within-clan reckoning of differential status women who may in their natal households be the eldest of their sibling set. Marriage at once makes women adults and transforms them into axiomatically subordinate wives in their husbands' households, which allows men in general to be ranked within clan according to their relative seniority as heads of households (see Toren 1994a).

In the ritual formulae quoted above, the first speaker, a man of chiefly rank, juxtaposes the terms *turaga* and *sautu*: 'that our chiefs [*turaga*] may be healthy, that our country may be one of peace and plenty [or that the *sau* be established in our country, *sautu tiko noda vanua*], a country of mutual love'. It is interesting to note, then, how the second speaker's use of *turaga*, and his not using *sautu*, implies a broader reference. *Dei vinaka tu na nodatou turaga, dei vinaka tu na veika kece e nodatou vanua.* 'Well established are our *turaga*, well established is everything in our country.' Spoken as they are by a high-status commoner of the clan that installs a high chief, they specifically imply that 'gentlemen' or 'married men' in general, and perhaps especially high-status men of the speaker's clan, have to be regarded as 'chiefs'.

In his excellent ethnography of Lau, Steven Hooper maintains: 'that decision-making about the succession and the organisation of the installation is *not* in the hands of the chiefly clans but lies with the landspeople, [is] a crucial factor which militates against the emergence of a chiefly dynasty wielding dictatorial powers counter to the interests of the people' (1982: 157).

This is true enough. I want to argue further, however, that the elective element in Fijian chiefship is what allows hierarchy and equality at one and the same time to inhere in the relation between people and chiefs; in other words, the position of paramount cannot be a matter of instituted lineal succession, for this would violate the idea of antithetical duality that informs all relations between people. In such a case, people would be faced with a situation where relations were not merely out of balance, but where it would no longer be possible to live in peace and prosperity. 'In Fiji all things go in pairs or the sharks will bite.' But the country where succession is out of the hands of landspeople clans would be a country where 'all things' no longer 'go in pairs'. It could not be described as *sautu*, as a country where the *sau* or paramount is 'established', if people in general are not, of their own accord, content to fulfil material ritual obligations to one another.

The fulfilment of these obligations of mutual service requires, for example, that men, as husbands, garden and build houses, and women, as wives, fish and make mats; that men of 'fishermen' clans provide big fish for feasts and men who are 'the hand of the feast' provide pig; that each clan undertakes particular tasks in relation to other clans in respect of births, marriages, deaths. It is the fulfilment of their prescribed ritual obligations to others that allows the people of a particular *yavusa* (group of clans), village, or country collectively to outdo another *yavusa*, village, or country in, for example, the exchanges that form part of life-cycle ceremonies, or in raising money for some community endeavour, or in amassing goods for the grand exchanges that take place on grand occasions - the opening of the Great Council of Chiefs, or a paramount's installation or death. Where, on such an occasion, a country's showing draws the admiration of people in general, then its people may properly be said to have 'shouldered the carrying pole of empowering the chief' (Hooper 1982: 228).

In considering chiefly succession, I am struck yet again by the thoroughgoing logic of Fijian dualism, by the way that sameness and equality is acknowledged and, at the same time, differentiated into the hierarchies of precedence that inform both domestic and chiefly ritual. In a situation in which all men who are married and the fathers of children are *turaga*, chiefs, where the fundamental unit of social organization is the house, and where balanced reciprocity characterizes exchange relations across houses and more inclusive groups (i.e. sub-clans, clans and *yovusa*), what requires that certain men be singled out as 'true chiefs' and accorded the status of paramount? The answer lies, I think, in the way that, in Fiji, equal and hierarchical relations invariably implicate one another - so much so that at times they threaten to collapse into one another, and the challenge is to keep them distinct.

Equality and Hierarchy

The competitive equality of cross-cousins informs relations between people whose countries are *veitabani* (their respective founding ancestors being represented as cross-cousins) and *veitauvu* (descendants of a common founding ancestor). Against this we have to set the idea that countries should be and are hierarchically ranked, such that the chief of a particular confederation may take precedence over another. This idea is generally held; but even in respect of the chiefs of the largest and most important confederations, there is no unanimity with respect to what the order of precedence might be.[11] So where men of the most powerful confederations are obliged to drink *yaqona* together, who takes precedence over whom is likely to shift according to context, and by virtue of an unspoken and mutual agreement that each will get his turn in the top central position of paramount authority and be served 'the first cup'. Certainly this is what happens when chiefs of smaller confederations meet, for example, at one of the bi-annual Provincial Councils.

Given that Fijian chiefship, and indeed all the minutiae of status differentiation between people in the collectivity at large, is at once expressed and constituted in *yaqona* drinking, where people are inevitably ranked according to their seating position on the above-below axis that describes any space in which the drinking occurs, it follows that there will, always, be an order of precedence.[12] That it *cannot* be a fixed order is a function of the way that the hierarchy constituted in chiefly rituals is bound to come up against the equal relation between cross-cousins that informs exchange across houses and clans inside a country, and across countries.[13]

In attempting elsewhere to explain what Hocart's informant meant when he said that, 'in Fiji all things go in pairs or the sharks will bite', I pointed out that 'given that all things go in pairs, a totality consists of a pair of pairs, which explains why, in Fiji, everything really goes in fours' (Toren 1994b).[14] This observation is crucial here, too, because it is the antithetical relation between *pairs of pairs* that makes equal and hierarchical relations play against one another and dependent on one another for their very continuity, as follows:

1. Equality between men and women as cross-cousins is in play against the axiomatic hierarchy between husband and wife.
2. Equality between cross-cousins across houses is in play against the precedence of the firstborn and seniority between siblings within houses.
3. Balanced reciprocal exchange across houses is in play against a within-in-clan hierarchy where houses are ranked according to seniority.
4. Balanced reciprocal exchange across exogamous clans is in play against ritual precedence where the highest ranking clan is 'chiefly'.
5. Balanced reciprocal exchange across clans and countries that relate to one another as 'land' and 'sea' is in play against the relation of tribute and redistribution that obtains between people and chiefs.[15]

Finally, the installing clan's prerogative of choosing a putative paramount and installing him (which implies that clan chiefs are one another's peers, each one a household head), is in play against the idea that succession accords with lineal seniority within the chiefly clan and that all statuses are hierchically ranked as a matter of divine ordinance.

It is the idea that a totality consists of a pair of pairs that allows equality and hierarchy to be implicated *at one and the same time* in those key kinship relations where hierarchy inside the house directly conflicts with balanced reciprocal exchange across houses. These key kinship relations are those between husband and wife (outlined briefly above) and between mother's brother and sister's son, who are also ideally father-in-law and son-in-law (*veivugoni,* a term that denotes the relation between children and their parents' cross-siblings).

The relation between mother's brother and sister's son is the most formal of respect relations between kin, and it is axiomatically hierarchical; the junior relative - the sister's son - owes unquestioning respect and obedience to the mother's brother. The junior avoids the senior, may not address him, sits at a respectful distance from him in any gathering, in general adopts a humble demeanour when in his presence, and is bound to respect his wishes. At the same time, it is this relation that allows the junior relative, as *vasu,* to *vasuta,* or, as I was told, to take without asking (*taura ga, sega ni kerea*) the property of men of his mother's clan. In cases of chiefly marriages across countries, this relation, traditionally and still today, creates powerful allegiances. Thus, as Ratu Laua remarked, women given in marriage constituted 'a war fence', a means whereby an ambitious village or country 'would be silent, because the girl was married there. Its pledge was the woman.' Traditionally, a powerful chief might exploit his *vasu* relation to his mother's country; but his own obligations of protection and redistribution of tribute had also to observed, if only because of the respect owed to his mother's brother.

It can be argued that the child's right as *vasu* is in effect a recognition of the out-marrying woman's rights in her natal clan (Toren 1994b). Note however that the *vasu* relation between mother's brother and sister's son is twofold: it combines the licence that is usually proper only to people or groups who relate to one another as cross-cousins with the extreme respect, avoidance and obedience that is properly shown by a real or classificatory son-in-law to his father-in-law. This makes structural sense, because the children of mother's brother are indeed cross-cousins to the sister's son; and mother's brother's daughter, who outside marriage is the peer of her father's sister's son, in marrying him is bound to become his subordinate.[16]

That antithetical duality also informs Fijian concepts of the person, especially in respect of existential effectiveness, is evident in the transformations that have occurred in this domain from the pre-colonial period to the present day (Toren 1998).[17] In brief, Fijians hold to a theory of the person that rests on recognition of one's relations to others and the obligations that reside in these relations. One distinguishes oneself to the degree that one demonstrates who one is as a function of what one is given to be in relation to others. And in each moment of relationship - be it hierarchical or equal - one strives to assert oneself as the subject of one's own acts, one *strives for* oneself and *against* becoming merely the object of the other's manipulation. So in any particular relation with kin - be it between cross-cousins, siblings, parents and children, spouses, or in-laws - ego *volunteers* the behaviour appropriate to that relationship, and in so doing compels an appropriate response from the other, that is to say a response appropriate to 'a life that envelops with love'. The willing respect and obedience of ego to his or her superior is *vakaveiwekani*, 'in the manner of kinship', and, by the same token, the evident assertion of another's superiority in giving food, clothing, money, or whatever is undermined by ego's asserting control as at once the implicit initiator and consumer of the gift. Thus one often hears someone say of others, of their parents, their older siblings, their mother's brothers - i.e. of persons to whom they are subordinate - 'they give me everything I want', and if one asks why, one is told 'because they love/pity me'.

Electing the Chief

Given the foregoing, it follows that if a particular Fijian chief is to be paramount of a country, then both his choosing and his installation *have to be* initiated by those who, because they take precedence in landspeople clans as 'owners' (original inhabitants of a land), are in a position to accord a paramount precedence in that *vanua*, country. The people (*lewe ni vanua*, literally, the substance of the country), by virtue of fulfilling their own obligations, at once empower the paramount and compel his fulfilment of obligations towards them all. Only if they have chosen the paramount can the people's initial allegiance to him be known, and only in this case can they effectively withdraw their allegiance should they find him inadequate.

A formally installed high chief is a living instantiation of the immanent power of the ancestors, which today comes under the aegis of the transcendent Christian God; as such the *mana* of a paramount inevitably and properly harms any one of his people who refuses him due service. But if a paramount fails in his duties towards the people, if he holds on to goods and valuables that are given him in tribute and is not seen to redistribute them, then his word is evidently no longer *mana*, effective, and the people have nothing to fear if they in turn withhold their services. In other words, Fijians *know* that it is they who, by virtue of their service and willing tribute, empower their chiefs. This idea extends both to the ancestor Gods and to the Christian God: the ancestor Gods no longer have malign power because 'no one attends on them any more' and by the same token the Christian God is all-powerful because of his many millions of worshippers.[18]

It seems fitting to quote here the words of Ratu Sir Kamisese Mara, President of the Republic of Fiji, on his own selection and installation in 1969 as Tui Nayau, paramount chief of Lau.

'The concept of primogeniture - the eldest son automatically inheriting the title and possessions of his father - is not Fijian. It is a European import. In Fijian tradition it was the most able and suitable of the line who received such honours... he was made chief by the people, and by their acclamation and permission only. If he proved unworthy, he did not last long ... It was the British era, with its concept of inheritance as a right, instead of a privilege, which froze (or fossilized) the chiefly system ...' He went on to relate that he had at first been undecided whether to accept the titles himself. He finally agreed - as the most expedient means of changing the present concept. 'Actually it is not a change, it is a return to the past idea which was much more democratic. The rigidity of the chiefly class is only a hundred years old. It is not what was meant at all' [*Nation*, Alliance Party magazine, vol.1 (5), July 1969, quoted in Hooper 1982: 158].[19]

It will be apparent to the reader that I cannot agree with Ratu Mara's remarks concerning the 'rigidity of the chiefly class', for people who are by birth chiefly do not now, and never did, constitute a class in the analytical sense of the term; they are *mataqali turaga* - of chiefly kind, and as such, form one of the seven kinds of people (*mataqali*, clans) who together, as in Sawaieke country, constituted a traditional Fijian *vanua*: 'Chiefs (*Turaga*), Raitena (the owners - *itaukei* - of the land), Priests, Heralds, Warriors, then the sea people and the landspeople ... [W]hen there are seven statuses like that, then you have a government.' The material in this chapter has obvious implications for the military coups of 1987 and the subsequent recent history of Fiji. One can argue that, so far as ethnic Fijians are concerned, Dr Timoci Bavadra would not, despite his election by a majority of the electorate and however excellent his personal qualities, be allowed to continue as Prime Minister of Fiji. Here I should note that Fijian villagers do not consider the post of Prime Minister to be political (*vakapolitiki*) in the sense that it is purely a matter of election; rather, they consider it to be a form of high-chiefly status (that is to say, only those accorded this status should be nominated for election as Prime Minister), and this is apparent, at the outset of this chapter, in Ratu Laua's explicit analogy (in 1983) between the installation of a high chief and a European Prime Minister. In a Fijian perspective, were Dr Bavadra to be accorded precedence over all, then the government could no longer *be seen to be* properly constituted. This cannot be the perspective of Indo-Fijians; thus Brij Lal's analysis suggests that Fijians were led astray by their chiefs, whose own interests required that the people be kept in ignorance:

For the first time in the modern history of Fiji, a paramount chief ... was not at the head of national Fijian leadership. Instead, a middle-ranking chief from traditionally neglected western Viti Levu had been elected to the highest office in the land. In a society where ascribed status, hierarchy and protocol are accorded great weight, and where traditional ideology holds that the business of government is the prerogative of chiefs, and chiefs alone, Bavadra's elevation posed troubling questions ... a successful performance on his part would discomfort chiefs who already felt themselves under siege from the corrosive effects of modern life and were struggling to reassert their authority over their people. Bavadra's pledge to educate his people to recognize the difference

between their traditional and their political obligations aggravated their fears...
at long last, after nearly a century of struggle, the western Fijians were within
reach of gaining a measure of the power they felt was their due (Lal 1992:301-2).

Despite my general admiration for Lal's history of twentieth-century Fiji, I
cannot find that he has any real understanding of the political sensibilities
of Fijians. For while it is true that 'traditional ideology holds that the business of government is the prerogative of chiefs, and chiefs alone', in a situation in which all married men are *turaga*, chiefs, able commoners
should also be prominent in government (as Ministers, top civil servants
and so on), and so they are; it is notable, too, that the present government
includes a number of women in the top posts. My main point here, however, is that Lal's analysis by and large focuses on class and regional interests that, I would argue, pale into insignificance as far as the majority of
ethnic Fijians are concerned, and here I include the 'urban-based professionals ... people of achieved status and essentially middle class values ...
[whose] social and material world had widened considerably, beyond the
comprehension of their kin who remained close to the communal culture
in the isolated villages' (ibid.: 302). My knowledge of such people is limited; nevertheless, those I do know well enough to have discussed these matters with them at once abhorred any violence against Indo-Fijians, asserted
themselves to be anti-nationalist and pro-democracy, and rationalized the
coups as understandable and their outcome as justified. Lal himself
acknowledges this when he points out, without any further comment, that:

> although the importance of class and regional factors in Fijian politics should
> be recognized, they should not be pushed too far. Many urban, middle class
> Fijians still supported the Fijian establishment and were active opponents of the
> Coalition government. Prominent western Fijians were among the leading
> members of the Taukei Movement [the extreme nationalist wing of Fijian poli-
> tics] even though they privately supported Bavadra's public criticism of eastern
> dominance in Fijian affairs (ibid.: 302).

Marcus's view that contemporary Fijian chiefship was shaped in part by
the deliberate efforts of colonial administrators concerned to establish
efficient indirect rule, and in part by the politics of ethnicity, is undoubtedly correct. Thus I agree with him that: 'the plural nature of Fijian society and the quite explicit atmosphere of ethnic politics cannot be
underestimated as factors accounting for the greater vitality of chieftainship, top to bottom, in Fiji than in Tonga. Cultural boundary maintenance
is thus an immediate concern among Fijians for whom, as elsewhere, the
chief is a central figure' (Marcus 1989: 200).

I end on this note in order to suggest that the antithetical logic of Fijian
chiefship is necessarily projected on to the institutions of the state. The
success of parliamentary democracy from the first general election in
1972, the inevitability of the coups of 1987, and the restoration of democracy in the general election of 1992 on the basis of a revised constitution
can be explained by this same logic. Democracy works well in Fiji when it

is seen to be under the aegis of Fijian chiefs; but, given that hierarchy itself has never been allowed to become an encompassing value, neither can the ethic of equality be allowed to predominate - as it would if men of high chiefly status were no longer seen to take precedence in government.[20]

I have argued in this chapter that the elective element in Fijian chiefship is a structural necessity, an expression of a polity in which instituted hierarchy and competitive equality are mutually constituted and, as such, have to be understood as *aspects of one another*. It follows that there has to be, as it were, a chiefly element in Fijian elections.

Appendix 6.1

1. RSL:... *Mai na gauna oya me vaka au sa tukuna vei kemuni na kena Bete o Tunitoga, sa vinakata na turaga e dua na ka qai tukuna vei Tunitoga, o koya sa qai tu vua na kena lewa. Sa tiko na matanivanua o Tuinimata, na i tutu vakaturaga qai tarava na sauturaga qo na Raitena. Kevaka sa yali tiko na turaga sa na rawa ni 'takeover' ko Narai. Turaga - Raitena - Bete - Matanivanua - Bati - qai ko ira na kai wai vata kei ira na kai vanua - na liga ni magiti. Tautauvata oya ni vitu nai tutu vaka oya qua dua na matan-itu ... E liu sa sega ni dua na vanua e sega ni vala. Veivala kei ira kece ga na veikoro ... Ia qo na gaunisala e liu, era dau vakaqara na turaga me ra kau na yalewa ki vakawati ki na dua na koro me rawa ni na galu kina na koro oya ni sa vakawati kina na yalewa. Kenai vakadei na yalewa. Io kevaka o na raica oqo mai Nukuloa, e dua na yavusa tiko e kea o iratou vata sara ga na yavusa qo nei Mitiele o Navure. O ira ya sa kau me ra laki ba ni valu. Ya na kenai vakadinadina. Oya na ... mataqali o Sisiwa, tokatoka o Sisiwa. Mai Nukuloa sa toka kina oqo ko ratou ko Naitalatala vakacegu ... Naitalatala sa mate, O Radini Italatala ga e sa bula tu. Sa buli me Tui Nuku ni sa lako na nona kaukaua.*

CT: *E na vuku ni cava sa sega ni buli tale e dua me Tui Nuku?*

RSL: *Vakatau sara ga vei ira na turaga ni Nukuloa. O ni sa raica tiko oqo eke na Takalaigau, sa kacivi wale tu ga e na Takalaigau ia sa sega ni se gunu, sega ni se soli vua na kaukauwa. Ia oya sa na qai vakatau vei iratou na Sauturaga (Raitena). Kevaka o ratou na raica ni turaga vinaka ni na lomana na vanua, sega ni bera e ratou sa na vagunuva. Kevaka ena via ca toka nona i vakarau ena via vakasuka toka me ratou na raica toka mada. Rawa in ratou na bokoca tale ka taura tale e dua tale na turaga.*

CT: *Tiko e dua na turaga mai Nukuloa sa taura rawa na i tutu oqo?*

RSL: *Io e tiko, ia na vakasama ga vakapolitiki e ra na raica ka kaya ni sega ni vinaka. Au kila ni turaga ni vavalagi talega era dau buli me vaka na Prime Minister ni veimatanitu vaka kina.*

CT: *Vakacava mai Navukailagi - Na Ratu?*

RSL: *Io, Navukailagi tale ga, ke sa dodonu nai lakolako vakavanua, e dua na turaga vinaka e tiko e dodonu me cicivaka nodratou vanua.*

CT: *A cava na nomuni vakasama? Eratou na bulia e dua na turaga me Takalaigau?*

RSL: *Io, au vakabauta. Ni sa tiko e dua na ka e ratou sa kila vata tiko na Takalaigau kei iratou na turaga ni vanua eke. Na turaga Takalaigau sa bale oti sa wavoki oti e na veikorokoro ka saga o koya ni sa buli e dua me Tui, na vanua oqo esa na dua ga na vosa. Kevaka e sega, sa na dui lako ga. Nai tutu vakavanua ni dua esa buli, sa yalataki na tamata, na qele, na co me sa kenai liua liu vakadua ko koya. Oqo e vakatokai na Sauvi, tu vakawawa. Qo o Sawaieke sa sauvi tu ga. Sa nanumi tiko, sa qui vakaraici e vinaka se sega. Na kena berabera, ia sega ni noqui tavi meu laki tukuna me caka ... Qo na ka kece sa saga tiko na matanitu me vakasuaka tale mai nai vakarau vakavanua. Kemuni sa mai dede ena vanua, kila ni dua na bula e ologa ena loloma. Ni dua na turaga vinaka ena tu kece vua na ka taucoko. Raica mada qo nai vakadinadina na vinaka. E so era na tauvimate - ia sega soti ni dau vinaka na nonai tovo ki vei ira na lewe ni vanua. E ra na raica ga ni davo tu, era sega ni kauwaitaka. Dua na kena vakadinadina au sa raica oti eke.*

2. *Au tara saka tu mada ga na wa ni tabua, ni bula vinaka na turaga e nodatou vanua, sautu tiko noda vanua me vanua veilomani, a rogoci tu mada ga na vosa. Mana e i dina [cobo].*

3. *Au luvata saka na wa ni kamunaga vakaturaga, kamunaga nai vakavinavinaka, kamunaga tale ga e cabo tiko yani vei iratou na turaga Raitena, kei na veimatabure kece e soqo tiko. Keitou ciqoma me kamunaga vinaka. Dei vinaka tu na nodatou turaga, dei vinaka tu na veika kece e nodatou vanua, soli tiko vei kedatou na leqa sa tiko me rogoci keda tiko na kalou, a noda i liuliu tu mada ga ko Karisito. Mana e i dina. Taba saka mai na kamunaga. I i [cobo]. A kamunaga saka e levu. Ka liu, ka liu, ka liu. E duo dosa, amuduo [cobo] muduo [cobo] amuduo [cobo] muduo [cobo]. Vinaka saka.*

Notes

1. Population 1988: 342,965 ethnic Fijians, of whom 31.4% lived in urban areas; 341,141 Indo-Fijians, of whom 42.4% lived urban areas (Lal 1992:217). Note that by 1988 Indo-Fijians had emigrated in large numbers and were now outnumbered by ethnic Fijians.

2. See, for example, Kaplan 1987, Kelly 1988, Norton 1990 and Lal 1992.

3. The ritual obligations peculiar to certain clans do not constitute caste-like distinctions; so, for example, traditionally any fit young man might fight for his *vanua*, and it was not only men called the 'hand of the feast' who gardened, nor only 'fishermen' who fished; today, as in the past, all men as husbands are obliged to produce *kakana dina* (true food, i.e. root crops such as taro and yams) for their families, and men of chiefly clans, like all village men, garden and fish. Note that two of the statuses mentioned by Ratu Laua - those of 'priest' and 'warrior' - no longer exist *as such*; nevertheless, their clans continue to be recognized.

4. Observations similar to those in this paragraph have been made by numerous other ethnographers of Fiji. See, for example, Hocart (1952, 1970), Hooper (1982), Turner (1986), Walter (1978).

5. George Milner, author of the *Fijian Grammar* and of a forthcoming *Fijian Dictionary*, informs me (personal communication) that '*Matanitu* is a mysterious word, especially the *tu* part ... *Turaga* may itself be a "fossilised" equivalent of Samoan *tulaga* "status, rank, position", a noun derivative from *tu* ("stand") ... "state" is a good non-committing gloss, but *tu* also has sexual connotations of dominance etc. as might be expected.'

6. Hocart lived in Fiji from 1909 to 1912 and did further fieldwork there in 1913.

7. Sahlins (1985) and (1991), following Hocart, takes a different view of Fijian dualism: in brief, he takes hierarchy to be an encompassing value, and places little emphasis on balanced reciprocity in exchange and the equality of cross-cousins. This may be because his historical essays primarily concern the period of the partial hegemony of the great chiefdoms of Bau, Rewa and Cakaudrove, whose chiefs seem almost certainly to have been concerned to establish, if they could, a vertical hierarchy. I have no fault to find with Sahlins's data, but I do disagree in part with his interpretation of them. My historical-cum-ethnographic analysis of the history of chiefship in the *vanua* of Sawaieke shows that Fijian chiefship - past or present - cannot, as 'value', encompass the pervasive antithesis between hierarchy and equality. Rather, its efficacy and its continuity *require* that hierarchy and equality remain in tension with one another as opposing, and equally important, aspects of social relations. The 'General History of the Country of Sawaieke' (*Na i tukutuku raraba ni vanua ko Sawaieke*), recorded by Lands Commission officials in 1916, covers a time-span that begins some 150 years or so earlier and ends at the period that Fiji was ceded to Britain in 1874. It includes an account of the origin of the title *Takalaigau* that is in many respects a classic tale of 'the stranger chief', but one whose implications are, I argue, rather different from those understood by Sahlins in respect of Lau (see Toren 1994b).

8. In respect of my argument in this chapter, George Marcus's comparative analysis of chieftainship in Polynesia demands to be addressed virtually line by line - especially, so far as I am concerned, in respect of its consideration of Fiji, where I find myself often in agreement with his analysis - agreement that is often nevertheless of the 'yes, but ...' variety. To take just one example, Marcus views the Fijian polity as being more similar to the Tongan than to the Samoan, whereas (as will become increasingly plain) I would argue that, in different ways and in equal measure, it is remarkably similar to both (see Marcus 1989).

9. He was at the time a young man of 22 years old or so, who had just returned from a tour of duty with the United Nations forces in the Middle East. His views were made plain as a group of young men and women and myself were drinking *yaqona* - i.e. they were expressed in front of his peers. No one else present ventured to agree with him,

and, according to my experience, he was highly unusual; most young men, while they may refuse 'to attend on' a chief who does not personally have their respect, hold entirely conventional views about the desirability of everything that is properly *vakaturaga*, chiefly.

10. See Note 5 above.

11. The growth in the eighteenth and nineteenth centuries of the large confederations of Bau, Rewa, and Cakaudrove was achieved in part through actual warfare and in part through the way that smaller chiefs sought the help of bigger ones in order to avert war (see Sayes 1984). In the contemporary polity, the chiefs of important confederations are likely to fill high offices of state such as Governor-General (when Fiji was still part of the Commonwealth) or, today, President of the Republic. It seems, however, that such titles are bound to rotate, as it were, across chiefdoms. So, for example, Ratu Sir George Cakobau of Bau (great-grandson of the famous Cakobau, called Tui Viti, King of Fiji, by Europeans) was the first Governor-General, and he was followed by Ratu Sir Penaia Ganilau (Tui Cakau, paramount of Cakaudrove, who later became the first President of the Republic). The current President is the former Prime Minister and high chief of Lau (Tui Nayau), Ratu Sir Kamisese Mara. Election of men to these offices of State is in the hands of the Council of Chiefs.

12. My initial work on Fiji is an exploration of how, over time, Fijian villagers constitute an idea of hierarchy as a fundamental principle of social organization, via their understanding of people's disposition in space, relative to one another, whenever they are gathered together to eat, to drink *yaqona*, to worship, to observe life-cycle ceremonies and so on (Toren 1990). For further analyses of *yaqona*-drinking and some of its manifold implications, see, for example, Toren 1989 and 1994b.

13. All chiefly rituals entail an initial offering of *yaqona* root as tribute (*i sevusevu*, a ceremony that requests, as it were, chiefly acknowledgement of one's presence) and the subsequent redistribution of *yaqona* as drink to all those who are present. *Yaqona*-drinking is at once the most everyday and the most sacred of Fijian rituals; it is by virtue of drinking the cup offered by the chief of the installing clan that a man is made paramount. Fijian chiefship is constituted, on a day-to-day basis, in a struggle to transform in ritual (paradigmatically, in *yaqona*-drinking) balanced reciprocity and equality between cross-cousins into tribute and hierarchy between people and chiefs. That this struggle is in principle unending is a product of the fact that all dynamic, fertile and affective processes are founded in the relation between cross-cousins.

14. For example, the first phase of all life-cycle ceremonies (birth, circumcision, marriage, death) lasts for 'four nights', and a herbal remedy prescribed by a healer has usually to be followed for 'four nights'.

15. The term for chiefs here is *na malo*, 'the cloths'; it refers not just to men who are, by birth, 'chiefly', but to the recognized leaders of all the

leading clans of a *vanua* (country), including the paramount.

16. A situation that recalls Lévi-Strauss's (1977, 1978) brilliant observations concerning the possible array of complementary oppositions that is inevitably entailed in 'the atom of kinship'.

17. Toren (1998) analyses pre-colonial sacrificial and consumptive practices in Fiji to reveal their implications for ideas of the person, together with historical transformations in these ideas as a function of the impact of conversion to Christianity. The antithesis between hierarchy and competitive equality pervades production, exchange and even tribute. But consumption is at once the end and the beginning of these processes, and in pre-colonial Fiji was the privileged site of existential agency.

18. The malign power of the ancestor Gods may be unleashed through witchcraft; see Toren 1995.

19. Steven Hooper prefaces his extract from this article with the observation that Ratu Mara 'was clearly the heir apparent and was immediately recognised as Paramount Chief on the death of his father. However, Ratu Mara himself was well aware that sucession was a matter of selection and not of right' (Hooper 1982: 157). Note that Hooper also records that neither Ratu Mara's father, nor his grandfather, 'had been formally installed in the proper manner as Sau, though they were accorded the respect due to the holder of that office'. Toren (1994b) includes a discussion of why it is that a putative Sau is often named and never installed.

20. The course of the relationships between Colonel Rabuka, who of his own accord instigated the coup, Ratu Sir Kamisese Mara, the Prime Minister whose government had been ousted by Dr Bavadra's Coalition, and Ratu Sir Penaia Ganilau, at that time Governor-General, can also be understood to accord with Fijian ideas concerning the responsibilities of warriors and chiefs (see Mara 1997, Milner 1997, and, for an alternative view, Lal 1992).

Part III

House and Heir

7

Aristocratic Succession in Portugal (From the Sixteenth to the Nineteenth Centuries)[1]

Nuno Gonçalo Monteiro

Successor, Succession, Immediate Successor

Unlike the situation in contemporary Western societies - where such terms are generally used by analogy with earlier historical contexts - in the period between 1600 and 1830, in Portugal, the terms 'successor' and 'succession' were in general everyday use. We will start, therefore, with a discussion of the meanings that were attributed to them at that time.

Bluteau's Portuguese dictionary of 1727 defines successor as 'he who succeeds another in his place, dignity, office, or wealth and property' (1712-29). But in the terminology used by the Portuguese aristocratic elites of the time these terms had rather more specific meanings. Despite the fact that we only possess a limited number of diaries, memoirs, volumes of correspondence and other records from the period, those we do have allow us to assess the extent to which these categories were clear primary definitions for classifying individuals and their relations to each other in society.

The first and fundamental distinction between persons among the aristocracy was that between first-born heirs and others. Even outside the circles of the main court nobility, among the higher municipal elites in the provinces, eligible persons could be thus classified: on the one hand, there was the 'lord of the house' or 'eldest son, successor to the house' (Viana 1808); and, on the other hand, there were situations where it was said 'he is a second son' (ibid.) or 'he lives on rent provided by his brother' (Ponta Delgada 1787).[2]

To 'have a succession' meant guaranteeing the existence of successors. This was a fundamental duty for presumptive 'lords of the house', and required that they marry and have many children, just as in any reigning family. One of the best accounts of this commonplace and obsessive obligation is to be found in the memoirs of the last Countess of Atouguia, the wife of one of the accused in the Conspiracy of 1758. Right at the start, she tells us that 'as the Count of Atouguia was an only son, no sooner had I married than I began to invoke the names of many of the saints, that they might prevail on God to give me succession for the house', an objective that she achieved after ten months of marriage. But it was not enough: 'as two years went by without my having any more children other than this one son, the Count of Atouguia started to want very much that the house should have more successors'. And this too would be fully achieved: 'while married, I had three sons and three daughters, all of whom were living when my father-in-law arrived from Baía and I presented them to him with much pleasure, hoping that with this number of descendants his house would be free of the danger it had faced at the time when there was only one single heir, of passing into the ownership of another' (Atouguia 1916: 5, 9, 13).

The status and responsibilities of successors were passed on to 'immediate successors', even if these were not biological descendants. As Martim Correia de Sá, fourth Viscount of Asseca, stated in the middle of the eighteenth century:

> I find myself without succession in my House, and with no grounds for hope in my own House, my brother Luís José Correia is my immediate successor, and he is not of an age where he can afford to wait very long: both from the political, and from the Catholic point of view, I must have him married. Politically, because I have to preserve the splendour of my House, since this is the purpose for which they are founded. And from the Catholic point of view, because I am burdened with debts (...) and must therefore seek a successor who out of mercy will wish to do the same that I did for my Father's debts, rendering me a service by taking on my debts.

And about the same time he added, in a letter to the Prime Minister, the Marquis of Pombal, with reference to this same brother: '(he is) my immediate successor who should be regarded as my first-born son'.[3] At around the same time, the Countess de Atouguia, whom we have already encountered, wrote on this same subject:

> When I was little, my parents told me that I would become a Sister of the Mother of God, and I expected this to happen; but they said this to me because they did not want to talk to me of marriage until they had settled me, because since I was the immediate successor of their house, it is certain they did not intend me to become a nun (Atouguia 1916: 4).

Successor and 'immediate successor' are terms that have a clear origin in the laws that provided for entailment. It is precisely in that body of · rights that the figure of 'immediate successor' is to be found. He or she was granted ample rights since, amongst other things, the immediate successor had to be consulted whenever loans or obligations were undertaken with guarantees given by the first-born or heir to the entailment, and he or she could request additional means of subsistence. These terms, therefore, allow us to establish something that is of fundamental importance: the group under study looked to the rights of entailment as one of its fundamental points of reference.

Entailment Rights

The genealogy of entailment in Portugal generated a huge body of legal literature. The most important Portuguese jurist at the end of the *ancien régime* summarized it thus:

> ... whatever analogies may be made between the earliest Constitutions based on legal rights and the rights of primogeniture ... their model, type, and origin, such as we now admit, have as their fundamental basis and prototype the Laws and Customs of our Nation ... The first fundamental Laws govern the succession to the Kingdom as a true entail (Sousa 1814: 9); ... our basic Law was similar to that of the Kingdom of Spain, and our entailments were established in imitation of our monarchy, just as there they were also the imitation of the Spanish monarchy (Sousa 1814: 14).

In fact, the first Portuguese legal compilations (the *Ordenações Afonsinas* of 1446 and the *Ordenações Manuelinas* of 1512-14) made no mention of this subject, which was only introduced in the Philippine compilation (1603, book 4, article 100). 'The Taurine laws of 1505, and the New Recompilation of the Kingdom of Spain ... were in part the source and model for our own ordinances' (Sousa 1814: 14). In summary, Portuguese entailment rights were modelled directly on the model of succession used in the monarchy, and very closely resembled entailment rights in Spain or, more precisely, in Castile.

In fact, in the Iberian peninsula, entailment rights as practised in Portugal were probably those that most closely resembled the Castilian example. Even though it relates back to a remote feudal legacy, best illustrated by the famous words of St Bernard,[4] Castilian primogeniture in a way shows a resistance to the general European trend of the period. It represents a re-assertion of the principles of primogeniture within a wider doctrinal context where the acceptance of the European *jus commune* was tending to favour the division of inheritance among all the heirs. In most European countries, after the sixteenth century, there was a tendency for the rights of entailment and primogeniture to weaken: in legal terms at least, they persisted in a mitigated form, or gave way to less restrictive rights of succession (like strict settlement in England).[5] In the Iberian peninsula, on the contrary, the rights of entailment, supported by an ample body of legal treatises, were perpetuated as an extreme form of primogeniture among the nobility, and were recognized as such in the legal literature of the period. Bartolomé Clavero wrote in this connection that

'Castilian primogeniture was to become the European model for an anthropology of the nobility' (1989b: 588).

Thus the *mayorazgo*, a late legal construct that went counter to the general trends in Europe and was characteristic of the Iberian peninsula, can be defined as 'the right to succeed to the assets left by the founder of the house, on the condition that they remain perpetually indivisible within his family, so that the first-born in order of succession may take and possess them'.[6] While the principles of perpetuity, indivisibility, primogeniture, primacy of male heirs and the right of representation can be regarded as being of a very general nature, the reality was that the specific form of succession was defined by the founder. In the case of Portugal, prior to the Marquis of Pombal's legislation of 1769-70, which imposed the Castilian model of regular entailments as the only model allowed, there was in fact a great diversity of rules of succession. It was possible to make entailments in favour of second-born children or of freely chosen or nominated persons. In addition, there were a great many different types of clauses and rules. Nevertheless, it should be emphasized that entailments in favour of the first-born male heir were always by far the most common.

If we move on from the legal history to the social history of the institution of entailment, the chronology is rather different. Although the first entails in Portugal were created in the late Middle Ages[7] by the Portuguese *fidalgos* (nobles, who represented about 1 per cent of the total population at that time), they were a long way from being commonplace. It was only in the sixteenth and the beginning of the seventeenth centuries that most of the entails of the various different branches of the Portuguese nobility were founded. The members of this class were engaged in intense competition for status, wealth and power. As in the case of Naples, we can probably assert for Portugal that 'Primogeniture was adopted at the beginning of the sixteenth century by a somewhat restricted group of feudal families, and became more widespread from the second half of that century onwards' (Visceglia 1988: 37). The practice of strict family discipline required by the entail model of reproduction, which we shall discuss below, also became the norm during this period[8], even though the granting of *comendas* (commanderies) to the second-born, which later became very rare, still persisted (Olival 1986-1991: 574-5). The only available demographic study suggests, moreover, that there was increased social differentiation within the *fidalgo* population between 1383 and 1580, with an increase in celibacy and the gradual social disqualification of the second-born branches, precisely because primogeniture was becoming the norm (Boone 1986).

It must be stressed, however, that the entailment model did not become totally dominant, owing to the remarkable fluidity and mobility of the society of the nobles in sixteenth-century Portugal. We can identify a number of factors that contributed to that. For example, at that time it was still possible to accumulate large fortunes in India and the Far East, and the hierarchy of the nobility was relatively poorly defined. The Crown was the institution that was most crucial in defining the structure of the titled elites, but political instability (e.g. the crisis of 1580) adversely affected its capacity to give continuity to its actions. We must, therefore, briefly devote some attention to the operation of those factors that prevented the full establishment of the entailment model.

First, a distinction must be made between succession and inheritance. Unlike the situation in other European contexts, there was no difference here between the transfer of status and the transfer of property (Augustins 1982). They were indivisible, and the rights to succession to both were vested in the 'successor' or heir. However, in each generation, the new property accumulated by the lord of the house in his lifetime (including improvements in entail property) was to be regarded as free assets (*bens livres*). Unless any of his sons or daughters expressly renounced their right to these free assets (for example, by reason of entering a convent or receiving a dowry), they were to be equally divided among the children, except for the *terça* (one-third of such assets). Despite the provisions made at the time of the founding of the entailments (requiring the inclusion of the terça) and the strength of the culture of the aristocratic house (which encouraged the other heirs to renounce their rights) this issue remained contentious, and even led quite often to legal actions. But throughout the eighteenth century the effects of this situation were greatly lessened by the fact of aristocratic indebtedness: in many cases, the free assets of the inheritance were insufficient to cover the debts of the deceased lord of the house, so that there was nothing to divide.

Secondly, the fact remains that throughout the sixteenth, and through part of the seventeenth, centuries not only did the amounts given over as dowries increase, but entailments were also joined by way of marriages that deliberately sought to tie together two entailed houses, despite the existence of both general and specific legal provisions to the contrary. In fact, the legislators often protested against this practice. Furthermore, at the end of the sixteenth and during the seventeenth centuries, repeated complaints were presented to the Cortes (Parliament) arguing that the ranks of the nobility in the service of the Crown had decreased owing to the reduction in the number of 'houses'. Moreover, the last compilation of ordinances of the Kingdom, in 1603 (book IV, article 100, 5 and following), clearly condemned these practices, and required that entails that had been joined by marriage in this way should once again be separated whenever the income of one of them was greater than a certain amount, in a similar fashion to Castilian legislation on this matter. But, as in the neighbouring kingdom, these measures had only limited success (Clavero 1989a: 247-59).

From the middle of the seventeenth century, and along with the dynastic change of 1640, significant developments took place in the hierarchy of the nobility. It was at this time that a 'first (or higher) court nobility' came to be defined, which was made up of those with titles and other holders of office in the Palace. This group was to acquire tremendous stability after the end of the war with Spain and the consolidation of the new dynasty in 1668. This change of dynasty had a fundamental effect on the behaviour of the aristocratic elites. The kings of the new Bragança dynasty granted very few titles or other honours. The existing ones, therefore, became a sign of undisputed social pre-eminence. In actual fact, it seems that these titles granted the 'lords of the houses' who held them such a strong personal claim to identity as to allow them to contemplate the possibility of the eventual disappearance or absorption of the house into other titled houses. In this new context, therefore, the rights of entailment, long since incorporated into the body of general law, took on new and more restricted forms.

The Nature of Assets Transferred

In the case of the higher court nobility (from the seventeenth century up to 1832), assets transferred by way of succession were threefold in nature: First, there were entailed assets. By definition, the original and oldest assets of the houses were tied up in entailment, even when they included lordships and Crown property donated in medieval times.

Secondly, there were assets or property of the Crown and military orders. Being gifts of the Crown, these assets were governed by specific legal provisions and rules of succession, as defined in the *Lei Mental* of 1434. The grant was subject to confirmation in each new lifetime or at certain specific moments in time. The assets of the Crown and the orders included all the lordships, commanderies, and titles, and even Palace offices.

Before continuing, three general comments must be made about this second type of asset. In the first place, this was the factor that most strongly identified the 'house'. By reason of the status that they granted, it was the lordships, the Palace offices and, if they existed, the titles that served to designate an aristocratic house. In the second place, the relative weight of the assets of the Crown and the orders in the total income of the houses increased consistently over the period under study, finally reaching an average total of over 54 per cent of all income. Finally, something must be said about the famous *Lei Mental* and what it implied for the development of the law of succession. This law defined strict principles of indivisibility, inalienability, primogeniture and male succession, and gave no recognition to the right of representation. In theory, it favoured not only the reversion of these assets to the Crown (in the case of female succession) but also defined possibly different destinies to be given to entailed assets and Crown assets respectively. Instances of both of these did occur, however. After 1640, the Crown granted the request of the representatives of the nobility in the *Cortes* and made a permanent change to the initial version of the law, agreeing that preference should be given to lineal descendants over lateral (indirect) lines in the succession to Crown property. Above all, it accepted the tacit principle that female succession was not subject to the *Lei Mental*, even although exemption still had to be requested on a case-by-case basis, and also conceded exemptions in many cases for collateral succession. In practice, succession to entailed assets and to the property of the Crown and military orders nearly always passed to the same persons.

The third and final form of asset to be taken into consideration here is the top civil, military and Church offices of the monarchy (appointments such as Council Presidencies, to military and colonial governorships, and the main dioceses). With some notable exceptions - which, however, disappeared in due course - none of these offices ever became subject to formal succession. However, in accordance with the prevailing political culture, the choice of appointees during this period nearly always ended up falling within a very restricted group of aristocratic houses of the higher court nobility. Moreover, the services performed in the execution of these official duties were rewarded with new royal grants.

House Codes and Vocabulary

In his will, written in 1632, Fernão de Sousa wishes 'that there may be no disagreements, or opportunities for such, between my heirs ... in this way they will continue to improve and increase the house of their ancestors, a duty that binds us all to hold nothing in greater respect than its renown ... it is not my intention to give advantage to one son over another, but only to preserve and improve the house and family of my ancestors'.[9]

At the outset, we should bear in mind the distinction between the house (*casa*) and the lineage (*linhagem*).[10] A nobleman was identified by his surname. This family name was important in so far as it established a connection with an old medieval lineage and because it was associated with a coat of arms, a *fidalgo* family. That was precisely what made up the lineage of the Portuguese aristocracy, a concept for which Severim de Faria put forward the following definition in 1655: 'an order of descent which, having its beginning in one person, continues and extends to children and grandchildren, so as to form a parentage or lineage; which since ancient times and for clarity of definition has been called noble' (Faria 1740: 8). The origins of Portuguese higher aristocratic families and their respective family names are the subjects of a vast literature, which also contains descriptions of the deeds of their founders and the variations in the respective coats of arms. The primary sources of identification for these were the richly informative Portuguese medieval 'books of lineage', but the truest definition of the group is perhaps contained in the 72 coats of arms painted on the roof of the Sintra royal palace at the beginning of the sixteenth century (Freire 1973). In fact, there was a qualified and perhaps reluctant admission that there were more noble families than those mentioned in Sintra, either because some had in the meantime arrived from abroad or because they had subsequently been elevated to the ranks of nobility. But the truly significant lineages were always very few, and corresponded to the older lines or to those whose founders had provided significant services to the monarchy.

Belonging to a particular lineage was achieved by way of the male line of succession (*varonia*), albeit with some restrictions. In effect, there was in the system of parentage that prevailed among the Portuguese aristocracy, as in others in Europe, a combination of elements of patrilineal and of bilateral descent. Portuguese law (in particular the Philippine Ordinances, book 5, article 92) unequivocally adopted the principle that nobility and peerage could be inherited either through the father or the mother: 'From which Ordinances can be deduced that whether by way of their mothers or by way of their fathers, nobility can be passed down to the children, who may freely use the family names and the arms of one as of the other' (Sampaio 1725: 30). Thus, it was also the case that the more common form of proof of noble origin relied on the 'four grandparents' test. While the institution of entailment helped to reinforce the principles of primogeniture and male succession, the reality was that the normal form of succession in entailments included the 'right of representation' (or, in other words, it granted preference to grand-daughters who were daughters of the first-born over uncles who were second-born), so that entailments involving a strictly male line of succession were exceptional. Despite the importance of the male line of succession, 'good' and 'bad blood' could be inherited as much from the mother as from the father, a fact that had major implications for marriage policy.

However, the importance of lineage declined after the fifteenth century, a time when it was still the basis for alliances among the aristocracy. The decline of the importance of lineage was caused by the increase in the number of houses using the same family name. This was due to the adoption of names associated with the old lineages. Sometimes these names were transmitted by the women. But sometimes people just started using them without any real right to do so. In fact, Portuguese nobles in the seventeenth and eighteenth centuries were born into a particular 'house', founded in more recent times, and initially associated with a coat of arms belonging to a particular lineage and a family name (which all the subsequent heirs were required to use) and identified by the possession of certain entailed property or assets, of a *comenda*, of a lordship, of a Palace appointment or of an aristocratic title. Particularly after the dynastic change of 1640, the notion of *lineage* gradually came to be devalued in favour of the notion of the *house* (especially if the house had been granted an aristocratic title), although at no time did the notion of the family (which corresponded, in name only, to the idea of the male line of succession) disappear completely.

The basic entity for the study of aristocratic behaviour in the period under study was therefore the 'house', a term that conveyed a cohesive collection of material and symbolic assets to whose extension and reproduction all those who were born in, or depended on the house, were compulsorily committed. At that time, the house represented a basic value for (nearly) all social elites. The family, in the sense of a noble lineage of ancient origin, as evinced by the family name (and/or the male line of succession), came to be just one of the elements that identified the house. As has been stated previously, even though at the outset the aristocratic house generally had a connection with a particular place and building - a name taken from the entailment, the lordship or manor, or even the military order (*'comenda'*) - and even if the house sought to perpetuate that name in its various titles, the fact is that the name of the original place continued to exist only as a remote allusion. It was even possible that the house might lose the right to the property but continue to use the name unchanged.

Moreover, even though it was normal for lords, immediate successors and collateral (indirect) heirs (including sometimes members of the Church) as well as a host of servants (who were commonly also called the 'family') to live together, one should be careful not to confuse the house with the residential palace building. During the period in question the latter was invariably located in Lisbon, even though the original seat would have been elsewhere.

One of the most crucial implications of this notion of the aristocratic house was the destiny that was mapped out for each child. The prevailing ideas in this domain were still perfectly clear at this time. The choice of whether to marry or place in the Church the daughters and later-born sons was a function of the strategic options of the house into which they had been born. Those who were destined for marriage, starting with the presumed heirs, were governed by the rules of politics of alliance between houses. If the other children remained celibate, it was expected that they would seek to increase the power and wealth of the house that had given them their being.

The destiny of unmarried daughters had always been the convent. As the troubled Portuguese ventures in India and the Far East began to have ever more uncertain results in the course of the seventeenth century, so too the houses began to contemplate an ecclesiastical career as the normal destiny for their second-born sons. They were brought up from infancy for this. They were sent to the two royal colleges at Coimbra (the Colleges of St Peter and St Paul), where most of the boarders since the middle of the seventeenth century were the second-born of the grand aristocracy, sons of the highest nobility of the realm.

It was expected that those who had gone into the Church, especially those who had reached the status of high dignitaries and rendered significant service to the king (bishops and cardinals) would donate, if not all their 'free assets', at least their services (which were, after all, their most valuable capital) to the houses of their brothers and sisters or nephews, so that the houses' endowments in tithes and benefits (*comendas*) would increase. Most of them did so. Many houses substantially increased their income and their distinctions in this way. Moreover, the houses not only capitalized on the services and associated incomes of their second-borns, they also sought to capture, by all means at their disposal, the prestige that went with these positions.

The aristocratic houses supported their daughters and second-born sons, or alternatively, they provided them with the amount needed for a dowry or the endowment required to enter a religious institution. One of the features of the seventeenth and eighteenth centuries was indeed the levelling off of the amounts of aristocratic dowries, which meant that, in real terms, the amounts of those dowries actually declined.

The Practice of Succession Between 1600 and 1830

The group of houses that will be studied here was basically formed in the middle of the seventeenth century around the nucleus of about fifty grand aristocratic houses and a roughly similar number of houses from the higher court aristocracy, all of which ended up, almost without exception, becoming titled houses as well. The total number of titled houses in 1640 remained practically unaltered up to the last decade of the eighteenth century, although there was an appreciable recovery between 1640 and 1668. The remarkable stability achieved in the approximately 130 years after the end of the War with Spain (1668) has probably rarely been equalled by other European aristocracies. Moreover, it contradicts many very common notions about the inability of aristocratic groups to perpetuate themselves through time.[11] Over more than a century very few houses were created and very few were abolished, and the central nucleus remained highly stable. Of the 50 titled houses that existed in Portugal in 1750, the date when they reached their highest level in terms of status (and also the year of D. João V's death and the entry of the Marquis of Pombal into the government), 34 had been granted their titles over a hundred years earlier and, of these, 7 dated back to the fifteenth century.

It should be emphasized that, between 1670 and 1832, no titled house was extinguished or removed from the life of the court as a result of the decline in the economic fortunes of the holders of the title. Neither was any house extinguished by reason of its only direct legitimate succession's having been female. Where there was direct succession, whether male or female, the titles were always renewed.

We can obtain a more detailed picture of the actual ways in which succession was passed down by studying the process of inheritance in 60 titled houses (elevated to the titled nobility before 1775) in the period from 1600 to 1830.

Apart from the virtual non-existence of succession by an illegitimate heir (of which there was only one case), there is one feature that stands out from the above picture, and that is the large proportion of male heirs. There is no doubt that the numbers are very high, contrary to conventional wisdom on this subject. There were many houses that managed consistently to produce a male heir over a period of more than two hundred years. But even when that did not happen, their capacity for survival was remarkable: more than half the houses under study managed to last as such for over two hundred years. And it should be emphasized that in

Table 7.1: Inheritance of Estates in Titled Houses (1600-1830)

Years	A	B	C	D	E	F	G	H	Absolute Numbers
1600-1650	77	6	3	3	11	0	0	0	35
1651-1700	76	0	6	2	10	2	2	3	62
1701-1750	75	4	7	2	8	1	0	2	85
1750-1800	54	3	13	0	15	0	0	16	80
1801-1830	74	0	9	0	6	4	0	8	53
TOTAL	70	2	8	1	10	1	0	7	315

A – Direct male heir; B – Male succession - grandfather to grandson; C – Direct female heir; D – Female succession - grandfather to granddaughter; E – Collateral (indirect) male succession; F – Collateral (indirect) female succession; G – Illegitimate heir; H – Extinction or union.

three cases they perished for political reasons (high treason connected to the conspiracy of 1758) and not for lack of biological heirs.

This unusual stability was the result of the combination of two factors: the choices made by the Crown in this matter, namely the systematic authorization of female succession; and the houses' own strategies for perpetuation and increase. I shall now focus on these.

First of all, we should consider the demographic aspects. Nearly all male and female heirs succeded in getting married (on average, always more than 92 per cent of them), with very rare exceptions indeed (in fact, all of those who did not, died very young). The percentage of titled aristocrats without surviving heirs fluctuated between a minimum of 13 per cent and a maximum of 26.1 per cent, even though it tended to rise over the period. Moreover, the percentage of those who had surviving male heirs was always over 61 per cent, and in the earliest period under study (1600-1650) it was over 80 per cent. Titled aristocrats with surviving children had to place on average between 4.2 and 5 children, though the tendency was for the number of children to decline slowly. This remarkable statistic was the result of three closely-related factors: the very early average age at which young girls got married (it went from a minimum of 17.5 in the seventeenth century to a maximum of 21.7 years at the beginning of the nineteenth century), the non-existence of any contraceptive methods, and the lack of breast-feeding by the mother - this task was always entrusted to wet-nurses.

However, when the succession failed, other elements of the aristocratic model of reproduction could be brought into play to guarantee the much-sought-after continuity of the noble house. For a start, the sons and daughters who were not heirs often went into the Church. Up until the spectacular fall in the numbers of those entering the Church (in Portugal as in other Catholic countries of Europe) in the second half of the eighteenth century, a total varying between a third and more than one-half of the daughters of the nobility remained unmarried. And up to 1760, over two-thirds, and at certain times over four-fifths, of the sons who were not heirs did not marry.

It should be added that homogamy in marriage was a fundamental aspect of the reproductive pattern followed by the group. Up to the end of the eighteenth century, both heirs and daughters married within the circle of the grand aristocracy in 95 per cent of cases. This choice was fundamental in order to preserve the social identity of the group and thus to contribute to maintaining their monopoly over the principal high offices of the monarchy and their corresponding remuneration in the form of royal grants. Indeed, it was this line of thinking that dictated that the houses preferred to channel some of their daughters and second-born sons into the clergy rather than marrying them off 'beneath their station', possibly without a dowry and significant allowances. But this homogamy in marriage did have one potentially negative effect: it increased the risk of annexation of one house by another.

To counteract these risks the aristocratic houses adopted a pattern of behaviour that was widely publicized among them and perfectly standardized.

First, if the master of the house had no heirs, and was unlikely to have them, an immediate attempt was made to marry off the closest heir. Sometimes this only occurred when that heir had already reached an advanced age. There were frequent stories of clergymen who renounced their vows in order to get married, in the sometimes desperate attempt to produce descendants for the houses of their brothers.

Secondly, when the succession fell to ladies, they would marry a second son with no house of his own almost without exception. Preferably this would be an uncle, so as to keep the surname of the male line. Even when no uncle was available and a suitable marriage partner had to be sought in another lineage and another house, the general rule, with a few exceptions, was to try to pass on the family name to the heir of the next generation. In any event, the husbands of these female heirs were to all intents and purposes adopted by the houses that 'took them in'. Their status, and in particular their economic status (food, lodging, etc.) was generally exactly the same as that of most married women in the aristocracy.

Finally, whenever there was a perceived risk of potential union between houses, the dowry and marriage contracts were drawn up in such a way that they would be separated in the succeeding generation. These clauses were hardly ever observed; but at any rate they provide evidence of the house's intention of preserving its own separate identity.

Choice and Succession

Recent developments in the social sciences in general, and in social history in particular, have witnessed a growing mistrust of the reified use of the various categories of historical analysis and of rigid behavioural models.

Even for those who distance themselves from the post-modern apologetics of the 'dissolution of society', the options are nearly always a renewed attention paid to the language used in documents and even a prominence given to individuals, to their experiences and to the way that their social identity has been formed. It is, therefore, perhaps understandable that I find it difficult to try to emphasize, as I am in fact doing, the rigidity of a particular social model and the surprising regularity with which the actors involved in that model reproduced the social roles allocated to them, which were markedly asymmetric.

In this context, I can make two very general observations. First, it should be recalled that the social order at the time of the *ancien régime* contrasted strongly with contemporary Western individualism. Political and social culture and the institutions of the day embodied an idea of the social order based on a hierarchy of its different members, sanctioned by history. This essential truth had a number of implications that we have to take on board. Secondly, it should also be emphasized that, unlike unilinear notions of change and development, the case studied here is in no way illustrative of a transition from collective solidarity to individualized behaviour and personal destiny. Quite the contrary. Among the the higher levels of Portuguese society in the fifteenth and sixteenth centuries, behaviour was much more highly individualized than in the two centuries that followed. On the one hand, the destinies of individuals were less strongly influenced by the estate they were born into. And, on the other hand, the constraints that derived from groups of family relationships were a good deal less severe. The strengthening of the discipline in the aristocratic houses, with an *ab initio* prior imposition of a status on each of their members, went along with the emergence of the grand aristocracy of the court as a closed and almost inaccessible social group. It was only towards the end of the eighteenth century that the rigid patterns of behaviour in these houses would start to show signs of breaking, just a short time before we witnessed the first signs of some easing of the restrictions on access to the highest levels of the hierarchy of the nobility.

In a system where individual destinies were in large measure already laid down at birth, the margins of choice were very limited. Furthermore, it was well known that one of the ways to ensure the desired outcome was to make a decision concerning a child's future at a very early age. Picking up old formulae from collective wisdom, people would say: 'our Portuguese normally destine their children for various different occupations. The first is a soldier, some follow a career of letters and others the Church. Parents know what the children want ... and right from the earliest years they allocate to each one that which will be his lot. To learn any trade takes a long time, and life is short.' And with respect to daughters, they would add: 'like household pests, girls are thrown out as soon as possible. They are sent to be educated in the convents, or to take on the role of daughters in the houses where they are eventually to be mothers.' But, in spite of everything, there was still a degree of choice, even as far as inheritance went. In these circumstances, such a choice was, nearly always, exercised by a refusal to marry. During the period under study, most successors still married within their father's life-time, and it is in fact remarkable how usually everything went off smoothly, with few situations of open conflict. Contemporary reports and correspondence do give us accounts, now and again, of the tensions to which marriage negotiations were subject. The many sources from the first half of the eighteenth century also show that relatives still had an important role to play in these matters. But it was rare for any conflicts to arise directly as a result of any unwillingness or resistance on the part of the betrothed. Because they were the exception, the situations where individual choice was directly and openly opposed to the destiny that had been mapped out for the persons concerned were comprehensively documented in historical records and were in later years much publicized. Amongst these was a celebrated episode with the third Marquis of Gouveia, who, having married the daughter of a titled Spanish nobleman in 1718, ran off a few years later with a married Portuguese noblewoman.

Daughters had little opportunity for opposition or resistance to the plans laid out for them. To marry or to go into a convent were practically the only acceptable options. Very few refused to accept the husbands suggested for them. By contrast, sons who were not in line for succession had a much wider range of alternatives. The vast majority were destined for the Church; but they could change their lives. They might find some female heir to a house and marry her, or they might risk a military career in the Indies, despite the fact that the chances of success there were by now rather slim. Whenever a war broke out on the European stage, many of them abandoned their ecclesiastical living in the hope of providing some valuable military service to the king, thereby receiving some royal grant and, consequently, obtaining their own separate income. A good indicator is provided by the list of student boarders between 1601 and 1727 at the royal schools in Coimbra, whose pupils were exclusively the sons of the higher nobility of the realm destined for a career in the Church. In fact, only 60 per cent actually died as churchmen, since a quarter of them became soldiers and a fifth even married. However, even in these cases, unless they had found a female heir within the court nobility, the alternatives nearly always meant a decline in social and/or economic status. To marry someone from the provinces or the daughter of a merchant was to lose status. And a military career in the East rarely allowed them to generate sufficient income to 'have their own house' at the level of the court aristocracy. A good ecclesiastical living provided a rather more secure income and a social position compatible with that into which they had been born.

The indicators we have analysed above relating to the destinies of the children of the house can only be properly understood if we bear in mind the crucial significance of the idea of the 'house' for the group we are studying. The efficiency and stability of the system relied both on the restrictive legal framework, which set the limits to what could and could not be done in terms of succession and inheritance practices, and on paternal authority, which defined at an early age each child's place within the system. But the system also relied on a number of less obviously compulsory conditioning factors. First of all, it relied on the existence of a set of institutions (namely the ecclesiastical institutions) that were essential to the continuation of the universally applied reproductive model of the aristocratic house. Secondly - and this element was of crucial importance - it relied on the social actors involved absorbing certain values, namely the values of the house, thus enabling them to view their destiny as a natural destiny, at least at the earlier ages at which the important decisions were usually taken.

Furthermore, levels of intra-family conflict were relatively low. Sometimes younger brothers and sisters would argue with the first-born about their allowances, or would take legal action to claim their percentage of their parents' free assets (those that were not part of the entailment or donated by the Crown). But such cases were never very numerous. And most of the unmarried siblings, that is those who had not been 'taken into' another house or had not founded another house, left their property and services to the house of the first-born or to their nephews - in other words, they gave their wealth back to the house in which they had been born.

The remarkable stability achieved by this model of behaviour began to break down in the second half of the eighteenth century. First, because of the crisis that affected the world of the European elites as careers in the Church became less and less desirable. This was reflected in a drastic fall in the numbers of noblemen entering the Church. Within the space of a few decades after that, the very discipline of the house began to be questioned. Sons who were not in the direct line of succession, and even some daughters, began to marry into the families of holders of large fortunes who were clearly outside the restricted circle from which, up to that time, the choice of a spouse had been made. The twilight of the grand aristocracy was already visible before the Liberal Revolution of 1832-34, which hastened its decline. In spite of this, the model that is presented here, and that until then had been seen as a reference point for all ennobled élites throughout Europe, has endured as a stereotype of aristocratic succession to this day.

Notes

1. Based on: Monteiro 1993a, Monteiro 1993b, Monteiro 1998.
2. Those quotations were taken from local lists of eligible citizens, to the Municipal Councils of Viana do Castelo (1808) and of Ponta Delgada, Açores, (1787).
3. Arquivos Nacionais/Torre do Tombo, Ministério do Reino, maço n.º943.

4. 'Si sunt nobiles, melior est quandoque aliorum filiorum dispersio quam hereditatis divisio; si sunt laboratores, faciant ut velint; si mercatores, tutior est divisio quam communio, ne infortunium unius alteri imputetur', quoted in Clavero 1989a: 438.

5. About the inheritance and succession practices of European aristocracies the best overview is still Cooper 1976.

6. Luís de Molina quoted in Clavero 1989a: 211

7. The first Portuguese entailments were studied by Rosa 1995, although in a different perspective from the one we use in this chapter.

8. Having described the practice of dividing inheritance amongst the heirs of the great houses in the fifteenth century, A. de Sousa Silva Costa Lobo emphasized that entailments became widespread 'from that century onwards' and that out of this process there emerged 'the class of the second-born, who were noblemen, but had no living other than that which was strictly necessary for their sustenance and who, because of the rules of society, could not redeem themselves from this fate and from the tutelage of the first-born, other than by entering the service of the state, or the idleness of an ecclesiastical office or a monastery ... while daughters who had no dowry ... retired to the convent' (Lobo 1903: 490-1). In actual fact, solidarity among members of a noble line age (identified by their surname and by the coat of arms) and the division of inheritance amongst close relatives seems to have been a good working model in a context where the accumulation of men and horses was decisive, given the remarkable fluidity of military and political events in the fifteenth century. It is a known fact that the house of Bragança itself adopted this model in an early phase (cf. Cunha 1990). But, later on, the widespread implementation of the practice of entailment and its reproductive models would prove to be irreversible.

9. From the will of Fernão de Sousa (1632), Arquivo da Casa de Bragança, Vila Viçosa.

10. These words had at the time a meaning similar to that given by J. Goody 1983: 16 and 224-8.

11. Cf. bibliography in Cooper 1976 and Monteiro 1998.

8

Family, Power and Property : Ascendancy and Decline of a Rural Elite*

José Manuel Sobral

Concepts and Objectives

I begin this chapter with a brief definition of some of the main concepts used in it. In using the term 'family', I am referring to domestic groups that succeed each other in time as representatives of a given continuous family line. When dealing with succession the term 'family' will assume another sense as well: that of a more or less broad group of persons who identify themselves as relatives and share a memory of a common ancestry.

Concerning the concept of 'power' I will draw on some of the ideas that belong to the established traditions of social thought - for example, the Marxist idea of power, in which power derives from structural relations, such as class power (the capacity to control people and material goods as a result of ownership of the means of production) and state power (the latter seen as an instrument of class domination). Another important influence is the Weberian conception of power, as expressed in his theory of stratification, which has a number of points of similarity with the Marxist idea, among them the idea of power as being intrinsic to social inequality, even though he also puts an emphasis on individual action - the capability of imposing one's will regardless of the resistance that may be encountered. In Weber's system of stratification, the basic groupings - 'classes', 'status groups' and 'parties' - are seen as forms through which power is widely diffused in the community (Abercrombie et al. 1994; Lukes 1978; and Weber 1922). I also took into account two more recent contributions to the study of power, those of Anthony Giddens and above all Pierre Bourdieu. While Giddens defines 'allocative resources' - property - and 'authoritative resources' - authority - as sources of power/domination, Bourdieu provides a more diversified analysis in which the social classes are characterized by the distribution of various different forms of capital - the economic, the cultural, the social, and the symbolic - and the various ways in which these relate to each other (Giddens 1979; Bourdieu

1979, 1984a). To simplify somewhat, *economic capital* is that which derives, for example, from property or income derived from the carrying on of an occupational activity; *cultural capital* is that which derives from possession of (high-level) education, as well as of knowledge that goes beyond the world of formal education; *social capital* is that which is inherent in the value of one's (personal or family) social position; and *symbolic capital* is any property or quality that is acknowledged or recognized by others (Bourdieu 1994). This chapter will show how all these forms of power are to be found in the history of the families of a local property-owning elite.

I define the term 'property' as a set of rights that people have over things. Property rights imply relations between people, in that they define who is, and who is not, permitted to have access to resources. That control over property confers power over others. In summary, the perspective I adopt here is similar to that of Hann, who states: 'the word "property" is best seen as directing attention to a vast field of cultural as well social relations, to the symbolic as well as the material contexts within which things are recognised and personal as well as, collective identities made' (Hann 1998: 5). The identities I am considering here are both the family and the individual identities, as well as the elite group itself.

The power that is derived from property is to be found at the heart of the family. It is held by the older generations and, either formally or informally, is controlled by someone of the male gender (a father, for example). This determines the relationship between family members. Property may also be a form of power exercised by the family in its local social space, and may form the basis for the acquisition or consolidation of other forms of power, such as political power. Or it may represent the success and confirmation of certain social strategies.

In carrying out the research on which this chapter is based, I took into account all these forms of power that are inherent in the idea of property. This is precisely because one of my core objectives was to study the so-called *process of social reproduction* in the linkages between family and society (Fortes 1958; J. Goody 1976; Bourdieu 1994). I have tried to analyse the ways in which members of each family succeed each other and how property rights (namely those over land and buildings) are handed down from one generation to the next. I also aim to study how succession and the transfer of rights are dependent on social position. The trajectories and strategies of these families are examined over time.

Thus, I have sought to establish how the distribution of property rights within the family relates to situations of inequality within it, how those same rights affect matrimonial choices, and what role family inheritance practices play in the production and perpetuation of the relationship between family and property.

I will focus on a local *power elite* and its evolution, from the end of the *ancien régime* to the present day.[1] In fact, the history of that elite is an excellent observation post for looking at the 'internal' and 'external' dimensions of the relationship between family, power and property and the linkages between them. By 'internal dimensions' I mean the ways in which resources - particularly property - are distributed within the family. By 'external dimensions' I mean those that are brought in from outside the family. These include two aspects. Firstly, those that derive from matrimonial alliances, strengthening the social and economic position of families, mainly by compensating for the fragmentation of wealth that occurs as generations succeed each other. Secondly, those that have their origin in non-economic spheres, like political events, which may consolidate the family's power, benefit it socially, and even bring economic advantages.

Brief Description of the Local Social Space and its Origins

The setting of this study is a rural parish in the *Beira Alta* region, in the district of Viseu in central Portugal. This area today has a population of about 1,300 inhabitants spread over three villages. The main local activity, agriculture, is broadly speaking divided into two main sectors: one is a diversified form of agriculture primarily aimed at family subsistence and only secondarily producing a surplus to be sold to market, such as potatoes and wine; the second is a market-oriented sector that basically produces wine, fruit, and olive oil and practises pig-breeding.

To simplify matters we can state that these types of agricultural activity are in a direct relationship with the strongly asymmetrical distribution of property. There are a fair number of families - around one-third - that do not own any property at all. Another one-third own property of 0.5 hectares or less. Only 8 per cent own land between 0.5 and 1 hectares in extent. There is an intermediate sector made up of ten families whose properties are between 10 and 20 hectares in size. Of the remainder, there are five families that own land ranging from 35 to over 130 hectares in extent. Ownership of modern technology is also typically concentrated in these large landowners.

The parish is situated approximately in the centre of the Dão demarcated wine region (*Região Demarcada do Dão*), one of the most important wine-producing areas in Portugal. It has good road links, is close to a main railway line, and has for a long time been part of the international market: for example, parish council records show that the area was already exporting corn and wine to Brazil in the first half of the nineteenth century.

It was not just the products that travelled. The local elites also travelled - to Lisbon or to Coimbra University, as did workers and small landowners, who went first to Brazil and then later to the United States, from at least since the second half of the nineteenth century. In the twentieth century more and more of the members of these latter groups went abroad, as emigration to the rest of Western Europe increased. Emigration is a clear reflection of the asymmetrical nature of property distribution and of the inadequacy of resources in the local economy. Even today, a large part of the income of local families does not derive from the primary sector, but from the salaries that members receive either from work in the construction sector in Portugal or from working abroad as emigrants (together with income from domestic work in the case of women). Salaried workers and small landowners - chiefly males under 50 years of age - are today above all part-time farmers: very often the farming work is left to the women of the family. Agriculture has declined in importance in the local economy, as it has in the whole country. This is one of the key elements in the progressive weakening of the position of the old local elite we are studying here and its loss of influence.

Many of the structural features of the local social space today - such as the unequal distribution of property - were already visible to some extent at the end of the sixteenth century. At that time, an aristocratic family became established in the region as the lords of the município (*donatários*)[2] and of two other neighbouring municípios. They established an entail. In 1597 they built a wall that laid down the boundaries of a *quinta* (a farm) here. Today that farm still has more or less the same boundaries, covering a little over 70 hectares. Under the system of emphyteusis, with over 300 long-term leases, they also had control over a large part of the income from the cultivation of land in the município. In 1609 they built a vast manor house, unparalleled in the region, and in 1637 they founded the local *Misericórdia* (charitable foundation),[3] which they endowed in perpetuity. In the seventeenth century (probably), we find two more entailments being established here, though these are of lesser significance, and yet another at the beginning of the following century. In other words, the uneven structure of property ownership associated with the presence of families from the major or minor aristocracy was already at that time a key feature of the local social space and of its network of social relations. Within these families there were other powers beyond those that derived from property ownership. The lords of the manor and first superintendents of the *Misericórdia* were for a time the governors of the region. Other families that owned rights to entails, but which were much less important, provided members of the local Câmara or town council (a political and administrative organ of a município, which is a grouping of various parishes).

Property distribution in this region did not change substantially after the end of the *ancien régime*. The rights of the only family from the grand aristocracy established in the parish remained intact, even though the family no longer lived there from the seventeeth century onwards. In other regions of Portugal, the Liberal regime disentailed the ecclesiastical property and sold the property of the religious and military orders, the income from which had gone, by royal grant, to the grand aristocracy. In this particular region, however, there was no significant transfer of property ownership. At the beginning of the second half of the nineteenth century the main local property-owners were still the same families of the two seventeenth-century entails (together with the grand aristocratic family mentioned previously) - Their representatives today still occupy a position at the top of the social hierarchy.

Before proceeding any further, I would like to dwell for a moment on the issue of the relationship between space and power. First, it should be remembered that, in the case we are studyng, power emanates from the ownership of landed property itself - for it was around the land and its owners that most of the village life revolved, whether the people were workers or tenant farmers (*rendeiros*). So the large estates were genuine *points of rotation*[4] in local life. The whole territory was affected by the structure of property ownership, and the large estate delimited and defined the very form of local villages: the centres of the villages were occupied in large measure by the houses and properties that bordered on the large estates, which meant that there was a concentration of older houses in a relatively small area and that the more recent houses were built on the periphery.

To adopt Bourdieu's terms, the fact of being a property-owner is in itself prestigious and is a form of symbolic capital. In our own day, the estates of the elite - land and houses - are the reference points for two types of discourse that point to different values, but that have in common the fact that they elevate the status of those who own them. The first type of discourse values the modernity (productive specialization, use of modern technology, etc.) of their estates; the second type of discourse, which is the prevalent form of discourse about property-ownership and wealth, sees in the houses of the landed property-owning elite examples of something that has preserved the antique and the authentic (and has good taste). They are examples of tradition and of a past that lends prestige. This is a process that has been observed in many other contexts (Shils 1981; Loewenthal 1993, 1998).[5] In summary, for most of the population, economic domination went hand in hand with symbolic domination - and for a long time with political domination as well.[6]

I have described very briefly some of the dimensions of the local social space in order to show how it both produces and is a part of the relations of power (cf. Lefebvre 1974). I think that Anthony Giddens's notion of *locale* encapsulates very well the overall assessment I have made here of the spatial dimensions of power, as it denotes 'contexts of interaction, including the physical aspects of the context - its *architecture* - in which systemic aspects of interaction and social relations are concentrated' (Giddens 1985: 12-13). At the same time, it enables us to understand some of the significance of property ownership for the local elite, apart from its purely economic aspects.

Elite, Family, Property and Power

The fundamental basis of the local elite's power is still today landed property, although the degree of power varies according to family. In some cases the land in question was purchased centuries ago; in other cases, the ownership or consolidation of ownership dates from the nineteenth century. Four of the five families of today's large landowners had ancestors who were in a similar position when the Liberal Revolution took place in the 1830s. According to data from internal tax revenue sources, the largest landowner was the Casa do Paço, which was owned by the heirs of the lords of the sixteenth and seventeenth centuries. Their local assets were administered by a general receiver of rents. Everything leads us to believe that this grand aristocracy family of absentee landlords did not *directly* exercise any power in local life at the end of the *ancien régime* - in that they controlled neither the governing body of the município nor the militia (*Ordenanças*) in the years immediately preceding the Liberal victory in 1834. By contrast, the two owners of entails whose rights dated from the seventeenth century were at the top of the *local* landowning hierarchy, still at a great distance from the grand aristocratic family of *Casa do Paço*. In 1852-53, the income from the município of this house was some four times greater than those from the other two entailments. However, the grand aristocratic house paid 11 per cent of all taxes raised by the município, which were borne overall by 1,435 taxpayers. But, as they lived locally, the two smaller houses had power in the council of the município, in the local militia, and in the religious fraternities. One of them, an ancestor of the largest landowner in our own time, was Mayor at the beginning of 1834. He was also Commander of the militia and Superintendent of the *Misericórdia*.

Before analysing other families in the local elite, I would like to look at the families of these two owners of smaller entails, who also administered other entailments outside the município. Their political fate was crucially affected by the advent of Liberalism. Although they welcomed the new regime that was established in 1834, it was at this time that they left - or more likely were removed from - their posts in the *Câmara*, never to return. Their names do not appear in the lists of citizens put forward for council offices in the decade of the 1840s, and yet those lists contained the names of other local notables. At least in the early stages of the Liberal regime this group was not trusted by the authorities of the new regime. However, it should be mentioned in passing that this did not mean that all the small district nobility was anti-Liberal. Curiously, it was only some hundred years later, under the ultra-conservative regime of the *Estado Novo*[7] (1933-1974), that an administrator of one of those landed property entails came back as mayor (*Presidente da Câmara*). This situation is undoubtedly a reflection of the fact that control over resources, as represented by property-ownership rights, continued to give its holders social prestige a hundred years after the establishment of the Liberal regime.

Despite their removal from public office, these administrators of landed property continued to be influential in the *Misericórdia* - which, it should be recalled, remained the main financial institution in the area until the twentieth century. They were also predominant in the *Confraria do Santíssimo* (Fraternity of the Most Holy One), another Catholic institution that was of lesser local significance, and in the Parish Council from 1836 onwards.[8] The fact that these families were part of the aristocracy must be seen to explain the particular trajectory that they followed, as well as the strong element of segregation in relation to other landowning families whose history was very different from their own. Besides the position at the top of the social hierarchy that property-ownership gave them, these families had another point in common - the absence of any alliance by marriage with families that were not part of the aristocracy.

In one of the cases, although the family did not belong to the grand aristocracy, it was related to it, and had been an aristocratic family for many centuries. It owned an entail founded in the fourteenth century, and was part of a network of family relationships that even included among its ancestors members of the Portuguese royal families. It owned a family vault at a local church that was under its patronage, and used the ancient Portuguese royal emblem in its coat of arms. Of the brothers and sisters who reached adulthood in the second half of the nineteenth century - two male and three female, four of whom would live on into the twentieth century - none would get married. They had plenty of wealth in the form of landed property, which included in particular various manorial houses in the region and a manor house with land in northern Portugal. After the Liberal regime abolished all entails, those assets could quite easily have been used as marriage endowments. Whatever the reasons for their celibacy, the maintenance of a link between the family (a blood line and name) and the ownership of property (Saint-Martin 1993) was ensured. In the 1920s, the vast majority of those assets ended up passing down by inheritance to a cousin who was the closest relative in the paternal line. This person, however, was a childless bachelor who, in the 1970s, donated the property he owned to the descendants of the kings of Portugal, thus ending the centuries-old relationship between this particular family and this property.

The other family could not lay claim to such an eminent aristocratic lineage. The entailment was founded by a cleric. Documents from the *ancien régime*, which grant varying status to people in accordance with their social position, do not give the members of this second family the deferential and pre-eminent treatment accorded to the one just mentioned. In 1868, following the death of the former head of the family, the inheritance was divided. The heirs were three siblings, two brothers and one sister. The way the property was handed down and the paths the members of the family subsequently took are quite different from those taken by the earlier family. The first-born had already married - he would in fact be the only one to get married - and so acquired a title through marriage. The other brother and the sister received property from the estate of their parents. However, under the law of the *terço*[9] the parents had already endowed the first-born as lord and effective successor by leaving him the main house and its surrounding lands. In other words, they had left him the most important spatial components of the family's identity and its most important symbols - in particular the family's house with their coat of arms itself. Ownership of the family property, at the local level, was diluted to

some degree, but that which had the most symbolic and material significance for the perpetuation of the family name remained, as was normal in
the aristocracy, with the first-born. We can say quite fairly that there was a
separation between inheritance and succession, since the assets were
divided in the form we have related above, but the first-born son kept his
position as the link that provided family continuity leading from the past
to the future.

He then married outside the district into a family of the minor aristocracy, and would see his son consolidate the local position of the family still
further again by marriage. He married the daughter of a great capitalist,
who had been ennobled but was of humble origins, and who was a shareholder of the Bank of Portugal. His vast economic resources enabled him
to marry his daughter into a family that was undeniably weaker in this
respect, but that would bring into the overall equation of the marriage
alliance the prestige of its ancestry and possibly even the condition of
being a former landowning family. Here, as in other contexts, marriage
took place between those who had resources, or capital, that could be
regarded as having equivalent value (Bourdieu 1980). It was their heir
who, in 1876, bought the sixteenth-century farm that was part of the estate
of the former grand aristocratic lords. That property today is still in the
ownership of the same family, and continues to be the largest property in
the district. This has provided that family with prestige, power and influence that have extended right down to our own time. All this is immediately visible in the way the physical space is organized, since that particular
estate was next door to the house where the heir of 1816 lived and was
annexed (joined) to it, thus enlarging the territory identified with the
family. Since the 1950s, this family has also held the Superintendency of
the *Misericórdia*, which, despite being a shadow of its former self as a charitable foundation, continues to be the most prestigious of all local institutions.

The first-born of this second family was the only one to get married.
However, his brother, who received by way of inheritance a substantial
legacy, sufficient to build a vast residence, had two daughters whom he
recognized as his lawful heirs. Nevertheless, he always accepted playing a
subordinate role in relation to his elder brother. His mansion did not display any aristocratic symbol, nor does his family grave, by contrast with the
enormous coats of arms and stone-built vaults of his brother. The family
has extended down to our own time through the family of the first-born,
and to this date no problems of division of the inheritance or of succession have occurred, since there was either only one (legitimate) son or
there was no son, so that ownership of the rights and the position was able
to pass down to one sole heir (a nephew), who in his turn passed them
down to his only daughter.

Of the four mayors appointed in the turbulent year of 1834 when the
Liberal regime was established, three were wealthy landowners from the
parish. From 1832 to the present day the property-owning elite of the

parish was the sector that supplied the largest number of mayors (13). I think this fact clearly establishes the importance of the local elite in regional politics. It was an elite made up of property-owners, but also included priests and later graduates of Coimbra University. I think I can therefore rightly call it a rural bourgeoisie, to adopt the term advanced by the historian Albert Silbert (1968).

Let us take a closer look at the trajectories of some of the more important, but not aristocratic, families in this elite sector, which were in the ascendant throughout the nineteenth century thanks to their political efforts. We can best study them by looking at the history of the *Casa do Outeiro*. The man who runs it today counts among his maternal and paternal ancestors and relatives not only the most important local political leaders, but even some important national leaders. His paternal great-grandfather, a graduate of Coimbra University, was born in this same *Casa do Outeiro*, became Mayor, district administrator, superintendent of the *Misericórdia*, several times member of Parliament and vice-president of the Chamber of Deputies. One of his brothers was Portuguese consul in Newcastle. This great-grandfather was not one of the greater local landowners, though he was reasonably wealthy. The fame he achieved in politics - as well as some presumption of being of aristocratic origin - made it possible for his only daughter to marry a rich graduate from a neighbouring parish, of humbler origin, from a family of landowning and money-lending priests, with a fortune acquired on their father's side in Brazil. This couple had already reached the top of the local property-owning hierarchy in the second half of the nineteenth century. The son-in-law, a Law graduate like his father-in-law, took over from him in the political sphere. He was to be one of the local leaders of one of the two major parties at the time (the Progressives), Mayor, Justice of the Peace, superintendent of the *Misericórdia*, civil governor and one of the founders of the Nelas Agricultural Syndicate, an association of landowning farmers dedicated primarily to defending the interests of the region's wine-growers. This couple had three children - their daughter married and took a country manor donated by a spinster cousin as her dowry, while each of the sons took his own manor and the lands attached to them.

Their two sons were to pursue a political career. One, an agronomist, was to become Minister of Agriculture and Governor of Angola during the First Republic (1910-26). The other, who graduated as a lawyer and became a magistrate, was also under the same regime Mayor, Governor, and superintendent of the Misericórdia.

This latter, father of the current manager, was to marry into another family that achieved a prominent position in the last quarter of the nineteenth century. His father-in-law's family was wealthy, but not part of the aristocracy. The father-in-law, Dr Joaquim, was the son of a local trader who lent money and was also Mayor, the nephew of a priest and of other bachelor uncles, owners of agricultural lands who also dealt in money-lending. Their wealth all flowed together into the person of Dr Joaquim, their sole descendant. The wife was the daughter of a rent collector of a grand aristocratic family, the owners of *Casa do Paço* a wine merchant who was the main private local moneylender and the ancestor of another family of large local landowners. Dr Joaquim became Mayor like his father, superintendent of the *Misericórdia*, member of Parliament, founder of the Agricultural Syndicate, and local head of another important political party of the time (the Regeneration Party). As in the previous case, this graduate landowner established himself as a landowner and politician. Apart from his son-in-law, Dr Joaquim was to have a son who became an agronomist, and who was also a superintendent of the *Misericórdia* - and the political enemy of his brother-in-law.

Let us now consider the personal careers of the members of these families. The three entailment families, which owned most of the land at the beginning of the Liberal period, withdrew from the political arena, and one of them did not seem to invest locally in anything other than landownership. By contrast, these newer local dynasties consolidated their position as landowners in other ways - by money-lending, by seeking fame through political activity and by holding public office and, in all likelihood, through networks of captive 'clients' as well. Apart from this, they invested in the acquisition of educational capital - for example, by qualifying in Law at Coimbra. Given their lower starting-point for resource accumulation, the rise of the graduates was only made possible by bringing in other family resources in the form of legacies left to them by unmarried relatives in their wills (both these graduates inherited from two uncles who were priests). The existence of unmarried relatives was a key element in enabling someone to join the elite. Another difference in this sector by comparison with the entailment families was the fact that they tended to marry locally. While the economic position and above all the aristocratic status of the entailment families reduced their available options within the region and meant that they could choose a marriage partner anywhere in the country, these latter families found their partners locally in more than one generation, thus bringing together those with significant educational capital and those who possessed economic capital in their own right, joining, for example, a graduate with no fortune to a wealthy heiress.

The concern with maintaining the economic and social capital represented by the ownership of property and with perpetuating the family at the top of the social tree to some extent brought the aristocratic and the non-aristocratic segments of the local elite closer together. But there were nevertheless significant differences, which have to do with those elements of their family identity that they prized most highly, as well as with two temporal factors: the specific moment in time that their families were founded, and the duration over time of that recognizable family unit. The members of the aristocratic segment managed to stay at the top after the abolition of entails by employing strategies to overcome possible critical moments when their asset base might have been reduced, for example by dispersal of property through marriage and division of inheritance. Thus they preserved the essential aspects of property-ownership and of family representation in one sole heir. This led them not only to try to counterbalance the division of inheritance, which diluted income, with marriages that would bring in new income, but also to remain celibate in disproportionate measure, as well as refusing to grant any rights to illegitimate children (this would only change with the constitution of 1976).

Whereas with one or two partial exceptions, property-owners of non-aristocratic origin started out by not having any illustrious ancestors or genealogy to call upon. The family had acquired prestige in that same generation or shortly before. There were no restrictions on marriage - and in particular on the marriage of female members of the family, perhaps because there was never any problem in finding a suitable marriage partner for daughters. At the beginning of the twentieth century the various heirs of the two graduates I have mentioned were able to establish *houses* - a label that associates a given family with a given property.[10] This was undoubtedly a result of their many activities, particularly in the political field. At a time when agriculture was the main economic activity, to be a landowner was to have the highest and most prestigious social status. The founding of *houses* in this way, therefore, represented the high point of their local consecration. These houses were handed down to their various heirs, with the one that had belonged originally to their parents remaining always, with its neighbouring lands, for the oldest son. The spatial dimensions of the family's presence and power were also taken into consideration in the way in which they perpetuated their presence in the cemetery founded at the end of the nineteenth century, by means of family vaults or permanent stone graves, which set them apart from ordinary people. Their memory is also a form of capital.

However, celibacy - and the non-recognition of illegitimate children - also served to keep intact the property of the other two local houses that represent the remaining large landowners today. In their political activity, the members of these families were also much more discreet, even though they held one or two formal offices and exercised some informal influence. One of these families was founded at the beginning of the twentieth century by the brother of a grandmother of the current administrator of the house of Outeiro. Here the property and social position were handed down from an uncle (who refused to recognize his illegitimate only daughter) to a niece. In the next generation, a brother's part was bought out by the first-born. In this way, the descendants of this household managed to preserve the relationship between property, house and a prestige-giving social continuity.

The other house is of humble and more recent origin (the second half of the nineteenth century), and was established after the successful emigration of its founder to Brazil. The latter had only two children: one remained a bachelor, while the other married. The one who married did not have any children. The bachelor had one child, who was legitimated by the marriage of his parents *in articulo mortis*. The two brothers kept the property undivided, so it was passed down to the sole descendant. This man married a niece of the wife of his uncle, who was also the heiress to the wife's estate. With these marriages property was acquired elsewhere, and the house was kept in the same family right down to the present day.

The above-mentioned house of Outeiro owes its present survival to the fact that it was not *physically* divided. It was managed by the first-born son, who was an unmarried accountant, as a legally constituted farming enterprise (corporation). Currently it is he, as the major shareholder, who retains control. He is trying to ensure that his nephews, who own a fourth of the company and live outside the community, do not inherit the ownership of the company. In his view, this would signal the end of the family's position in the local community, in economic and symbolic terms. The various nephews, who are faced with financial difficulties, are not amenable to arguments and strategies employed to maintain the family's ties to the ownership of landed property. Apart from anything else they have never lived in the local community. They belong to other social spheres, and presumably have plans and values that are different from those that have constituted the guiding principles of the local landowning elite over at least the last two centuries. Similar reasons can be found to explain why, during the last twenty years, two of the *houses* of relatives of the house of Outeiro have disappeared from the local community.

Concluding Remarks

My main aim in this chapter was to emphasize how property-ownership was in many aspects the basis for the local power of families belonging to the elite. It should be recalled once again that prestige was bestowed by the mere fact of owning property. The categorization of the various classes of those who were eligible to vote and who were eligible for election to office in the census system introduced by the Liberal regime was in itself an explicit acknowledgement of the political value of being identified as a landowner.[11] Later on, that same status was the basis for obtaining academic degrees - in Bourdieu's terminology, increasing one's educational capital. To be identified as a landowner also enabled the person who was so identified to become a philanthropist by means of the *Misericórdia*, or by contributing to the spread of education, thus cultivating an image of generous Christian charity and of enlightened citizenship. Through property-ownership these people acquired a privileged life-style associated with educated culture and the cultivation of good taste. In our own day their residential buildings stand out as examples of that good taste, and are seen as a part of the local *heritage* that must be preserved. Landownership was also the basis on which they were able to become the local political leaders *par excellence*. In summary, property-ownership was a fundamental factor in the accumulation and preservation of various types of capital by the families of the local elite and in cementing their power.

I would like to conclude by just mentioning briefly once again the relationship between this elite and local political power. That relationship may give us some clues about the changes in the relationship between elite families and property-ownership. For this purpose, it is necessary to take into account the life-paths of the families involved and the impact of the relative decline of agriculture on those life-paths and on their condition as rural landowners.

The absolute local dominance of these elite families in regional terms came to an end with the founding of the Republic in 1910. Most of them were not sympathetic to the new order, and the new regime brought about open conflict between the two brothers-in-law who supported it, one of them a supporter of the more radical faction, the other a conservative republican. With the Republic came a plebeianization of public office: leaders were sought out from those more humble backgrounds in which they were likely to find greater electoral support. Thus, between 1910 and 1926, only one Law graduate became Mayor, in sharp contrast to the situation that prevailed before 1910. But apart from the specific changes in the political field, the elites also gradually withdrew from the local community. For example, whereas the parents of those who were alive at the time of the Republic had been landowners and graduates, but had not carried on any profession in connection with the Law they had studied, their children entered the professions for which they had received a university education - even though they did hold on to the farms. Little by little, as income from work became significant or indispensable, they stayed more and more away from the local community. The ever-declining importance of agriculture meant that their income from farming declined by comparison to the income that they could earn from other activities. The process is somewhat similar to that in which average property-owners, less well-endowed in terms of land, became involved - they invested their all in the education of their sons from the end of the nineteenth century onwards.

Under the *Estado Novo* (1933-1974) there was a total withdrawal from the local community. Various factors came together here. One of them was the fact that the elite actually left the local community. Its members no longer lived there permanently. They left for the capital, where they had jobs. Then there was the decline of the primary sector, which led to a widespread decline in the political importance of landowners. The dictatorship did not require the specific support that some local political boss or other might be able to give it, given the control that it exercised over the whole nation. As the room for electoral competition diminished, so the clienteles associated with competition between political parties declined too, and the elite also withdrew from local public offices, which were directly controlled by the government.

As their power to act at a supralocal level diminished, so too there was a reduction in the range of favours that the local elite could dispense. Their sponsorship role therefore also declined. Even as employers they lost ground, because the limited modernization of their farms lessened their ability to recruit labour and consequently reduced their power over the contingent of potential salaried workers. At the same time, the number of available workers also declined drastically, as a result of emigration, from the mid-1960s onwards.

Under the *Estado Novo*, therefore, changes that had taken place at a more global level were reflected locally, in that the Mayors were no longer the large landowners but rather professionals - doctors or lawyers, for example, who sometimes remained in office for lengthy terms - a clear sign that the role of Mayor had become a bureaucratic one. Being Mayor, moreover, enabled the holder of that office to muster a much wider clientele of people who owed him favours than the clientele he might have obtained from using the limited resource of property-ownership. Local positions also lost some of their attraction for members of families who had held those offices in earlier times. All these factors, but particularly the decline in farm incomes, together with the increasing significance of urban employment made possible by the accumulation of educational capital, led to a decline in the elite's investments in the rural world. By contrast to what had occurred in the previous century, the members of the elite did not buy more property, with the result that in some cases the link between the *houses* and large-scale landownership was broken. However, it should be said that neither of these cases extended to the aristocratic families.

With the advent of democracy in 1974, bureaucrats and professionals now compete for public office. None of them come from families that were eminent because they owned large landed estates. The Parish Council is run by small landowners and officials, and even in one exceptional case by an ordinary worker. These people occupy positions that, a century ago, belonged to the large landowners. Today the latter no longer have any important role in local political life - if indeed they have any role at all.

Notes

* The documentary sources for this article are identified in the author's book, *Trajectos. O Presente e o Passado na Vida de uma Freguesia da Beira*, Lisbon, ICS, 1999.

1. The term *ancien régime* refers here to the state under the absolutist monarchy and to a society in which the pinnacle of the social hierarchy was represented by a grand aristocracy (cf. Monteiro, this volume, chapter 8). The *ancien régime* terminated in Portugal with the onset of the Liberal régime in the civil war that ended in 1834.
    This is a very different context from the one in which the expression 'the power elite' was coined - C. Wright Mills used it to describe the connection between the political, economic and military leaders of the USA after the war. The term 'power elite' is here used to denote a concentration of different forms of power, in this case the power that

is concentrated in a small number of families. Cf. Mills 1956.

2. The *donatários* were the local lords, members of aristocratic families - a position that could be handed down from one generation to another, by royal permission - who had a certain number of powers granted to them by royal decree (of a judicial nature, for example). This gave them certain rights over the production and distribution of certain goods, and these rights in turn gave them income from rents.

3. The *Misericórdias* were fraternities whose aim was to dispense Christian charity. They were generally dedicated to assisting the poor, the old, the widowed and the orphaned. Created by the elites, and having at their disposal sometimes very large amounts of capital that they lent out with interest, they represented for those in charge of them an important source of economic, symbolic (in terms of prestige) and political power.

4. For Simmel a 'point of rotation' is an object of interest that is fixed in space (a building, a church, etc.), and that gives rise to certain types of relations around it. Cf. Simmel 1986 (1908): 661 ff.

5. At least, this is how it appears to those who are ignorant of the houses' origins, because their history contains some surprises (in the twentieth century, houses were rebuilt in order to give them an air of antiquity and a unity of architectural style).

6. Symbolic domination, according to Bourdieu, is that form of domination that is exercised by way of the acceptance of certain postulates, axioms, assumptions, etc., that benefit those who occupy a certain class position. In this particular case that means those who own buildings and artefacts that are associated with good taste and tradition. Cf. Bourdieu and Wacquant 1992: 116-49.

7. The *Estado Novo* was the name given to the regime of the political dictatorship that ruled Portugal from 1933 to 1974. It was strongly influenced by the Roman Catholic Church and by Italian fascism. Its anti-liberal stance was opposed as much to the monarchist-liberal regime (which, broadly speaking, had been in existence from 1834 to 1910) as to the First Republic (1910-1926) that succeeded it.

8. *Junta de Paróquia* (later on *Junta de Freguesia*): the Parish Council is the local political and administrative unit in the Portuguese state. Several parishes make up a municipio, the executive organ of which is the *Câmara Municipal* - The Municipal Council or 'Town Hall'.

9. In donating or leaving property in his or her will, a person was entitled to dispose freely of one-third (*um terço*) of his or her estate. The remaining two-thirds formed part of the *legítima* (legitimate inheritance) of his or her heirs, and he or she was therefore not able to dispose of it freely.

10. Bourdieu 1961; Flandrin 1976; Lévi-Strauss 1984; Saint-Martin 1993; Monteiro 1995.

11. In that system, only a small minority of males who had a certain level of income were entitled to vote.

José Manuel Sobral

Part IV

Monopolies and Enclaves

9

Re-serving Succession in a British Enclave[1]

Jean Lave

Introduction

Grape Britain: The dynasties who have controlled the port industry since the seventeenth century live in a corner of Portugal that is forever England.

This is the headline of an article about British port shippers in the *Sunday Times Magazine* (London, 3 August 1997). The article notes the visits of a variety of celebrities and royalty to 'the Taylors' and 'the Symingtons', portrayed respectively as the oldest and the largest of the port firms, as the pre-eminent port families and as in perennial rivalry with each other over the production of vintage port. The headline reflects faithfully the story that follows: its subjects are described as aristocratic (those 'dynasties'), as unchanging (since the seventeenth century), as British ('forever England'), as heads of port-wine families and firms, and as if they are *the* British in Porto. The article gives a skilfully decontextualized rendering of 'long-unbroken elite succession' among the British port-wine merchants. The 'Taylors' and Symingtons certainly would not object.[2] This chapter examines how the port gentry produce such a decontextualized vision in practice, its *raison d'être* and its effects.

Stories similar to the one in the *Sunday Times* are told in many venues: the port gentry families are described with reverence in the literature and the free tours for hordes of visitors to the port firms tightly clustered in Vila Nova de Gaia. Firms regularly produce commemorative volumes for anniversaries marking their founding or for decades, or centuries, of port-wine production. There are frequent luxurious and elaborate tours for journalists and substantial customers that start at the Port 'houses' in the historical trade entrepôt in Vila Nova de Gaia across the Douro river from the city of Porto (it is in Vila Nova de Gaia that almost all port is aged, blended, and bottled and from which it is shipped), swing across the river to the exclusive male port scions' weekly luncheon for themselves and their guests at the British port firms' private club, the Factory House, and then travel 80 km. up the river for a weekend of elegant meals, excellent port, and tours of wine-making centres at the firms' guest lodges among

167

the vineyards in the demarcated zone of port grape production. These tours are hosted by the old port families associated with particular firms, who entertain their guests as if presiding over house parties at rural estates. A crucial component of their claims to social standing and power is fashioned through these tours. Large orders of wine result, and also a constant flow of articles that reiterate facets of the port gentry story amid wine reviews and society gossip in the popular and trade presses. The journalist's picture of the families and their lives is typical of the genre:

> Although there are now many Portuguese companies, British port houses still dominate the market and their members live up to the image of the Englishman abroad. Jim Reader, production manager of Cockburn's, came out to the company as an oenologist and now looks every bit the colonial gent, with his ruddy cheeks and twirling moustache. He recalls, 'At my interview all they wanted to know was whether I played cricket.'
>
> Oporto may not have any obvious trappings of the Empire, but the few hundred Brits in the trade live as if they were in Britain. *The Telegraph* or *The Times* land on their desks every morning. The men favour tweed suits in winter and Panama hats in summer, eat Marmite for breakfast, and speak execrable Portuguese. The women subscribe to *Country Life* and *Tatler*, grow rose gardens, make jams for the annual bazaar, keep braces of pheasant in the freezer, and join quilting circles and amateur dramatics groups.
>
> Hospitable to a fault, their houses are done up as English country homes with lots of flowery chintz, hunting prints and stags' heads. The children are sent to public school in Britain. At weekends they go to the Oporto Cricket and Lawn Tennis Club where they play, watched by intrigued Portuguese children who gather on the wall. On Sundays they attend the English church in the morning, then walk the dogs: Dalmatians for the Taylors and springer spaniels for the Syms. And of course they all claim to drink a bottle of port a day.
>
> 'We're strange animals', admits James Symington over white port and tonic at his country estate, where a wild boar's head takes pride of place.
>
> 'I feel that Oporto is home and have a great love for the country, but one's way of life is largely British. Most of our socialising is with the other British because one shares the same outlook, the same set of ideas. Portuguese men tend to like roaring off on motorbikes at weekends, which is something I can't imagine doing, while I can't imagine the Portuguese women getting down on their hands and knees with a trowel in the garden like my wife, Penny' (ibid., p. 45).

The Sunday Times version of the port gentry story sets the scene as a colonial enclave, with its 'colonial gents', as a 'small, isolated community where until recently the only way home [Great Britain in this context] was by boat', in which 'many British port traders have married into each other's families'. Here, 'members live up to the image of the Englishman abroad' in spite of not having the 'trappings of empire'. A series of vignettes describe men who stand for the colony of old port-wine families and familiar brands of port. The vignettes tell us from whom these men have inherited their port-shipping mandate and which of their sons are to follow. Alistair Robertson, James Symington, Rupert Symington and Peter Cobb are subjected to this treatment. Specific issues about grooming successors in the next generation are presented in the article as a preoccupation in family, not corporate, settings. The Annual Ladies' Day Lunch at the Oporto Factory House 'is an occasion for matchmaking, discussing the best public schools to send one's offspring to, and comparing outfits in turns of phrase Jane Austen would have appreciated' (ibid., 42).

By contrast to the framing of succession in individual terms - in discussions of public schools or spouses - community *institutions* for producing and sustaining family life are scarcely mentioned - indeed, only as historical accomplishments of the colony.

Practices of succession refer in part to antecedents that entitle the bearer (invariably male) and his family to elevated social position and an assured future. They seem to presume a future inhabited as they presently live it (if not better), and so avoid speculating about it. This flat, presentist vision is, in effect, ahistorical in character, like the one that depicts the port trade as dominated by Brits who in turn are dominated by the rivalry between Symingtons and Taylors as they try to outdo each other in the making of vintage ports. There are other sorts of 'histories' as well: the journalist's story sketches a whiggish 'event history' composed of internationally recognized benchmarks, 1703 (Methuen Treaty), 1812 (Napoleonic Wars), 1832 (Portuguese Civil War), 1974 (Portuguese Revolution), as an armature on which to hang the port gentry's distinctly self-congratulatory tale of the discovery, invention, fortification and improvement of port wine by generations of discerning Brits. There are excluded histories: drastic political-economic transformations in the centuries of the port trade and the changes these have wrought in the British enclave are practically invisible. So is Portugal, the host nation state that encompasses the port trade and the British enclave. In quoting extensively from the story in *The Sunday Times*, I have included all but one of its meagre references to Portugal and things Portuguese. A-histories, Whig histories, excluded histories - they erase and conflate the relations that produce port gentry entitlement.

Many of the authors in this book share a view that family succession to wealth and high social position is a complex and contradictory process extending across multiple places, generations, and practices. In this view, 'succession' treated as a matter of choice within an elite family or corporate entity appears problematic, too narrow a construction of the devolution of power and position and too limited a view of the significant participants and crucial actors. Bearing this in mind, Antónia Pedroso de Lima and João de Pina Cabral's insistence that we locate leadership and succession in shared contexts seems fundamental to understanding any and all aspects of social life in terms of social practice, situated as it is in spatial, historical, economic and political relations.

What '*elite* contextualization' might mean is crucial in pursuing ethnographic studies of succession among the powerful and privileged (and with them the powerless and underprivileged). There are special perils in carrying out research on those with more power to control their relations with the anthropologist than the latter has to stipulate the dimensions of her ethnographic inquiry. Among the British in Porto, at any rate, I found that much of the power to control what others came to know involved decontextualization of key conditions and processes for producing succession, in response to the surprisingly numerous others who would have liked to draw it into public view. Excluded, Whig and a-histories are examples of such practices. In such circumstances it makes sense to engage in an anthropology of recontextualization, exploring ethnographically the practices through which the prestigious and powerful erase and fabricate the conditions of their own production.[3]

The Problem

For the British historically connected with the port-wine trade who are locally recognized 'first families' in the British enclave in the city of Porto, succession to leadership in the community and the trade is in part a matter of demonstrating effortless entitlement to it. Their apparent ease paradoxically requires sustained hard work, including political struggle to defend positions of privilege. Much of the work goes into sustaining local institutional practices that are partially the means and partially the symbols of their success. Tensions between the requirements to demonstrate effortless ease and to engage in persistent labour are partially resolved as port gentry families participate in two distinct circuits of succession-production that they further arrange to keep apart.[4]

The first links the port firms in Gaia, the Factory House and the wine 'estates' in the Douro. How the port gentry inhabit these spaces raises questions about how a few families manage to portray themselves as first families, and obtain ratification as such, through their astonishingly practised interactions with the public, customers, and the press. A close examination of the port gentry histories in *The Sunday Times* will clarify what the story's tellers wish to make public and wish to erase.

If the first circuit is about displaying success, the second is about securing successors. The insular round of day-to-day life in the British enclave in Porto, including regular attendance at church, school and club, presents major sites of elite leadership in part aimed at the control of succession. The enclave provides women and children (and men now perhaps more than in the past) with reassurance that they have not become merely ghosts of their former selves. But they have far less control over other participants than in the Gaia-Douro circuit. For, in spite of the impression the port gentry seek to create, the British enclave in Porto is heterogeneous, composed of class-, gender- and nationally-differentiated factions. Work by elite leaders to secure their institutional trajectories in the enclave is a way to ensure succession for their desired successors while securing other social locations for those who are not. Indeed, as community leaders this 'guarantee' is in some sense their problem. Ethnographic exploration of their labour and political struggle in the British enclave is part of the recontextualization of port gentry succession.[5]

The Factory House is a pivotal institution that plays a part in each circuit. But there are many practices that segregate these circuits in space and time: common boundaries (that in most other social settings seem confirmed by mundane social arrangements) are here made differently, between commodity and persons, between public and private family life, and between firm and family. All are brought into the service of producing and sustaining family succession to power and influence in the British enclave and in the port trade.[6]

Background

British merchants first, and later their families, have been a presence, overseeing family life and port-wine export firms in Porto, Portugal (a city of two names, called Oporto by the British), since the late eighteenth century, and in small numbers for a century before that. As the English favoured Douro wines - when fortified with brandy, the grapes grown in the severe conditions of the upper Douro river valley produce a strong, sweet wine - English factors settling in Porto at the mouth of the Douro came to dominate a trade in 'port wine', as their successors still do today.

A lucrative trade comprising diverse constituents inevitably produced confrontations. Whether these arose from conflicts of class, privilege, religion, city versus country, or one of several other points of tension, as most shippers were British and most landowners and farmers Portuguese both contests and contestants were easily divided along national lines. In 1755, the Portuguese government was vigorously petitioned by British factors and Portuguese farmers. Each accused the other of running down the trade. Guided by the future Marquis of Pombal, the state established a monopoly company, the *Companhia Geral da Agricultura das Vinhas do Alto Douro*, with exclusive powers and effective control over the making and export of the wine. It also demarcated a particular area of the Douro, decreeing that the wine from that region alone could be exported as Douro wine, and granted certain privileges to the Porto exporters.

At the heart of the port trade is a changing but continual struggle between Portuguese family farmers who raise port grapes and merchant exporters, many, but not all of them, British, who export the wine and have relatively recently come to dominate its production as well. But dilemmas of the last fifty years look quite different from those of the first two hundred and fifty, as many of the British merchants have become more emblematic of, than central actors in, the port trade. There are problems concerning the continued hegemonic position of the old port families in the British enclave in Porto today, in the face of the declining contribution of the port trade to the Portuguese economy and its external trade balances. It is uncertain whether the port families can continue to sustain the community institutions they nonetheless control. And they face increasing control by the multinational owners and Portuguese managers of the 'British' port firms.

Indeed, what three decades or more ago were family partnership-based firms are for the most part no longer family-owned. The firms that control the port trade today are small subdivisions of multinational corporations in the global alcoholic beverages industry. The families face these changes with much at stake in re-serving a future for themselves and their children as scions of the port trade and as metonymic representatives of the British enclave. In the longer run the fragility of the position of the port gentry families of the enclave in Porto seems clear. A central question concerns how they are to sustain their power when this has decreasing resonance with their political-economic interpolation in the global corporate organization of trade.

Port Gentry and the Factory House

A prior question is, 'Who are the port gentry families?' According to the port gentry narrative, it should be easy to answer: these families have been in Portugal for three hundred years, founded port-wine firms nearly that long ago, own and manage these same firms today, and can trace unbroken descent from then until now. None of the port gentry families meets these criteria. There are historical reasons.[7] We also know that most firms that existed at the turn of the century and were still operating at the time of the Portuguese Revolution in 1974 were subsequently acquired by multinational corporations. If not their unbroken succession to ownership of port-wine firms, what does distinguish them from the rest? The key lies in the membership of some British port firms in the exclusive Factory House. A dozen or so firms belong to this club, officially known as The British Association, and are represented by men whose forebears worked up to influential positions in the port firms a generation or more ago, or whose families now own, or formerly owned, port firms or who have ancestral claims on connections with the port trade.

The twelve member firms in 1993 were Churchill Graham, Cockburn Smithes, Croft and Co., Delaforce Sons, W. & J. Graham, Martinez Gassiot, Robertson Brothers, Sandeman and Co., Silva and Cosens, Taylor, Fladgate and Yeatman, and Warre. Though the names appear to be Portuguese, Martinez Gassiot (English and Spanish originally) is owned by Cockburn's, Silva & Cosens by Symington. The individual members, including the port gentry, are eight Symingtons, D. G. S. Bain, Huyshe Bower, Alastair Robertson, R. A. Reid, J. K. Burnett, and I. A. Sinclair, three Guimaraens, Peter Cobb, Jim Reader, Johnny Graham, George Sandeman, David Delaforce (in London), D. A. Orr and among the honorary members, George A. Robertson and W. A. Warre, who live in Great Britain. Members of the Factory House officially include 'high-ranking managers or directors' of the firms, but for those who are the first generation to enter a port firm, the degree of port gentrification they assume is

Table 9.1: The Factory House

Members 1993	Member Firms	Owned By
J. Graham	Churchill Graham	J. Graham
Peter Cobb		
G. Guimaraens		
J. Reader	Cockburn	Allied Domeq
R.A. Reid		
J.K. Burnett	Croft	IDV then Diageo
David Delaforce	Delaforce	Croft
J.R.O'C Symington		
A.J, Symington	W. Graham	Symington
D.A. Orr	Martinez Gassiot	Cockburn
G. Robertson (Hon.)	Robertson's	Sandeman
G. Sandeman	Sandeman	Seagram
M.D. Symington		
P.D. Symington		
D.M. Symington	Silva & Cosens	Symington
A.B. Robertson	M.H.S. Bower	
D.G.S. Bain	Taylor Fladgate & Yeatman	Taylor's
D.F. Guimaraens (assoc.)		
B.D. Guimaraens	Fonseca Guimaraens	Taylor's
I.D.F. Symington		
P.R. Symington		
J.A.D. Symington		
W.A. Warre (Hon.)	Warre	Symington

modest and conditional. Bain, Burnett, Orr, Reader, and Sinclair, as 'newcomer' managers, are pillars of the British enclave, but not port gentry.

Whom Factory House members distinguish themselves *from* has a history: besides Portuguese port wine merchants, these include British merchants who do not trade in port wine, Brits whose class standing is less than that of the port gentry, and women. Each of these exclusions is elaborated in history, in the Gaia-Douro circuit and in the British enclave today.

The Factory House is a three-storey imposing, rather grim, granite building that fills most of a city block. It

stands at the corner of two busy streets in the City of Oporto, not far from the River Douro ... Two centuries ago these streets were in the centre of the commercial and residential area of the city; now their importance has diminished and their situation become unfashionable, but the Factory House continues to be a reminder of the British presence in the Port Wine trade, unbroken for more than three centuries (Delaforce 1989: xii).[8]

Within this edifice a grand staircase rises at the far end of an imposing entrance hall, leading up to several salons and dining-rooms and the ball-room. There is a multi-level, multi-room library, and a billiards room (both shut down, and derelict at present), an old kitchen done up as an informal museum, new kitchens and a caretaker's apartment. The Factory House was built between 1785 and 1790 under a lease from the Portuguese government to William Warre. Whether he obtained the lease in his capacity as Consul of the British Nation, or as head of a private association, was then unclear and/or later obscured, creating a nice ambiguity about who owned the building. In 1810 British trade factories were abolished by treaty with Portugal. The Factory House denizens promptly renamed their club The British Association, suggesting an inclusive stance towards fellow-travellers in Porto that they by no means espoused. After the Napoleonic Wars there was deep controversy over rightful ownership. A small group of port merchants in possession of the Factory House argued that their firms had paid for the building out of a special levy on their exports. In opposition, the rest argued that it belonged to 'The British Nation in Portugal' and should be open to all (Delaforce 1989: 44). Consul Crispin's report to His Majesty's Secretary of State in 1830 argued in favour of those in possession, ending, 'If the Factory House were to be open for general use by Right, to all British Subjects, it could not be closed to any individual of whatever Class, male or female.' (Delaforce 1989: 43).[9] It is not possible to tell whether Crispin was more horrified at the spectre of the lower classes or of women enjoying the use of the Factory House.

The quarrel went on for almost a decade before the excluded merchants finally gave up their quest. But it was not the last.

> An approach was made in 1902 to the British Association by a group of British residents, with the suggestion that a club be formed in conjunction with the British Association, to be based in the latter's premises in the Factory House … The proposal was given scant consideration and after a meeting of members of the Association, attended, it should be recorded, by only eight members, and these possibly the most conservative of the shippers, it was turned down in rather peremptory terms. In fact a social club was formed in 1902 with the name of 'British Union Club', shortly changed to the 'Oporto British Club' (Delaforce 1989: 40).

Over two centuries the uses and vitality of the Factory House have changed. The outsiders in 1830 were merchants whose business connections as well as social lives were adversely affected by their exclusion. By 1900 everyday business was conducted in Vila Nova de Gaia, and desires to belong revolved around the Factory House as a social club for the community. The Oporto Cricket and Lawn Tennis Club now takes that place in the enclave, and the only parts of the Factory House that are used by the members are those designed for entertaining (such as the dining-rooms and the ballroom), as opposed to the rooms meant for shared use and sociability (such as the billiards room and the library).

As the social institutional anchor of the port gentry it should not be sur-prising that the Factory House is a point of passage linking the Gaia-Douro circuit and the British enclave. But it plays a different part in each. On the one hand, as port gentry bring visitors to those exclusive weekly, men-only, Factory House luncheons, or on occasions like the annual Ladies' Day, vis-iting journalists, connoisseurs and wine buyers come as close as they ever will to encountering the inter-family social life of the enclave, mainly through the stories served up with dessert and port. So visitors like the journalist must rely on what the port family members choose to tell them about their lives in the British enclave. This implies several things: that the port shippers' elite position and succession is crafted somehow in divided lives; that visitors are furnished a picture of community life that supports elite claims, but is substantially inaccurate; and that the port gentry fur-nish a view of their lives that emphasizes a sort of 'late empire' ambience and themselves as the aristocracy of an otherwise homogeneous British enclave in Porto.

On the other hand, the Factory House members' families demonstrate their social power and exclusivity in the British enclave as they give the occasional private party, but more importantly, issue limited invitations to the annual Factory House Christmas Ball, and other special festive social events. Here the membership of families and firms is very much con-founded, and the effortless entitlement of the port gentry and their 'long unbroken succession' come into play in the enclave itself. At moments of high festivity they do seem to bring together their success, their successors, and selected others who have laboured on their behalf. In between the enormous old building stands eerily empty.

The Gaia-Douro Circuit

The Gaia-Douro circuit takes the port gentry and their families out of the contexts of their everyday lives. In this sense and taken as a whole it is a practice of decontextualization. How this is fashioned is surely part of what it means to be port gentry. As the port gentry move through the Gaia-Douro circuit they create claims to exclusivity both through practices that strip away the complex process of their production and through prac-tices that confound public, corporate and domestic spaces: decontextual-ization and conflation are two sides of a single coin. Each implies that families like the Symingtons and Robertsons have the resources to impose their interests and dispose of social arrangements and practices in their own fashion in circumstances they control with some ease.

Removal from the British enclave is also a move *into* other places and practices. In Gaia and the Douro the port gentry's families, the Robertsons, Symingtons and others, are multiply, directly enmeshed in the political economy of the port trade. In the circumscribed world of the Gaia-Douro, the port gentry have become demonstrators of the life, the class (gender relations and nationality), for which vintage port wine is suited and that it in turn symbolizes. In this productive consumption they contribute to the marketing and distribution of port wine. But this is part of the production of port wine for trade and profit. The port merchant families demonstrate the 'authenticity' of their authority about port wine as producers of port. At the same time they demonstrate entitlement to that authority by the lives they (appear to) lead as old gentry wine-producers, which are the very lives for which port wine is appropriate. These families' lives are forged in the dialectics of the production, exchange, distribution and consumption of port wine, that is, in intimate connection with processes of commodification.

This section first examines decontextualization practices that saturate convivial occasions throughout the Gaia-Douro circuit - erasures of economic struggles in the port trade, the creation of a vision of the port gentry as leaders of a homogeneous British enclave, and the dismissal or denial of their profound interdependencies with Portuguese vineyard-keepers, workers, colleagues, neighbours and the Portuguese nation. Then we will turn to that other sort of decontextualization by which working social boundaries are disguised or erased for purposes of establishing entitlement to a gentrified position.

Decontextualization Practices

The Sunday Times article describes a series of direct assertions of the Symingtons' and Robertsons' status in terms such as, 'the Robertsons "make an entrance", to the Annual Ladies' Luncheon at the Factory House, "befitting the first family of port"'. ... 'Holding court on the other table are the Taylors' deadly rivals the Symingtons, or Syms, as they are known.' Their position is underscored by contagion from those whom they know - celebrity visitors are mentioned repeatedly in the news, brochures and other accounts, in conversations among themselves and with visitors. The journalist reports that 'Visitors to the Taylors include US secretary of state James Baker and King Albert of Belgium; John Major spent his holidays two years running on a Symington estate.'

They occupy the headline, from which we learn, 'The dynasties who have controlled the port industry since the 17th century ... feud in a manner befitting the Carringtons and the Colbys.'[10] That is, the journalist organizes the story she tells around what her hosts convey as a compelling rivalry between Symingtons and Taylors over the quality and marketing of vintage ports. 'It's the 2% of sales that make or break your reputation', says Rupert Symington '… It's really between us and the Taylors.'

There are things askew in this portrayal of the port trade on the one hand, and of the relations among port merchant families on the other. Decontextualization has the effect of fetishizing vintage port and family prestige at one and the same time as it commodifies them.

Begin with the claim of a dominating rivalry over vintage port. There is a hierarchy of qualities of ports that runs downwards from vintage to 30-,

20-, and 10-year blended ports, to low-quality (but high-volume) ruby ports. All the firms make every type of port. Vintage ports are a very small portion of the wines sold by any of the port firms. The Symingtons' holding company and Taylors' do engage in competitive relations - over the low-end, inexpensive ports. Until the practice was outlawed a couple of years ago, some firms sold port *a granel* - by the tanker truck - wholesale to French supermarkets to bottle under their own labels. Opposed by many firms, including Taylors, the Symingtons were popularly suspected of being among the offenders. Yet another serious struggle within and among port firms is generated in a contradiction between rare, expensive and unpredictable vintage wines (and by contagion their producers), and the contemporary global-economic logic that insists on high-volume standardized production. From the multinational management point of view vintage ports are a disruptive, expensive distraction from mass wine production and sales.

In short, as the families' story of 'unbroken elite succession' directs us to their 'rivalry over vintage port' it erases the local and immediate economic contextualization of port wine, vintage and otherwise (and indeed, its further contextualization in the alcoholic beverages industry). We are left with a view of the port trade as a matter of noble families in conflict over noble wines.[11]

This theme of competition between rival elite families is developed with an emphasized distinction between intense competition in the trade and peaceful - even boring - community life, where matchmaking is the only form of 'hunting' still indulged. Erasure of the production of elite positioning is made in practices that displace attention from the British enclave and its participants' daily lives and preoccupations. This exclusion is made in a deeply spatial way as movement around the Gaia-Douro circuit is provided and controlled by one host firm/family; it is limited to corporate offices, the Factory House, and the Douro *quintas*. It brings visitors into the places where their hosts apparently take a whole-hearted stand in the world. It invites visitors, obligates them with seductive hospitality, to adopt that point of view. Traveling the Gaia-Douro circuit also discourages visitors from making opportunities to spend time with other participants in the production of port wine and its gentry. In terms of preserving their entitlement to the position they enact, itineraries restricted by their hosts to the Gaia-Douro circuit prevent peripheral participants from moving around in the everyday lives of the port shippers' families in Porto.

There are undoubtedly more general ideological and political-economic relations that make that other, 'not real', not-commercial world seem unimportant to those drawn into the port gentry's 'world'. It must be difficult to question, since intimacy is implied in this shared public 'private life' without calling attention to that other, more private mundane life in the British enclave.

There are still other effects of the process by which port gentry hosts draw others into confirming their entitled way of life, and erase or exclude the effortful and complex processes that help to produce elite succession. When the families portray themselves as engaged - only - with an opponent-other, it is as if a mirror is positioned so that each reflects the other, and as rivals they fill the narrative frame. This surely is one of the attractions of describing family life in terms of a rivalry among equals, a feud.[12] Adversaries become the only context for each other, as they portray their lives to visitors as two 'dynasties' in competition. Persuading the unwary to rivet an intense focus on relations between two families is a convenient way to make the rest of the world seem irrelevant.

At the same time, the emphasis on just the two families, and their feud, is wielded in such a way as to imply that the British enclave is a homogeneous community. 'While they dine together, play cricket together and worship together, out in the real world the British port-wine families are locked in battle.'

This description, like most points concerning 'the British community' is interestingly inaccurate, in ways that serve interested parties. First, the story names the two 'first families'. A very few others are portrayed as in the second rank; then by extension follow an unnamed number of others of supposedly lesser stature. The whole 'few hundred families' in the British enclave are assumed to be like these, though only their pale imitations. Reciprocally, this implies that families like the Robertsons and Symingtons are 'naturally' entitled, superlative representatives of the colony as a whole. The headline of the article offers an example when it announces that the two families 'control the port trade' - as if the two were all there is of the port-wine trade and the British community.

The 'real world' in the quotation above is contrasted with community life, which apparently is not real. Such claims are possible in the circuit that links the port firms and Gaia and the *quintas* in the Douro, but only because they segregate visitors, who never come in to contact with the heterogeneous fractions and really conflictual politics of the British enclave. Further, in the enclave in Porto there may be a brisk exchange of dinner invitations between families within a given social fraction, but even the port gentry families are divided between Anglicans and Catholics. Symingtons are Catholics, while many other port gentry families are Anglicans. An admission of religious differences among the elite would establish that there is deep social, cultural heterogeneity among them, and would lay 'the feud' open to harsher connotations than a joust among (co-worshipping) co-equals. But, finally - an issue that is probably of greater concern to the port families - an admission that some are Catholic would suggest the possibility of a fatal Portuguesization.

Which brings us to that other major context-stripping aspect of the Gaia-Douro circuit, the erasure of Portugal, the land in which they live, where their ancestors resided for some generations and where their lives in every aspect depend on Portuguese people, labour, practices of port production, and other connections too numerous to mention. Indeed, although the article's author inexplicably claims that, 'Were it not for the Portuguese terracotta roofs and cobbled streets, members of the oldest British outpost in Europe could fancy themselves back in London', the myriad crucial ways in which life for the Brits in Porto is dependent on and enabled by Portuguese persons, relationships and institutions is never mentioned. How do the elite port families erase Portugal from 'their' story? 'Unsurprisingly for a small, isolated community where until recently the only way home was by boat, many British port traders have married into each other's families.'

'Home' is England, not Portugal, and that they are 'isolated' implies a segregated enclave life within Portuguese society. Indeed, perhaps this accounts for the emphasis in the article on matchmaking as a preoccupation of British women. The story does not offer an explanation, however, for the matchmaking or for sending their children to public schools in England. 'Topping up British blood,' and 'sending their daughters to England to look for husbands', as those quoted in the story describe their practices and intentions, convey a fear of assimilating, or fear that others in the community might fracture or blur its national gate-keeping 'standards' by becoming Portuguese and ceasing to be British.[13] Perhaps most startling in this respect is their cultivation of 'execrable Portuguese', which effectively protects them from being mistaken for Portuguese.

There is another literal form of erasure of Portugal tucked into a paragraph introducing the Douro valley, where the demarcated zone of port production lies.

> The families spend most weekends during summer [untrue - it's too hot] at their wine estates in the Douro valley. It is 80 miles east of Oporto, and the oldest demarcated wine region in the world. It is here that the grapes are grown, the terraces bulldozed out of impossibly steep granite cliffs over which eagles circle. *One of the most silent places on earth for most of the year*, during harvest time in late September the hills echo with voices of hundreds of pickers. (Italics mine.)

The disappearance of Portugal from this description of port gentry family life is deft. Almost all those 'bulldozed terraces' were actually hand-hewn by Portuguese and Spanish vineyard workers over many generations. Is there really nobody there but the Brits and 'their' estates until harvest time? Not so. This may be a useful image in portraying them as lords of all they see, bolstered by references to migrant wage labourers as 'peasants'. But in fact the population of the Douro consists of between three to five hundred thousand Portuguese residents, who own much the greater part of the land, and who are occasionally known to raise their voices, pick up their guns, gun their pick-ups, and of course dwell among and labour in their vineyards.

On the other hand, Portuguese children in Porto are pictured sitting on the wall of the Oporto Cricket and Lawn Tennis Club. The image is very colonial and complete nonsense - it is a middle-class neighbourhood, there's nothing to watch. The implication is that Portugal, outside the British enclave, is a Third World country.

Family members' quoted opinions about the Portuguese are effortlessly rude, intended to establish social and cultural chasms between Brits and their host country (reassuring themselves that no visitor might plausibly suspect them to have 'degenerated' into lives more Portuguese than British). There is another quotation in the article, this time from Penny Symington, the wife of James, the paterfamilias of the Symington Group. Deriding the inconsiderate behaviour of the Taylors' guests to exhausted grape-pickers at the end of a long day, she says 'There is a huge disparity between the way we live and the vineyard workers. One resisted having a pool at all for a long time because one doesn't feel good swimming and lounging while peasants are labouring in 38° heat.'

The particular decontextualizations produced by the port gentry matter: no Portuguese life or labour, and scarcely even Portugal. No heterogeneous British community. Concealed dependencies on Portuguese and British 'others' displace attention from the British enclave and their strenuous efforts to produce their own succession. Exclusivity takes on new meaning here - not simply as a matter of snubbing people or denying them access to some social club, but by denying that the practices and processes of their production involve anyone but themselves.

Conflating Categories, Blurring Boundaries

Claims to ownership of history, landed estates, merchant houses, and the status associated with different brands of port wine lend glamour, wealth, and entitlement to the port gentry. Appearing effortlessly entitled is not all and only a matter of decontextualization, then, but often also its opposite. That project is advanced by invoking as their own riches of lineage, tradition and history that may or may not 'belong' to the families. For instance, the article headlines 'dynasties who have controlled the port industry since the 17th century' and, in the article, 'little ... has changed in 300 years'. These claims wield magical influence without requiring historical justification: 'Three hundred years'? 'Unchanging since the seventeenth century?' 'Dynasties?' Port wine was not produced in its present form, was not fortified nor made into a wine akin to contemporary port, until 1840. Of what relevance is it to the wine or the families that Peter Bearsley travelled the Douro in 1727? And if this tenuous ancestor did not get there until then, why date 'Taylors' back to 1692? Further, 'the dynasties who have controlled the port industry since the 17th century' could not include the Symingtons, who did not come to Porto until 1882 (as the article confirms, without drawing attention to the discrepancy). And more generally, the very idea of a port dynasty of three hundred years is meaningless, since the history of any of the port firms has involved frequent shifting partnerships, forms of business organization and participants' families. The complex histories of these families and firms and of the changing trade do not inform today's families' claims on founders' privileges, which surely assume continuity of something substantial across all those generations.

We must ask which histories count for whom. Visitors do not hear disputed the common story of 'founders' and 'centuries of common tradition' in the lodges in Gaia nor in the *quintas* in the Douro. Residents in the British enclave are also ignorant of its history. Claims to hundreds of years of connection deep into the past of the trade hold up well - where access to contrary evidence is not easily available, especially in a community that makes a mini-industry of producing congratulatory Whig histories for and about itself.

Port gentry families have not owned land until recently, and own very little now. Yet they portray themselves as the owners of country estates. '...other English merchants became shippers, building lodges in Gaia and acquiring large stocks of wine, *and eventually their own vineyards*.' (Italics mine.)

'The families (we lose sight of workers, journalists, wine buyers, and other clients) spend most weekends during summer at their wine estates in the Douro valley.' The possessive 'their' is massively misleading. In addition to the fact that they have every reason for, and long traditions of, not owning land in the Douro - leaving the fluctuating risks of climate and crop to the Portuguese vineyard-keepers - most do not own 'their' *quinta* guest 'houses' either. Almost all are owned by multinational corporations, certainly the *quintas* to which commercial/publicist 'guests' are invited. In fact there is a whole cottage industry in mystifying who owns what.

The port scions present themselves to visitors by creating a sort of a publicly 'private' life, a seductive social accomplishment, in which visitors are invited to participate as guests at the 'homes' of the port 'families', and learn to talk of 'the Syms' and the 'Taylors'.[14] But in fact during *quinta* weekends the port families are 'on' as representatives of their firms, re-creating a way of life, a sort of 'natural habitat' for the convivial imbibing (and selling) of port wine. The location and practice of private life in Porto is not accessible from the public practice, that disjunction being a key facet of their elite decontextualization.

Somehow the Syms and Taylors further manage to persuade the visitor of their privileged place among the British port families on the basis of claims to the unparalleled nobility of their wines: the names of brands of port wine, elite families and major 'British' port firms are constantly conflated, so that each is employed as if it stood for an alignment of all three, drawing parallels between a hierarchy of families and a hierarchy of port wines: 'Taylor's is the oldest family firm ... and the brand name is so strong that all the clan members are referred to as Taylors. It dates back to 1692 and produces some of the world's finest vintage ports. Alistair took over in 1967 at the death of his uncle Dick.'

It may well be that no one was knowledgeable enough to explain to the journalist that Joseph Taylor bought the firm in 1823 when he was a junior partner in Campbell, Bowden and Gray. The latter went bankrupt, and sold him their stock at *10 milreis* the pipe (at a time when the going price in Gaia was around *120 milreis*) (Duguid and Lopes, forthcoming).

Although the Symington family name never appears on a bottle, they are the largest port dynasty and produce familiar brands such as Graham's, Warre's, and Dow's (firms named for old port merchant families, before they were bought out by Symingtons). Yet the Symingtons insist that they are the only real 'family company'. This skirts the issue of what that might mean, and the issue that in fact they have never been a family firm, but rather a (mostly) privately-owned holding company whose direction is in family hands.

> Seated around these two often explosive epicentres are members of all the big families of port familiar from bottle labels: Delaforce, Sandeman and Croft.

> Their names are written on the roofs of the lodges across the river at Vila Nova da Gaia, where the barrels are maturing, as they have ever since the British first began shipping port 300 years ago. (*The Sunday Times* Aug. 1997:95)

Conflating the names of families, firms, and brands of wine is not only a project of a few fortunate families. Everything possible is done in Gaia to mask the multinational ownership that has overtaken earlier 'family firms'. Banners along the Quai in Gaia advertise the port 'houses', playing on the relations among family names, familiar port brand names, and the notion of ancient, traditional family vintners. '[W]hen flagging port sales forced them to sell out to multinationals ... many family members stayed on: the famous surname and family history is good for sales.'

In the end, given that it is part of their job to entertain visitors in order to sell port wine, free ratification in the British media for themselves as old British family dynasties in a colony in Portugal is also free advertising for the multinational corporations. This is of course another conflation of family and firm. They are at one with their multinational corporate bosses in selling port by selling themselves as exemplars of the life-style of the rich and the upper class.

There are, then, three dense points of mystification in which the families impersonate, borrow, or appropriate the trappings of upper-class life. They conflate their family position, wealth and home with the *quintas* and guest houses, staff and entertainment budgets of the multinational corporations who own the port 'houses'. They appear to be 'landed wine gentry' even without significant land or vineyards. Further, the notion that it is possible, especially through that commodified notion of the 'brand name', to conflate families, port wines, and port firms, further conflated as port 'houses', does to family reputation what the *quintas* do to apparent established wealth. The upper-class base and way of life they assume (double meaning - take on, expect) depends upon erasure and/or conflation of divisions that depend on and conventionally reflect political-economic, legal and social distinctions between families, family firms, multinational corporations, landowners, homes/houses and more. Where the erasure and conflation occurs may well be in the hearts and minds of family members, in their habits of dwelling in and occupation of corporate guest houses that may once have belonged to their families and 'feel like home'. It occurs with the collusion of the firms, and/or as the managers simply assume them as perks of their jobs (as well as being part of their job descriptions). But the line is also erased with art and contrivance to advance the personal claims of these families to embody the essence of the local British community.

When, without calling attention to it, their common histories conflate Portuguese, port gentry and multinational ownership of vineyards, confound 'old port family' and corporate ownership of guest lodges, and further conflate family, firm and vintage port, there is surely a case being made for the aristocratic nature of the port 'dynasties'. Talk of family tradition, history and ritual, landed estates, country weekends and famous names of famous quality bring such a story together.

But further, I think they are portraying themselves, as an elite of a certain vintage, a colonial elite, not much changed since the turn of the century. They portray themselves as displaced in time to the heyday of empire, in which many of the port community's anchoring conceits are stuck, as a device for purveying nostalgia for the 'good' old days of empire. The sort of gentry they are is being displaced towards a not-too-distant past, as a metaphor for, or confusion with, their displacement in space (not too far from England, but provincial, a colony, as well as a colonizing presence in Portugal; a rural aristocracy because removed from metropolitan Great Britain, but further, because removed to country estates.) Also, the notion that the gentry build their great houses in the country historically distinguished the British upper classes from those of the Southern European gentry (for instance in Italy, Spain and Portugal) who located their mansions in cities. This may be another way the port gentry affirm that they are emphatically British and emphatically not Portuguese. So, if the author mocks them gently throughout her telling of this story, underlining their slightly quaint and provincial ways, it may well be that the Brits in question do not mind: they want to appear rather 'old world' in both senses - it is their market niche.

The Porto Circuit: Labour, Preparation and Political Struggle

Within the British enclave in Porto, we will see not only some of the practices that the Gaia-Douro circuit excludes - most of the conditions of possibility for elite positioning in the community - but also the challenges to the 'old port families'' community identity, institutional practices and personal trajectories that follow inevitably from the heterogeneous character of the enclave. For, despite long-standing differences, port gentry families combine forces when seriously threatened, in order to sustain the community identity, its institutional underpinnings and the privileged personal trajectories this implies for their families. This may help to explain why Peter Cobb remarks that his worst enemies in the trade are also his best friends.

Dilemmas in the British enclave in Porto are in some respects complementary to those of the Gaia-Douro circuit. The port gentry lead more robustly unreified everyday lives, but their entitlement is more vulnerable because the work of producing it is more visible and more strongly challengeable. There are also greater possibilities of running into a harder-edged reality, possibly in the guise of their own children, and finding themselves confronted or ignored as ghosts of a world gone by.

The British Enclave in Porto

Contrary to the vista of Porto from the distant Douro, the Porto enclave circuit, with its school, church and social club, and the heterogeneous fractions that compose the community, is only partly enmeshed in the port-wine trade. It could also come as a surprise, given the exclusive focus on the Gaia-Douro circuit to this point, that Porto is the major industrial city of Portugal, with a population of over a million. If there is a 'little corner of Portugal forever England', it is not the city as a whole. There is a small area of the city in which the British port-shipping (and other) families in the nineteenth century located their church and graveyard and their social club, and a neighbourhood, Foz de Douro, along the ocean at the mouth of the Rio Douro, where a number of British families lived and where they eventually located the Oporto British School. But this neither was, nor is, a literal enclave. Rather, there is a thin scattering of British people and activities across a dense Portuguese city. Some still live in Foz. Most British families in Porto live elsewhere than in the nineteenth-century locations identified with the British. It is their patterns of association with each other, and self-segregation from their Portuguese neighbours and colleagues, that give the word 'enclave' meaning today.

The British in Porto arrange their lives so as to live principally in relation with each other, in a yearly round of community activities. Some of those families have names, and a few have occupations associated with the port trade. Many British live in Porto for other reasons. Some Portuguese families send their children to the Oporto British School (OBS), where a majority of the pupils are at present Portuguese. A number of Portuguese families are members of the Oporto Cricket and Lawn Tennis Club. Probably all Brits in Porto are aware that the enclave has a portentous history. All versions of the story woven so often and effectively into public trade relations and the Gaia-Douro circuit give the British colony in Porto a unique identity as 'the 300-year-old port-wine shipping colony'. They know who is and is not invited to parties at the Factory House. At the same time, very few Brits in Porto know much about economic transformations in the port-wine lodges in Vila Nova da Gaia.

Claims to legitimate succession are established in part through participation in institutions that mediate between personal and community identities. The Factory House is a crucial case in point. The Oporto British School (OBS) is another, though it mediates community and participant identities in quite different terms. It is one of the main institutions that ground everyday assumptions that there *is* a British community in Porto. Just about everyone born in the enclave has gone to the Oporto British School. Attending the school is a step in producing new members for all groups within the community. The OBS serves the elementary needs of most families in the community for primary schooling conducted in English. But its history and present priorities make it principally a feeder school for British public boarding schools. As such it has played a significant part in the production of British 'gentlemen' in Porto: it had its origins in the heyday of empire at the end of the nineteenth century, and has been implicated in the production of Britishness for families that have resided for several generations in Porto. The OBS provides an institutional trajectory that flings the children of port gentry with fair automaticity from Porto into the UK for formative years in public schools that inculcate British culture and stances on class, gender and nationalism/racism along with a forgiving admiration for their class-cultural credentials. Finding spouses to 'bring back', many return to take up life as well-off British gents (and ladies) for yet another generation. Both education and marriage strategies seem to ratify the natural entitlement of the existing elite port families.

Another such site, but of less broad importance to the enclave as a whole, is St James's Anglican Church. It was built in 1818 after years of conflict with the Inquisition and other authorities in Portugal. This church was designed from the plans for the Factory House ballroom, and was required by the Portuguese Catholic authorities to have a high wall around it so as not to be visible from the street (Delaforce 1982). The church holds many concrete reminders of families with a history in the port trade - names on tombstones and pews, members who insist on sitting in their family pews, plaques on the walls in memory of those who died in two world wars, and stained glass windows dedicated to deceased family members. Port wine is served after services each week during a hospitality hour. The congregation these days is small, never filling the small church. But the same people show up at the Oporto Cricket and Lawn Tennis Club, where Church Ladies' Guild meetings and Annual General Meetings of the school and the church congregation are held. The port families' lives as well as those of other British residents in Porto are interwoven on a dense basis across these institutions.

The Oporto Cricket and Lawn Tennis Club is yet another community institution deeply involved in sustaining the enclave and in preparing succession among elite families. It is a private club with a large lounge, a formal dining-room, bar, lunch-room, guest-rooms, terrace, swimming pool and cricket pitch, hidden from the street, accessible only via a long driveway. It has a staff of a dozen almost entirely (English-speaking) Portuguese, with a membership committee (who must vote on new members nominated by existing members) and a governing board elected from the membership. These committees are dominated by the port gentry and other pillars of the community. Children meet their friends there. Young couples socialize at the Club, the new mothers' exercise group meets there several mornings a week, those with young children pick them up at the OBS at noon and come by the Club for lunch, and people meet for drinks at the end of the day, and sometimes arrange for a table in the dining-room, especially popular for family gatherings on Sunday after church. There is a yearly round of 'traditional' balls, parties, tennis and other sports competitions, and groups that meet regularly, including the Church Ladies' Guild, bridge groups, a quilting group and in some years the Douro Players or the local singing group. The Club is the centre of family social interaction and leisure activities for all those Brits in Porto who prefer to socialize with each other. Without it, I have heard teenage girls say, they would have no social life in Porto. As in the OBS, the Portuguese members, safely categorized as affiliate members, are suffered, indeed must be suffered, for they make vital contributions to the finances of the Club.

The British school, club and church, along with the Factory House, are the most central institutions for sustaining an identity as a community. They are the principal sites of institutional trajectories that pre-serve the port gentry families. But there are other community institutions that round out this picture of the enclave. There is a local branch of the worldwide British Council in Porto, with an English-language library, a roster of English language courses, occasional British cultural events, and a small British staff. There is an unusual British Consulate - situated in a huge house and gardens donated by an old port gentry family for this purpose some years ago. The Consulate is privately supported by the community, and would not exist otherwise. This too is a source of pride and identity, not to mention invitation-only garden parties, Queen's birthday celebrations, and receptions (and increasingly mundane efforts to advertise British products exported to and imported from Porto). There were until mid-century a British Hospital and a British Golf Club maintained by the British in Porto, now disbanded. The latter was given up by the British when they lost control of it to its Portuguese members.

Social Fractions

The significantly differing social/cultural/political economic groups that compose the British enclave in Porto include, besides the port gentry, their near supporters the dignified and responsible Pillars of the Community. They include peripheral and poor British residents of Porto, Anglophile well-to-do Portuguese families, and corporate managers out from Great Britain on three-year contracts, supervising production in

enterprises owned by multinationals. The social fractions are divided by
their deep political-economic differences, arrayed in a social hierarchy by
nationality that cultivates distinctions in radicalized terms and in a gender
hierarchy made in relation with the other two.[15] These translate into different stakes, desires, and positioning with respect to the structure, power,
resources and everyday practices in each of the community's institutions
concerned with processes of succession (principally the OBS, the Oporto
Cricket and Lawn Tennis Club and St James's Anglican Church).

Port gentry represent a certain version of the community's identity.
They are a living instantiation of it. That 'living' is what they do - they
inhabit an elite circle within a foreign enclave that views its national roots,
and the growth and development of its wines, commerce and culture in
Northern Portugal, as superior to those achieved by its host country. The
Factory House roster and exclusive practices underwrite the port gentry
families who form the social apex of the enclave. They consider the
enclave, the church, the school and the club to be 'theirs', accept the def-
erence that their positioning commands, appear glamorous in their care-
less focus on each other coupled with their dismissal of, or a marked
courtesy to, 'the rest'. They represent the enclave to visiting dignitaries
and Portuguese high officials, and act as stewards and decision-makers for
social institutions that pre-serve the community - and its elite families.
They are the arbiters of who is socially 'in', informally in their several generations, and quite formally, as the Factory House is accepted within the
enclave as *the* site of high social selection.

Portuguese families who applied to the OBS were given a cold recep-
tion until about 1960. Even then they were told without apology of a quota
system so arranged that only after all British children were accepted would
places be selectively made available for Portuguese children. Should a very
fundamental issue concerning School property arise at the Annual
General Meeting, only British members of the School can vote. Lunching
often at the Club, it would be difficult not to notice that British members
occupy the desirable tables next to the windows; Portuguese families sit
quietly in the inner row. British members hop from table to table talking
with friends and family, but only to tables with British lunchers. The membership roll of the Club is divided into members (British) and Associates
(divided further into 'other nationalities' and 'Portuguese'). The distinction is more serious than its connotations of less than full membership;
Associates pay equal dues, but do not have voting privileges in the most
serious decisions affecting the governance of the Club.

Given the exclusionary habits in the enclave, it might seem surprising
that Portuguese families are allowed in the School and the Club at all. But
without the participation of the Portuguese members, neither institution
could survive financially. So there is polite toleration along with visible
exclusion exercised by the British. This picture of the British families confirms the view that this is not a community self-sufficient enough to continue to close its doors to the 'native' population around it literally. The

picture is a more complex one, of mild seduction and firm rejection, of conditional invitations followed by renewed distinctions.

If Portuguese families are merely tolerated, there are more subtle ways in which other participants in the British enclave (defined in terms of its spaces, organizations, and activities) are to be found in its social hierarchy between the most prominent and sought-after families and the Portuguese. Two further categories of the unequal, both British, include 'pillars' (my term) and 'manager families on contract'. The pillars include high-level managers for British companies in and around Porto who, along with their wives and children, are British citizens. Some have lived elsewhere in British expatriate enclaves, having moved to Porto from Southern Africa or some other part of the British (or Portuguese) empire where their companies have plants or offices. They expect to stay in Porto until they retire or even for the rest of their lives. In several cases mentioned earlier (for example Bain, Burnett, Orr, Reader, Sinclair) the pillars have worked in managerial capacities in port firms and are members of the Factory House, but have arrived too recently to qualify as port gentry. Unequal gender relations, frequently justified in terms of traditions of excluding women from the Factory House, create another sort of pillar: the wives of port gentry - port wives, as they are known. The pillars, men and women, are respected in part because of their positions and long-term residence, in part because they are notable for their hard work on behalf of the community. The men are to be found on governing boards of community institutions, often as the secretary or the treasurer; responsible for the organization of a major community event (such as the recent centenary celebration of the OBS) or on the hiring committee to choose a new headmaster or Anglican priest. The labour they put in is necessary to establish a substantial position in the community. Both women and men are pillars of the community in one further sense as well. They defend the enclave as a venerable and very special one, whose current generation of influential port families carries the history and the spirit of the community, and whose desire that life should not change, or at least neither rapidly nor radically, is fully justified and appropriate. They defend the port gentry and their agenda against the families of British managers of multinationally-owned industrial enterprises in Porto.

The managers, on three-year contracts, are on average a bit younger than the pillars. The manager families are seen by port families and pillars as troublemakers. By definition, this would include anyone making suggestions about changes in the community who has not established long residence and contributions of labour to community activities. As old port family members and pillars characterize them, stereotypically, they sweep in and want to change things without any respect for those who have made the community what it is today and are responsible for it. Then they leave. Those who stay steadily on have to pick up the pieces and deal with the inevitably negative consequences of the 'thoughtless dissatisfaction' of short-term residents.

In sum, the old families exclude others, and pillars assist in this endeavour. Expatriate men in particular take a good deal of prestige from their association with the old families, and translate for them. In speaking on their behalf they sometimes appear to be of them, and the line is especially blurred for managers elected to the Factory House. Highly respectable British men do much of the community's 'executive' work, and their pillar wives do much of the 'other' work of institutional maintenance. The Portuguese, excluded within the community, remain a puzzle. It seems likely that it is in their relations with Portuguese families that are not members of the Club and do not send their children to the OBS that the advantages of their commitments come into play, by a sort of contagion of British 'cultural superiority'. In short, the British families who claim kinship in the port trade do not maintain the social superiority of their position by themselves. The Portuguese finance it as do the others, including manager families on contract; the pillars defend them, and the manager families on contract give service to the community, seek friends in it, send their children to the OBS, attend Church, and depend on the Club for their social life.

Battles over Institutions, Identities and Futures

Along with church and club the school offers one example of just what hard work it takes to sustain long processes of family succession. This school has taken leadership to produce; it produces leaders (whose responsibilities and privileges eventually involve governing the school) in an involuted process aimed at (apparently) self-sustained reproduction. To maintain continued succession among a small group of families takes ingenuity, implicit alliances, and of course many changes. To do so in the face of tensions and differentiations within the port enclave takes a certain ruthless political concentration. It requires the partial inclusion of many in order to secure their exclusion from succession to elite positioning within the colony. The School Charter of 1894 begins, First Resolution re: Scholars, Clause I: 'That the School be exclusively for British subjects [meaning boys] of the age of six years and upwards provided they can read and write.'

As late as 1989 the First Article of the OBS Charter simply copies a declaration brought along through many official revisions of the Charter:

> The Oporto British School is an educational association, formed by the members whose names appear in the corresponding register and whose object is to maintain a school to administer instruction and education to the children of British subjects, in order to prepare them for the entrance examinations to British schools, up to the 13 plus level.
> The principal, after consultation with the Board of Governors, may accept non-British pupils as long as the number of pupils from countries where the common language is not English does not prejudice the normal school programme.

When it opened, the OBS included families with surnames like Robertson, Standring, Rawes, Milne, Flower, Mason, Cassels, Ennor, Tait, Wright, Rumsey, Turner, Thom, Walker, and Vivian. Girls may have attended during the First World War; but there was an indefinite hiatus until they were again admitted in the early 1930s. The pupils at this time numbered around fifty, meeting in a house in Foz that is still part of the School.

How the families that started the school acquired the house and land is not entirely clear. School charters always have referred to the School as the property of the British community of Porto, and the steadily increasing property and physical plant of the School have been paid for by student fees, loans, and substantial contributions from companies in Porto - the majority of them port firms. With its ownership undefined, the school itself acts as a concrete reification of 'the community' that would (in fact it recently did, momentarily) come apart were rights to property ownership ever brought under discussion with the intention of clarifying membership. This may be one of its strengths as a kind of social glue.

Notable about this whole process is the incredible amount of effort, worry, work and struggle it has taken just to keep the School (and club and church) alive. It has been perennially difficult to find and keep teachers, bring them 'out from England', and then persuade community wives to step in at the last minute when new arrivals fled back to England without giving notice. There have been repeated efforts to designate and furnish school materials and school uniforms. There have been fights over raising school fees, subscriptions for building, building itself, dealing with more or fewer children as economic and political fortunes waxed and waned, and fights to hire and fire headmasters. The school committee even struggled to rationalize school management and cede day-to-day power to the School Head, create a Bursar, etc. But they were unable to withdraw even so, by their own account. All this before we even start to consider fights about the organization and mission of the school.

The School governing committee always involved, among others, those scions of the port firms described in the common narrative of 'the old British port enclave', including Robertsons and Symingtons galore, as well as Cobbs, Delaforces, Guimaraens, Reids and others. Port scions and their wives "two female members" became a by-law of the Board's standing rules in the late 1950s) have been major contributors of labour. The Finance Committee has long been composed of three men, virtually all port firm pillars, and the treasurer was for many years, the Controller at Sandeman's.

Seeing to it that their own children, above all, are adequately prepared to take the Common Entrance Examination at the age of thirteen and gain placements in British public schools has been the principal mission of the school's port gentry-stacked school governing committee. But the school has much more complex social tasks. It supports similar trajectories of children of the pillars. It must sustain the trajectories of Portuguese children (who will leave to attend Portuguese schools at thirteen), poor

Brits, and British managers' children. They will succeed and fail, be included and excluded in particular ways, all of which is very important for those becoming port gentry in Porto as well.

The school must address the needs of a heterogeneous set of class and national fractions within the community because it is engaged in fixing them all in their places (as they fix themselves). The issue here is how struggles and fights, in the school and about the school, sustain and defend the port wine gentry and the present identity of the enclave, and how the school and the fights together generate other paths of succession besides those of the port gentry families.

Schools here, as elsewhere, are political arenas. The OBS is a dense transfer point of power between community identity and its embodiment in elite persons. And in the community, in the middle of the OBS schoolyard, at, yes, the central tables for the celebration of the hundredth anniversary of the school, we find a table full of young Symingtons, and another of Robertsons and their guests. They are the focus of admiring, longing glances from those present but excluded by their easy possession of those desirable tables, selves, the occasion, the school, and with these the continuing identity of the British enclave.

Their apparently effortless entitlement at such moments is not, of course. The excluded have visions of their own. Battles over the OBS are ongoing. These are struggles to strengthen or dismantle, transform or reserve to new social fractions, a defining social position in the divided, heterogeneous British enclave. The different fractions in the enclave all have serious stakes for themselves and their children in the OBS and the community it serves, and they cannot all prevail. All fractions are reserving and re-serving ways of life, some local, some not.

Who challenges families such as the Symingtons and Robertsons, and how? Where do they find allies in major battles? Two fights over the future direction of the OBS since 1996 provide a basis for addressing these questions. First, the port gentry families have a stake in keeping the OBS focused on its mission as a prep school for their children, but, as with the club, they cannot afford to do this on their own. The Portuguese families who send their children to the OBS favour the prep school aspirations of the port gentry families. They are seeking British class culture for their children, and care enough about it to submit to the hierarchical and prejudicial policies of the school. Relations of the port gentry with Portuguese participants in the enclave are rather like their relations with the multinational firms. In both cases, even though in some sense at their expense, the others need the Brits to purvey a high-class glamour and to convey a certain British class culture. On the other hand, the middle-class managers recently come from Great Britain, thoughtlessly confident in their British identity by comparison with the 'old British' and soon to move on to some other country, fight to focus the OBS on the International Baccalaureate Degree. This high-school degree program, originating in Switzerland, has a standard curriculum all over the world. In order to receive accreditation, schools adopting the curriculum must put expensive resources into books, laboratories, teachers and advanced high school level courses. The advantage for the multinational managers would be a high-quality international school in Porto, with full courses to the age of eighteen, and the possibility of a smooth transition for their children to similar schools in other countries. They are joined by poorer Brits in Porto, some of them long-term residents (for instance missionaries), who cannot afford to send their children to England to school.

The governing committee instituted the IB programme a few years ago, under the auspices of a very capable headmaster with high intellectual standards. But it was swept aside as the headmaster was fired, and with the school in financial as well as social crisis in 1996 attempts were made to sell the school to the British Council. Here the traditional Portuguese families, the port gentry and their loyal supporters, the pillars, fought together to prevent the 'loss of identity' (and control) that would follow. They were victorious. On their agreeing to erase the School debt, the OBS governing committee was handed over to a younger generation of port gentry men, more conservative even than their fathers. A moment of succession. What appeared a few years earlier as the political-economic writing on the wall, the fall of the port family dynasties and with them the British community as 'the old port enclave', was for the time being firmly repelled in the interests of the port gentry.

There is a second struggle over British schooling in Porto that engages and reflects other tensions in the community, as a new international school has appeared in Foz: the Colegio Luso-Internacional do Porto (CLIP), drawing influential and skilled teachers away from the OBS, and pointedly promising a British but non-racist education.[16] CLIP was started by a group of American-educated Portuguese MBAs who represent a newly wealthy and influential business class in Porto, perhaps indifferent to the class-cultural charms and demands of the port gentry and the British enclave. CLIP offers something new to long-term residents: a means of exit from the shadow of the Factory House, from the British port-gentry-dominated enclave in Porto. If Portuguese families and multinational managers join in moving their children to CLIP, the OBS dedication to the prep school preparation of children who are to take their places in the 'long unbroken' succession to British hegemony in the enclave in Porto would surely dissolve.

How do the port gentry families succeed, at present, in defending their position? What strategic resources of power and control do 'old port families' employ in re-serving their stakes in community identity, institutional practices and personal trajectories? Conflation of firm with family - the *sina qua non* of the Factory House - is involved in the enclave as well as in the Gaia-Douro circuit, but in the opposite direction. Rather than injecting family into a well-disguised work setting (the port houses, the *quinta* weekends), the institutional practices of everyday life in Porto inject the firms into the family life of their employees. In the enclave those in charge of community events routinely appeal to the port firms for donations, for folding chairs and school loans, and for quantities of port wine to drink, auction, give away, or serve after church. More impressive still, the port firms employ those who work on the school governing committee, and the school controller, all of whom give their time-consuming services 'for free'. Over the years there have been a number of offers to the OBS of large loans by the port gentry families at times of major financial difficulties, conditional on direct control over the school. They and the port firms (including the Catholic Symingtons) make substantial contributions to the Anglican church. The port families have long controlled the changing formal organization of the OBS governing board, and the church and Club boards as well. They work very hard to keep these institutions of succession working as they want them. As a last resort, there is an informal, misleadingly-named organization called Friends of the School, made up of Robertsons, Symingtons and a few other familiar families, who gather to plan strategies for controlling critical votes that affect the future of succession processes in the enclave. Finally, when absolutely necessary, as in the battles described above, they make reluctant concessions to poorer Brits, contract managers and traditional Portuguese families (Lave 1999).

The Sunday Times emphasizes the consuming competition between port families/houses, and repeatedly quotes port-wives on how boring life is in the British enclave. The latter is cast in peaceful contrast to the 'real world' of men feuding over wine. But in ethnographic terms this perspective is reversed. With respect to family success and succession it is the enclave, not wine competition, that looks the bloodier battlefield.

Conclusions: The Dilemmas of Fetishism and Ghosthood

It may seem odd to emphasize the robust hard work of the port gentry families with respect to their succession and successors in the British enclave, and at the same time argue that they are caught in dilemmas that leave them as if disembodied spirits, or echoes of a dead past. But the mundane labour and political tensions involved in sustaining the British enclave don't leave much room for self-reification of their effortless elite entitlement. In the Gaia-Douro they come recklessly close to taking themselves to be whom they fashion themselves to be. In the British enclave they are fighting in practical terms to hold on to who they have been, in part by concealing who they are (for example, as Friends of the School). There is something more sober and anxiety-producing about this direct engagement that makes self-commodification more difficult, perhaps inappropriate. Ratification by others in the enclave might be more reassuring to the port gentry than the admiration (and published mystifications) of visitors and clients in the Gaia-Douro circuit. The danger is that instead of confirmation of their position as old port gentry by others in the heterogeneous community, they may run into evidence that their port gentry market niche is a social anachronism. The Gaia-Douro's fetish-object may be the British enclave's ghost. This is the crack that the segregation of their lives between *quinta* and enclave papers over.

Fading away? There are declining numbers of families like themselves and fewer resources for pursuing pride of place and position. They live and lead the enclave in a pond that has shrunk to include fewer bourgeois peers in the city of Porto and made them more dependent on clients and other resources of their firms. They have helped reduce their social relevance further by their exclusionary habits. They may suffer the same fate as Colonial Williamsburg, becoming an outdoor museum of port houses in Gaia (West 1985). Possibly, the companies may be sold off by the multinationals, who have already transferred many of their functions away from Porto. It is not impossible that the trade will be reduced to one Portuguese and one British port company. The men face the 'end of an era' danger of being retired and not succeeded by their sons, but replaced by Portuguese managers with MBA degrees from the US and UK like those that founded CLIP. The CLIP offers, for the first time, a means for several of the heterogeneous local groups of British and Portuguese families to exit from the field of play established by and for the port gentry.

The Port Gentry face other sorts of anxieties besides the 'end of an era' arguments. They may fear being 'found out' historically, as they have made claims about past continuities that in most cases won't stand scrutiny. They fear being mistaken for - or becoming - Portuguese. This must be fed by fears (exacerbated by the presence of contract managers) that they may no longer be authentically British. The claim to long British pedigree - the most basic premise of narratives of 300 years of unbroken succession - conflicts uncertainly with the common recognition that today they are 'more British than the British' (Lave 1999). Yet both seem highly desirable. This is one facet of the dilemma of ghosthood. That is the hard work and political battle to keep everyone, including themselves, in their 'proper' places in the old British port wine enclave in Porto also works to place them anachronistically in the larger contexts of contemporary Portugal, Great Britain, the EU and the end of the twentieth century. By doing what they do they hold on to what they have; but doing what they do (having what they have) holds them in something like a turn-of-the century posture. They exercise ways of being British country gentry that can only be reconciled in the present world in the rare contexts where such a version of being British is taken to be the real thing.

The port gentry emphasize relations between their premier social position in the community with respect to its diverse and less influential members and vintage wines in relation to inferior ports. Entitlement to leadership, which in the port gentry's story flows from the quality of their Rolls Royce ports, in fact is more substantively connected to economic and organizational transformations in the trade, in Portugal and globally.

The appearance created by the Symingtons, Robertsons and others in the Gaia-Douro circuit of effortless entitlement to their position as port-wine gentry is fairly secure, not easily open to challenge in its carefully arranged settings. But the process of producing it is precarious, because its practices of decontextualization and conflation are those by which commodities are produced and fetishized, and because these families' economic history and present location in a different set of economic relations help to make a thin and doubtful line between their (g)hosting performances and their transformation into commodified emblems of port wine. Here lies one of the principal contradictions in the production of their succession. This transformation involves both aspects of commodity fetishism: the erasure of the real social relations of labour embodied in the production of a commodity, and the attribution of social animation to products or objects themselves inert (I am thinking here of the intimacy falsely promised visitors in the Gaia-Douro circuit, the Factory House balls in an otherwise deserted stone monument). The telling and enacting of their entitlement by port gentry can be seen as a work of reification or fetishization. Their practices of decontextualization and rearrangement of boundaries, spatial, proprietary, and categorical, produce the port gentry as effortlessly entitled rather than effortfully produced - in short, as fetish objects. When they act so as to produce themselves as wine gentry, under circumstances in which that is their waged labour, they may easily become part of that which is being sold - what might be called the Colonel Sanders effect.[17] Hard selling - self-reification or auto-fetishization - contains the possibility of commanding successful ratification of their elite succession, but also of being transformed into walking advertisements for port wine.[18]

The port gentry families find themselves in intimate engagements with changing political economic forces in a contradictory process of producing both their entitlement and their successors. On the one hand, they manage this through self-election, but in circumstances that place them in grave danger of commodification. On the other hand, they engage in the re-production of family succession in ways that place them in serious risk of superannuation. The various practices that create elite succession and its predicaments are not just divided and segregated, they are also interconnected and mutually constitutive. It is only because these processes are segregated in practice, but also only because they operate together, that elite family succession is successful.

Where in the very uneasy world of the port gentry is it possible for them to resolve their dilemmas and be at ease, at least momentarily? I'd guess it is at moments when they are seated around the luncheon table at the Factory House, telling their stories to journalists, who, like the gentry, have a stake in making them come true.

Notes

1.   João de Pina Cabral and Antónia Pedroso de Lima created an acutely considered problem for their workshop. Wrestling with it has transformed my understanding of the port gentry. I consider this a great gift from two wonderful colleagues. Colleagues and friends Penny Harvey, Jeanette Edwards and Elizabeth Bloomer kindly sent me

copies of *The Sunday Times* article. Many lively conversations with Gill Hart and Ole Dreier helped give shape to the argument. I have enjoyed and learned from years of intellectual interchange with Shawn Parkhurst and Susan Shepler, and I thank them for their serious critical readings of several drafts of the paper. I owe a deep intellectual debt and heart-felt thanks to Paul Duguid, who has read draft after draft, and inspired me with his inspired rereadings.

2. The quotation marks around 'Taylor's' reflect the fact that the family referred to is that of Alastair Robertson, head of Taylor, Fladgate & Yeatman. This usage is part of a pattern by which families and firms are onflated in the production of port gentry, as we shall see; but it is not common usage in the British enclave.

3. The production of elite succession, like the production of elite knowledge (Latour and Woolgar 1979), involves processes of exclusion, entitlement, a kind of smoke-and-mirrors claim to self-production, and erasure from public memory of the conditions of that production. This 'decontextualization' raises questions about relations among the politics of knowledge production as elite practice, the production of elites, and the production of knowledge about the privileged and powerful. We need specific strategies of research, therefore, to address exclusionary practices and the power to bring them about. It seems sensible not to confine research to sites where claims to entitlement to elite leadership appear to originate - whether in family business enterprises or family dynasties. Recontextualization of elite practices of succession should involve inquiry in and across multiple settings, and include those of our own choosing (though not of our own making). Second, it seems important to widen the study beyond its elite players. It is helpful to explore the plural character of elite succession, which also produces various kinds of not-elite succession and eliminates others. Third, we need to work at histories of various kinds, resisting self-congratulatory family histories, and - what amounts to the same thing in firms - production histories that calibrate time as progress by enumerating improvements in business productions, improvements in quality of products and steady expansion of corporate organizations. Finally, we might do well to hold on to a deep concern about the artefactual character of our understanding, under circumstances where high stakes and ubiquitous opportunities for practice lead to polished, skilful demonstrations of a particular history or a particular 'private' life for public consumption.

4. I use the term 'circuit' with some hesitation to invoke active travel through complex social terrains and spatial arrangements; to indicate that these travels are often repeated; and to imply that the ruts thus impressed on social life are plural, and in this case only cross in one significant place. Thus together they make a sort of figure 8, with the Gaia-Douro circuit longer in spatial terms, through smaller in temporal terms, but equally important and quite differently implicated in

bringing about elite succession in cultural-political terms.

5. After two preliminary field trips to Porto in 1991 and 1992, I spent a year there from August 1993 to August 1994, returning for two months in the summer of 1996. During that time my fieldwork was located in the British enclave in Porto.

6. This inquiry into the sustenance and transformation of British class culture in the centuries-old enclave of port-wine exporters is part of a collaborative anthropological-historical investigation of the port-wine trade and its families, entitled *Producing Families, Trading in History: An Ethno-Historical Investigation of the Port Trade of Northern Portugal.* The 'port project' began in 1992, involved three scholars focusing respectively on its history (Paul Duguid), especially with regard to crucial changes in the port trade in the period of the Portuguese civil war in the early 1830s, on Portuguese vineyard-keepers in the Douro valley (Shawn Parkhurst) and on British port shippers in Porto (myself). We have been interested since the inception of the project in how to capture generative processes that separate 'family firms' from 'family life'. The port trade 'colony', with its merchant capitalist partnerships and social enclosure, invites that question. We took it to be a theoretical question, one intended to contribute to critical assessments of naturalized 'public' and 'domestic' domains. We intended to inquire into the processes by which they are produced as distinct and separated phenomena. But in the present context I find myself inquiring into techniques of succession in the elite context of core 'old port families' that conflate public and private, family and firm, homes and houses, corporate property and private estates (in public). Unpacking these relations is one way to address relations between family firms and family life.

7. For instance, they elide business practices of the late eighteenth and nineteenth centuries by which firms were owned by partners who actually put up credit to run them, the partnerships shifting and changing practically year by year. The majority of these partnerships bought and sold other goods besides port wine. Complex partnerships make it difficult to establish, often, whether London or Porto was the 'main' office of a firm (Duguid and Lopes, forthcoming). Clerks rose in the ranks and married into their bosses' families, and sometimes became partners themselves. Senior partners 'made in Porto' went back to Great Britain. This means that roots of contemporary corporations cannot be traced back to precisely comparable eighteenth- and nineteenth-century economic entities. And there was no 'born to' aristocratic fraction that preserved its entitlement through exclusive intermarriage.

8. A Factory House member, John Delaforce produced several volumes of Whig history on the enclave. The principal aim of his book, *The Factory House at Oporto: Its Historic Role in the Port Wine Trade,* was to defend the right of the British port firms to its exclusive possession. He ends with

a flourish: 'The members are aware of the need to safeguard the character of this historic and unique House, but to ensure this some degree of exclusiveness is unavoidable. Meanwhile, it continues to fulfil the role for which it was originally designed, as the social headquarters of the British Port shippers and as the scene of many functions and entertainments' (Delaforce 1989: 104). Quotations like this one and his references to '300 years' and 'unbroken presence' must be read as part of the port gentry's self-presentation. I assume, however, that his quotations from Consul Crispin and the British Foreign Office are accurate, even while selected to support his point of view.

9. In November 1831 the Foreign Office wrote, 'It is possible that the Documents which were brought to England in 1807 may contain evidence to prove that the Factory House was a national building to which all His Majesty's subjects are entitled to have access, but in the present state of the information which has been furnished to the Secretary of State, Lord Palmerston is further advised that the claim of the general body of merchants resident in Oporto to free admission into the Factory House is not made out in such a manner as will render it advisable for his Lordship to disturb the parties now in possession' (Delaforce 1989: 43.).

10. Of Dynasty, a soap opera about the super-rich.

11. This view obscures another distinction between Taylor's and Symington's, as the former look down on the latter as parvenus. Thus, in a book celebrating Taylor's '300th anniversary': Taylor, Fladgate & Yeatman [...] [is] the only British port firm still totally privately owned ... Symington survived the most difficult times after the war by selling 20% of their company to the French group Pernod Ricard ... [The Symingtons] were the family that duing [sic] the 1950s and 1960s banked most on the revival of port - perhaps because they were originally traders not port merchants, and even today admit that they are faithful to their trading origins' (Foulkes 1992: 13).

12. This also suggests the elitist attractions of sports metaphors more generally.

13. In the first long quote from *The Sunday Times* (above p. 3), Portuguese men (on motorcycles) are characterized as too proletarian to get on comfortably with the port gentry, Portuguese women (who won't lower themselves, literally, to garden) as too aristocratic. This is surely an exotic excuse for exclusion, the more so since it inverts the class/gender conflations of the British speaker, who would no doubt assign himself and other port gentry men a class/gender position superior to that of their wives.

14. These terms of exaggerated intimacy with the Symington and Robertson families are not in common use in the British enclave in Porto, it should be noted.

15. Discussion of the Factory House earlier pointed to long-held princi-

ples of exclusion that still operate in specific contemporary ways today: women are not members and are not admitted to the Factory House except on rare social occasions. Non-port merchants cannot belong. Nor can lower-class British in Porto. Portuguese firms are not represented. These distinctions inflect social fractions and practices of exclusion throughout the enclave.

16. The pervasive derogation of persons and things Portuguese at the OBS includes quotas for Portuguese children and no Portuguese head teachers. Portuguese teachers are paid less than their British counter-parts. There is only token Portuguese membership on the school governing committee. Portuguese parents' voting rights at AGMs are restricted and the meetings are conducted in English. Monotonously, School Annual Reports explain that the 'lower accomplishment' by the children must be attributable to poor English on the part of Portuguese children.

17. The man who built up and then sold his fried chicken business became a sort of advertising puppet for the company he previously owned.

18. Port-wives may have known this intimately, if marginally, for much longer than the men.

10

How Do the Macanese Achieve Collective Action?

João de Pina-Cabral[1]

An ethnic community finds its definition in the course of individual situations of social confrontation where it is symbolically contrasted with others. The members of such a collectivity not only feel that they belong, they are also led to act in forms that reflect that belonging. And, in order to act out their belonging, they state their belonging. All of these are acts of social construction. From a series of personal decisions concerning 'who I am', one gets to answer the question 'who we are'.

In the words of Jaber Gubrium:

> Interaction in general and talk and language-use in particular, do not merely convey meaning, but rather, are ways of 'doing things with words' to 'create' meaningful realities. From this perspective, the orderly and recognisable features of social circumstances are 'talked into being' ... Descriptions ... are not disembodied commentaries on ostensibly real states of affairs. Rather they are reality *projects* - acts of constructing the world for practical purposes at hand (1990: 210).

In defining oneself as belonging one is staking a claim on a shared future.

Survival through time of ethnic belonging, thus, depends on shared sentiment, on collective action and on common expression. In turn, these require a complex interplay of power relations. In particular, when a collectivity finds its cohesion around the control of specific resources, by means of which its members acquire political power and/or material advantages, the transmission across generations of the control over these resources is of the utmost importance.

Personal unitary leadership is one of the means through which this process may be achieved. This is the traditional situation of succession. In many other instances, however, leadership is diffuse, and the instituting of successors is not a clearly personalized occurrence. Nevertheless, the collectivity's survival always depends on the achievement of some level of unitary action and of transfer of power across generations. In such situations, the collectivity may not have a corporate existence, being a function of the control of the resource that guarantees its survival.

João de Pina-Cabral

The present chapter attempts to show how an ethnically defined collectivity, without a clear corporate existence, achieves collective action through time, thus managing to hold on to the ethnic monopoly that has been its primary condition for survival for a number of centuries.

Macao and its Eurasian Bureaucratic Elite

In this chapter, I will focus on the Eurasian bureaucratic elite of Macao - the *macaenses* or to^2 *saang^1*, as they are known respectively in Portuguese and Cantonese. The 'Macanese' are the result of four and a half centuries of Portuguese presence in the Pearl River Delta. In spite of the major differences that have marked this long period, some things have stayed relatively stable that differentiate Macao from other ports on the China Coast. Firstly, the Portuguese Administration has always had to share power, in more or less informal ways, with the Chinese State and its representatives (cf. Pereira 1995). Secondly, the financial capital that has moved this city as a trading post and given their subsistence to the city dwellers has usually been either Chinese or, for a period, British. Thirdly, the labour force that has moved the city has always been Chinese.

The Macanese, living in relative isolation from mainland Portugal from the late 1500s to the late 1800s, developed a local creole culture - with its own language (not unlike most Portuguese maritime creoles), its own forms of dressing and its own cuisine. Apart from the heavy hand of the Catholic Church, they were left very much to their own devices and governed their city by means of a local parliament, the *Leal Senado*. From the late nineteenth century, however, Portuguese colonial administration was progressively installed. If they wanted to retain their privileges, the Macanese had to demonstrate their 'Portugueseness'. They were, therefore, forced to respond by dropping their Creole culture and integrating themselves into mainstream Portuguese culture. The *Leal Senado*, in turn, was demoted to the role of a municipal authority. The Lisbon-appointed Governor and his government have become the major political powerholders in the territory - at least in formal terms.

The Macanese have always been in close contact with the Chinese population and have always interbred with the Cantonese lower classes (cf. Pina-Cabral and Lourenço 1993). Their major form of subsistence, apart from administering the city and tapping the correlative informal resources, has been their capacity to function as intermediaries and *línguas* (translators) in business deals between foreign merchants and the Cantonese merchant elites.

In particular, ever since the British started taking an active interest in the China Coast, at the end of the eighteenth century, the Macanese have played the role of intermediaries. In 1840, in the wake of the Opium Wars, the British took over Hong Kong and established their own colony, abandoning Macao. This was a serious blow to the city, which forced it to rely increasingly on more marginal forms of economic activity: as a gambling centre (cf. Pina-Cabral and Chan 1997) and as a point of passage for internationally repressed merchandise, such as *coolies,* opium, gold bullion and the like (cf. Pina-Cabral 1998a).

The Macanese, however, found an important role in Hong Kong, where they again played the same intermediary role, both in the Administration (particularly of the New Territories) and in the all-important banking sector (their role in the Hong Kong and Shanghai Bank Corporation was legendary). Furthermore, they held a similar position in most other European footholds in China from the middle of the nineteenth to the middle of the twentieth centuries. After the Second World War, and particularly after the 'Liberation' in 1949, they were increasingly drawn back to Hong Kong and Macao. In Hong Kong, however, the *Portuguese,* as they were known there, found their niche in the state and financial administration challenged by the budding Chinese Westernized middle class that developed in the 1960s and 1970s. In Macao itself the conflict between these two middle classes took on the aspect of an open fight around the civil disturbances that accompanied the Great Cultural Revolution in 1966/7 (known in Macao as the *1,2,3,* cf. Dicks 1984).

After the Democratic Revolution of 1974, Portugal's desire to hand over Macao to the People's Republic of China became official policy. When the Portuguese State withdrew its military presence from the city in 1976, it became clear that Macao's days as a foreign-administered enclave were coming to an end. In fact, only in 1987 did the Chinese State finally devise a political solution that allowed it to prepare for the integration of both Macao and Hong Kong. Macao was handed over to Chinese Administration under the 'one country, two systems' policy on 20 December 1999, after which it became a Special Administrative Region, on terms somewhat similar to those that have applied in Hong Kong since July 1997.

Since 1976, therefore, the Macanese have been fully aware that the hold they have over the middle ranges of the administration of the city would be coming to an end. Their adjustment to this, both in linguistic terms (cf. Pina-Cabral 1994) and in terms of marital practices (cf. Pina-Cabral and Lourenço 1993), was particularly swift and efficient, considering that we are dealing with aspects of ethnic identity that involve deep personal investments. Ironically, however, the 1980s and early 1990s were a period of incomparable prosperity in the city. After Mao's death in 1976, Deng Xiaoping's policies of opening up the economy and of greater freedom of movement meant that Macao was swamped by a wholly new population eager to make a living (cf. Pina-Cabral 1998a). The fast development of the Pacific Rim during this period also meant that increasingly wealthier patrons as well as a growing number of Mainland Chinese visited Macao's casinos. The GATT agreements gave Macao export quotas that also opened up new financial possibilities. Finally, the Portuguese invested in a full renovation and modernization of the administration of the city. By contrast with Hong Kong, where the Chinese middle class expelled the

Macanese from their established economic niche, in Macao they succeeded in renovating their ethnic monopoly and reconstituting themselves as an administrative elite.

This chapter is based on materials gathered from 1990 to 1995, and focuses on the means through which the community achieved this process. It is a process that does not depend on the production of single successors to particular positions. As an administrative elite, the community's legitimacy depends on accomplishing universalistically defined administrative goals (cf. Cohen 1981). Thus, if the Macanese are to hold on to their 'privilege', they require both a diffuse production of successors to unspecified positions and the institution of an unstated structure of authority that allows for joint action.

Today, they are confronting a major new challenge: Macao's hand-over to China in December 1999 means that they will finally be replaced in their traditional role. To what extent this will occur and how they will reintegrate themselves into a polis that was historically grounded on their very existence, but that will henceforth be governed from Beijing, is something that only future studies will be able to determine.

The Macanese are an 'ethnic community' in the sense of a collectivity defined by reference to a common origin, whose members are closely linked by relations that constrain them to act in the interests of the group, being connected with each other by ties of long-term personal acquaintance and by a number of diffuse obligations (cf. Pina-Cabral 1994; Anthias 1990; Calhoun 1980). Moreover, they give evidence of the existence of a close network of personal relations of familiarity and of the corresponding 'reality projects' (cf. Gubrium 1990).

This sense of a belonging steeped in both shared experience and shared subordination is admirably captured by a member of one of the most distinguished Macanese families when writing for a local newspaper:

> If you take away from the Macanese his or her[2] environment, isolating him from his community, you take away his capacity for survival; and that, because being Macanese is above all feeling Macanese and part of a group. ... To be Macanese implies that one feels Macanese, but it also implies passing by the test of being considered Macanese by the other Macanese. Elitism? Perhaps. But things are what they are and there is no point in cloaking them, as that way one wouldn't get anywhere.
> This condition fully justifies the circumstance of someone's being able to consider himself Macanese who, in other terms, might not have all the necessary characteristics for that; and, on the other hand, the marginalizing of others who, whilst possessing those characteristics, have in some way betrayed the community. Betrayed, but rather in the sense of someone who doesn't work for the community, when he has every opportunity to do so.[3]

In more general terms, what is being said here is that, as a political entity, the Macanese community functions by means of a system of authority that, albeit informal, is fully determinant for the individual life of each member, quite as much as for the continuation through time of the community as a whole. The Macanese constitute an 'informally organised interest group', 'protecting or developing power for their members through informal organisation mechanisms' (Cohen 1974: 120). In order to belong to a group of this nature, as the quotation above amply illustrates, it is not enough to adopt a specific life-style that would externally symbolize group belonging. It is also necessary, on the one hand, to be 'hooked onto the dense network of interpersonal relationships between the members of the group' (Cohen 1974: 124) and, on the other, to show openly that one is willing to follow the dominant reality project, as legitimized by the collectivity's authority structure.

In the pages that follow, I will attempt to unravel the way in which collective action is achieved by means of this authority structure, grounding it both on the legitimization of informal power-holders and on the functioning of informal networks of sociability.

Although this is not the place to discuss the issue at length, it must be stated from the start that research in the Territory has indicated beyond doubt that phenotypic appearance is not an inescapable marker of ethnic belonging. Albeit one among other factors of Macanese self-definition, it is by no means a single determinant of ethnic group belonging (cf. Pina-Cabral and Lourenço 1993). Portuguese, as well as Chinese dispositions towards racial matters (cf. Dikötter 1992) have always differed considerably from those that characterized the British Empire in its heyday. They allow for a wider margin of ambiguity, where ethnic group belonging is not externally imposed on Eurasians by the fact of their phenotypic characteristics but is largely the result of identity options.

The Privilege

If we were to consider the fact that the Macanese have held until today a virtual monopoly over the intermediary levels of the public administration of a Territory whose population is mostly Chinese, we might be tempted to classify them as a typical 'colonial elite'. This would be a mistake, however, as it would be grounded on a superficial consideration of the apparent legalities, disregarding the complex political reality that has always characterized the city throughout its history and, most of all, since the uprisings of 1966/7. By contrast with what happened in Hong Kong at that time, the Portuguese Administration lost most of its capacity for independent decision-taking (cf. Scott 1989), governing the city since then through a system of complex negotiation with the mainland Chinese authorities.

Even although they fully exercise citizenship within the territory, the Macanese have lost their rights of sovereignty, both at the time of the 1966/7 incidents and later on, when the Portuguese democratic authorities declared that Macao was 'a Chinese territory administered by Portugal' (1976 Constitution - cf. Pereira 1995).

Thus, on the one hand, their condition as subjects of the Portuguese King (and later the Portuguese Republic) has shielded them from the worst insecurities that have befallen the population of South-western China through the chaotic political events of the past two centuries: from the Taiping Revolution, to the Opium Wars, to the various civil wars, to the Pacific War and finally to the series of tragic campaigns of the Maoist period. But, on the other hand, it has also implied considerable insecurity in the face of a Chinese state that has always been ambivalent to Macao and, most of the time, militarily dominant.[4]

The ethnic monopoly, therefore, has constituted an indispensable condition for the Macanese to cohabit with the Chinese population. The latter hold the rights of ultimate sovereignty as well as the greater military and economic power; but, in contrast, they have suffered from a 'deficit of social citizenship'.[5] Even today the full exercise of the rights of citizenship on the part of most Chinese inhabitants of the Territory is considerably limited by the transitoriness that has historically characterized their presence in Macao (what Hong Kong social scientists have called 'the stepping-stone syndrome' - cf. Yee 1989).

Thus, the monopoly is perceived as a 'privilege' - such is the very word often used by Macanese to refer to it, as it allows for a modicum of security within a region that has been subject to considerable political, sociological and financial turmoil. Furthermore, there are material benefits. By integrating itself into the Macanese ethnic field, a mixed couple from the lower classes (both Portuguese and Chinese) can gain for its children the considerable benefits that result from informal access to the ethnic monopoly. Characteristically, the children of such mixed couples are socially promoted by relation to their parents. But, although the Macanese ethnic condition usually brings with it a privileged access to middle-class status, the fact is that the very same condition imposes radical limitations for anyone who wishes to promote him- or herself above that middle-class layer.

Thus, in some aspects, to refer to the Macanese as an elite could be misleading: in the first place, because the 'Macanese privilege' is one among other possible privileges within the city, and involves a loss of other substantial privileges. For example, the Macanese have never been the dominant economic force in the Territory, the principal fortunes being in the hands of Chinese capitalists (gambling is the most obvious, but not unique, example). Small-scale commerce is also, with rare exceptions, out of their reach. The more recent development in industry, as well as in the service sector, is largely also in Chinese hands. This means, therefore, that the sudden expansion of the private sector of the economy that took place in the 1980s would have left them out, had they not succeeded in taking advantage of their control of the administrative bureaucracy for obtaining material gains.

And misleading in the second place, because the very notion of 'elite' is ambiguous. It is never very clear whether the term refers to the whole of a social group that controls a privilege (for example, an ethnic or a socio-professional group) or, on the contrary, whether it refers only to those members who, within that group, hold positions of authority, allowing for the informal enforcement of patterns of collective action. Abner Cohen, for example, who might be considered an inspiration in this field, hesitates over this issue.[6] In what follows, I shall rather opt for the second definition. The Macanese, therefore, will be treated as an ethnic community that becomes an informally organized interest group by means of the operation of a 'moral economy': that is, 'the slowly evolved but carefully maintained community consensus on many fundamental issues which orders and legitimates responses to the upset of the community's way of life' (Calhoun 1980: 121). And the people and families who hold a central place in the maintenance and management of this consensus - who hold authority within the community - will be more properly referred to as an 'elite'.

The Macanese community is not a formal group. As such, the authority to which I refer does not assume any contractual or official aspect. On the contrary, it inheres in the personal status of those people that hold it. One might best describe it by means of Bruno Latour's notion of translation: 'all the negotiations, intrigues, calculations, acts of persuasion and violence by means of which an actor or social force assumes, or confers upon itself, the authority to speak or act in the name of another actor or force'.[7]

Translation

Depending on the nature of the interests that each particular informal group aims to protect, so its elite will be primarily formed in the areas of social action where those interests are situated - that will be the primary locus of 'translation'. In the case of the Macanese, the determinant area is the Portuguese Public Administration of the city. Thus, we can define two profiles that constitute a disposition to assume elite condition, which may or may not be associated within the same person. The first is professional. That is, either people who hold jobs at leadership level in the Administration or the government or, alternatively, members of the liberal professions who function as interfaces between the Administration and the Chinese economic interests dominant in Macao and Hong Kong. I have in mind lawyers and solicitors, and, to a lesser extent, doctors, architects and civil engineers.

The second profile is familial: that is, loosely defined, families who both maximize the principal symbolic vectors of community belonging (Catholicism, Portuguese culture and Eurasian background) and have accumulated over time a number of members who correspond to the former critera of elite status. These are identified in the Territory as *famílias tradicionais* (traditional families). They have special claims to Portugueseness - being usually more proficient in Portuguese and often sending their children to Portuguese universities; they are staunchly

Catholic - investing symbolically in the Catholic churches and cemeteries; and they correspond to older Eurasian stock - discriminating against recent intermarriage.

On the one hand, therefore, we have the capacity for action in the area of interest of the ethnic monopoly; on the other hand, we have the capacity to represent the community through a maximization of the symbolic elements that most visibly define it historically. This polarization, however, has a somewhat artificial nature since both profiles are often combined in the most clearly marked elite elements of the Macanese community.

To be the child of a traditional family, to be married to an offspring of such a family, or have found the skills necessary to represent culturally the values associated with these families is often not enough to achieve 'translation'. But it is an important head start for someone who acquires university education, who is promoted to a leadership post in the Administration or who achieves some form of political significance in the Territory.

Similarly, to be a graduate, to be rich or to hold a leadership post is not enough to achieve elite status. But it is an important door, by passing through which one may come to form a new 'traditional family' or find a marital alliance that will associate one with an already existent family.

Thus the important official positions that a number of Macanese have achieved during the 1980s and 1990s are not necessarily a condition for the informal power that such people seem capable of exerting. On the contrary, these positions rather tend to be the result of the power they have achieved. Precisely because it is informal, this power is not grounded on a single factor (to be rich, to be the son of so-and-so, to be Director of this or that service, or to be elected to this or that political post). Rather, it corresponds to the integration of a whole network of relations and conditions that converge on a particular person.

What this means is that this elite condition is personal and non-transferable. No leader will ever succeed another, as the Territory's newspapers so often seem to presume when they comment on the death of particular Macanese leaders. The example of the death of Carlos D'Assumpção was paradigmatic. Before he died he came to be one of the most widely acknowledged mouthpieces of the Macanese ethnic community. One of the main questions the newspapers raised at the time of his unexpected death was 'Who will occupy the space he left vacant?' This question, however, is wrongly formulated, for his position was genuinely non-transferable to the extent that it depended directly on his own personal conditions and his individual life history. It combined, (1) being the offspring of an old and numerous 'traditional family'; (2) having a distinguished career as a lawyer; (3) having collected a vast network of informal links of amity created throughout the various moments of his life in which he exercised his notable skills as mediator - from being President of the Students' Union in the University of Coimbra at the height of Salazar's power, to being on the winning side of the negotiations that led to the new

Gambling Contract in 1961, to mediating the ending to the 1966/7 incidents both with the local Chinese magnates and then with the People's Liberation Army, to the conflict between the Macanese old-fashioned cadres of the Administration and the governor who launched the process of modernization in the early 1980s (Almeida e Costa), to being central in the negotiations with the Deng Xiaoping period Chinese authorities that led to the Joint Declaration and, subsequently, to the drafting of the Basic Law that will govern the Territory after 1999.

This impossibility of replacing the figures with specific capacities for 'translation' contributes to a sentiment that I have come to recognize in Macanese conversation and in the Macanese press as *the mirage of the community's death*. When an informally organized interest group feels that its power base is under threat, as was the case for the Macanese community throughout the 1980s and 1990s, the death or disappearance of such 'translators' assumes menacing aspects, as the equilibrium of forces that that person incorporated can never be precisely reconstituted by any other person. This feeling, nevertheless, may be characterized as a 'mirage' to the extent that the community, with the passing of time, has also renovated itself. The new dynamics that have arisen require new equilibria, which other people will come to personify. In the case of the Macanese, however, this feeling is justifiably more intense, owing to the lack of ultimate rights of sovereignty to which I have referred earlier on.

Macao's Elites

Throughout the 1980s there was a significant renovation of the Macanese elite. Starting from a small group of young graduates who were called from Lisbon by the first governor of the Territory after the 1974 Democratic Revolution (Garcia Leandro), a nucleus of cadres with university education was formed that assumed roles of increased importance. A major crisis occurred in the early 1980s at the time of Almeida e Costa's governorship. His attempts to adapt the Administration to the growing demands of population increase, of increased demands for citizenship rights on the part of the Chinese inhabitants, and of the new financial possibilities resulting from renegotiations of the gambling contracts, led to a fear that the ethnic monopoly might be broken. This, however, was not to be.

The demands of the Chinese government for greater 'localization' of the Administration were systematically circumvented by the promotion of Macanese rather than of Chinese cadres. This was facilitated by the unavailability of Portuguese-speaking educated Chinese residents. Owing to the 'stepping-stone syndrome', the young Chinese candidates to middle-class status see Portuguese as a less worthwhile investment than English. The Administration being in Portuguese, it was therefore easy for the Portuguese authorities to circumvent the repeated pressure exerted by the People's Republic, particularly after the signing of the Joint Declaration.

With the passing of the years, and particularly since the governorship of Carlos Melancia (1987-1990), Macanese people assumed a growing number of leadership positions in the Administration, the Municipality and the liberal professions. The number of Macanese who were directors of services and members of government or of the Legislative Assembly was greater at the beginning of the 1990s than in most periods during the previous century - and certainly far beyond anything that their numeric presence in the Territory would justify.

Some of these people originate in traditional families or are associated to them by marriage alliance; others have succeeded in forming a name for themselves independently, owing to their personal qualifications. A common characteristic of practically all of them is that they opted for a public image that associates them with some form of Portugueseness: they are mostly graduates from Portuguese universities and they all speak Portuguese far more fluently than the common Macanese person. This is interesting, as in fact during the 1980s most Macanese families went in the opposite direction: Cantonese became the domestic language of most families, and proficiency in Portuguese tended to decrease.

Notwithstanding, while the older elite members are noted for their poor Cantonese and are illiterate in Chinese, among the younger ones we have witnessed a greater effort to avoid Chinese illiteracy. Some were even undertaking concerted efforts to learn to write Chinese. Another noteworthy aspect of these younger 'translators' is that, in the construction of their public image, they have become less dependent on Portuguese-style symbols of prestige, adopting more readily a language of prestige that is clearly associated with the Hong Kong Cantonese-speaking mass media.

Characteristically, the Macanese whose careers of success have been in the private sector of the economy tend to assume a smaller public visibility. This confirms our reading of the Macanese as an informally organized interest group whose privilege lies in their control over the Administration. By contrast, among the Chinese of the Territory, the figures with greater capacity to 'translate', who are therefore also those whom the local media follows more closely, are invariably associated with the private sector.

In broad terms, the elite profiles among the Chinese of Macao are associated either with commerce (for example, the people surrounding Ho Yin and their successors) or with the new industries (magnates such as Susana Chow or Eric Yeung). The heads of the triads have had a more discreet public profile in the past, even although they have always been most influential. The recent public prominence of Wan Kwok-Kui of the sect named '14 Carats' is not characteristic (cf. Pina-Cabral 1998a). Finally, a complex profile such as that of Stanley Ho - the Hong Kong Eurasian who is the figurehead of the casino industry - would require a study of its own.

How do the Macanese Achieve Collective Action?

There is, therefore, a vast difference between the two ethnic elites of Macao. The Macanese elite finds its following among an old middle class, and is grounded in a control of the Administration, for which it relies on what one might call a 'capital of Portugueseness'. The Chinese elite finds its power base among a recent middle class, and is solidly grounded in the private sector.

The old alliance between the Macanese elite and the Chinese elite, which was forged at the time of the challenges that marked the beginning of the 1980s, was represented by persons who have died in the meantime, such as Carlos D'Assumpção and Ho Yin. The 1990s have seen a rapidly changing scene. The 1992 elections to the Legislative Assembly showed that the capacity for political mobilization of this alliance was still considerable. Furthermore, the new prominent figures that have emerged among the Macanese are still associated to the classic terrain (such as the member of government Rangel or the Speaker of the Legislative Assembly Anabela Ritchie).

Finally, however, by 1996/7, the Administration started appointing Chinese people to positions of leadership. This will inevitably lead to a change, even if it turns out to be less radical than some Chinese people in the city presently hope. The struggle for position among different Chinese elites appears to be still undecided. The recent incidents, known locally as 'the Triad Wars', have shown that the terrain is moving very fast.

As the Macanese grip on the Administration loosens, will their identity die out in the Territory? I believe that a number of Macanese public figures have already started the process of trying to shift their role towards that of mediators both with the historical past and with the international networks that that historical legacy facilitates. These are advantages that the city holds over the competing Chinese cities of the Pearl River Delta.[8] The way will then be open for greater prominence for those Macanese 'translators' who have been investing in a more 'cultural' profile (such as the designer Conceição or the painter/architect Marreiros).

For the Macanese, the period between 1987 (when the future of Macao was finally determined) and the mid-1990s (the 'ethnographic present' of this paper) can be characterized by two diverging tendencies. On the one hand, there was a slight decrease in the rhythm of growth of the Administration and an increased pressure on the part of the Chinese middle class to penetrate it. On the other hand, however, since the initial launching of the reforms was based on Macanese cadres, this meant that by the mid-1980s they had been promoted to positions of seniority that granted them the means necessary for 'translation'.

The Macanese elite of the mid-90s was a relatively uniform group of people in kinship terms (their association to the traditional families), in educational terms (being graduates from Portuguese universities) and in linguistic terms (being predominantly Portuguese-speakers but very fluent in Cantonese). It is also worthwhile noting that there was a solid presence of both genders, even if men were in a majority.

211

Which Kind of Community?

In the 1980s and 1990s, the Macanese have represented an ever smaller percentage of the population (by the late 1980s they constituted approximately 1.6 per cent of the population of the Territory).[9] In spite of this, they have given ample evidence of managing to hold on to their ethnic monopoly and of being able to continue to negotiate it politically. This means beyond any measure of doubt that they have achieved collective action. In turn, that shows that their elite has successfully managed to 'translate'.

That being the case, then, our next step is to attempt to describe the processes by means of which the community both invests certain members with authority and then agrees to follow their authority. This is less simple than it may seem, as the Macanese have no official structures of community leadership, nor could they have, as these would have placed them in an awkward position vis-à-vis both the Chinese majority and the Portuguese governing minority. Thus we also have to explain how the people who hold the capacity to 'translate' achieve some sort of coherence among themselves.

As an informal interest group, the Macanese form a community - that is, their social interaction is based on a series of criss-crossing links of long-term personal acquaintance.[10] As such, we must not search for formal processes of integration, but rather for processes based on what Abner Cohen calls a *network of amity* (1981: 222). These networks of criss-crossing interpersonal identification link people together; but above all they function as vectors for the diffusion of the 'reality projects' without which there can be no legitimate authority and, therefore, no successful 'translation'.

Having said this, it must be stressed that there is no unanimity of opinions or interests within the community. On the contrary, conflicts internal to the community frequently arise, even concerning the most central aspects of the management of their 'privilege'. For example, in the summer of 1993 there was a public conflict in the Legislative Assembly concerning the maintenance of the relatively high level of salaries obtaining in the Administration in relation to those that were offered by the private sector. The principal contenders were both distinguished members of the Macanese community.

This conflict, as well as so many of those that occupy the pages of the local Portuguese newspapers, are a sign of the growing difficulty that the Macanese elite experienced during the 1980s and 1990s in adopting openly exclusivist attitudes. We may look at this under the light of the opposition between the *particularistic* and the *universalistic* interests of elites adopted by Abner Cohen (1981). In their quality as members of the political or the administrative structures of Macao, these people feel obliged to assume universalistic positions. Seeing that the Macanese are a numerical minority in the Territory, however, such positions will often conflict with the particularistic interests of their own community.

This growing difficulty in assuming publicly attitudes of exclusivism vis-à-vis the Chinese must not be taken as a sign of the disappearance of the Macanese as an ethnic community or of an increased irrelevance of the label of Macanese to their personal sense of belonging. This willingness to operate with moving and porous community boundaries is nothing new to the Macanese. For a long time their relation to the Portuguese from Portugal was precisely of this nature. In the days before the 1966/7 incidents, they claimed a greater permeability with the Portuguese (calling themselves proudly 'the Portuguese of the Orient' - *os Portugueses do Oriente*) and assumed openly exclusivist attitudes towards the Chinese.

By the mid-1990s all this had changed, however. The symbolic relevance of their 'capital of Portugueseness' (cf. Pina-Cabral and Lourenço 1993) had diminished considerably, whilst the age-old competition with administration personnel coming from Portugal became more intense. Contrariwise, there was a greater facility of cultural contact with the new Chinese middle class. This meant that the boundaries with the Chinese ethnic group lost much of the clarity that they had formerly possessed. The awareness that, after 1999, the future of the community, as well as of each individual Macanese that stays behind, depends on a negotiation with the Chinese, means that any form of public manifestation of exclusivism became clearly undesirable.

This explains how, progressively, there has been a reduction bordering on total disappearance in the Macanese *arenas of community*, by which I mean the public spaces and occasions where community belonging was openly staged before non-community members and where community members openly performed their own internal hierarchies of prestige. The clubs, private beaches, theatre performances, café meetings, religious ceremonies, brotherhoods and kermesses that played such a central role during the first half of the century progressively vanished. The famous *chás-gordos* (the Pantagruelian tiffins they offered at their homes), the exclusive club balls, the 'Portuguese-style' weddings, the spontaneous evening meetings of the local youth bands (*tunas*), the theatre performances in Creole (*patuá*), all of these are today nostalgic memories that, when exceptionally enacted, only serve the purpose of creating a sense of a shared past. Books are written about these things, restaurants are opened where this type of cuisine is now available to all customers, the Administration subsidizes *tunas* where the musicians may well no longer be Macanese, poetry books in *patuá* are published that only a learned few can read, local literati are busy writing lengthy and abundantly illustrated studies of local culture, and voluminous genealogical studies are compiled and published at great public cost where all sorts of genealogical acrobatics are performed, with ample if not always accurate biographical detail. But the Clube de Macao was sold, the D. Pedro Theatre was closed for over a decade and was then re-opened by the Municipality as a public service, the Tennis Club was taken over by the Chinese middle class, and of course there are no longer restricted areas of beach front.

None of this means that the community has vanished, of course; nor that it has lost its capacity for collective action. In order to undertake an overall assessment of the intensity of community links among the Macanese, we will follow Calhoun's suggestion of measuring three dimensions of community:

1. the *density* (does one observe all possible links?);
2. the *multiplexity* (are people linked in more than one way?);
3. the *systematicity* (are people integrated within a unifying system of corporateness?) (1980: 118).

As to the first dimension, density, one can observe almost total coverage in terms of personal acquaintance. There are, of course, areas of lesser relational density associated to internal socio-educational stratification.

Nevertheless, very seldom can one find two members of the community between whom there is not some sort of a link: be it of kinship, of marriage alliance, of professional association, of school peers or of neighbourhood youth gangs. Seldom do these links involve more than one intermediary person. That is, if we were to include cousins of cousins; colleagues or boyfriends or affines of siblings or cousins; students or subordinates of parents or children of students or subordinates, we would easily cover the whole community. In short, in terms of *density*, one can consider the Macanese community resident in the Territory as probably well above average.

Let us now consider Calhoun's second dimension. If we try to assess whether community members are individually connected by more than one type of relation, the conclusion will definitely be that the Macanese evince a high level of *mutiplexity*. Work colleagues are either relatives, children of relatives, old school friends, affines, or simply neighbourhood cronies. This dimension, however, needs further consideration, for it covers two considerably different aspects. On the one hand, we may ask ourselves if people are linked by more than one type of relation. As we have seen, the Macanese are. On the other hand, however, we may want to assess to what extent the different roles combine with each other and interpenetrate. For example, do the roles of cousin and director of services, or the roles of employee and old school colleague, tend to interpenetrate? Here the answer would not be so clear-cut. Macao is a modern city, with a complex bureaucratic administration, whose legal framework obliges people to measure their gestures by means of univocally expressed legal principles. In other words, whether a person is or is not my cousin, sibling or friend, I have the same obligations towards him or her as towards any other of my colleagues. In this second sense, pre-modern communities and peasant communities, such as have been described by many ethnographers, show considerably higher levels of multiplexity than the Macanese.

Nevertheless, whoever has lived in Macao for any length of time knows fully well that the 'administrative culture' that is dominant there allows for a considerable margin of permissiveness towards the interpenetration of roles. Most people tend to look away whenever they encounter what elsewhere might be criticized as nepotism. As a matter of fact, as we shall discuss further, in a multiethnic context such as this one, the maintenance of any sort of ethnic monopoly depends precisely on a careful management of multiplexity.

As a bureaucratic elite, the Macanese elite must preoccupy itself with the efficiency of the Administration (a universalistic value); thus it must circumvent the effects of multiplexity. As an ethnic elite, however, it has a strong particularistic interest in preserving its 'privilege', which often is contrary to the universalistic rules of bureaucratic procedure.

Finally, concerning *systematicity*, we must ask ourselves whether the Macanese are integrated within a unifying system of corporateness. This does not seem to be the case. Community boundaries tend to be porous, and there are no open arenas of community. The Macanese community is not defined by clearly demarcated borders. Rather, it forms itself around a publicly identifiable elite nucleus by relation to which each individual member situates his or her individual (and/or familial) belonging. Notwithstanding this, there are some organizations that, without being ethnically exclusivistic, wind up representing the interests of the Macanese. In the period under study, perhaps the most important of these was the *Associação dos Trabalhadores da Função Pública de Macao* - the civil servants' trade union. In the mid-1990s, this was still fully controlled by the Macanese.

We can conclude that the Macanese community is relatively intense, even although it does not possess strong public arenas of community and has low systematicity. This being the case, we must turn to private relations in order to search for the processes by means of which the community acquires its internal structure of authority. In the pages that follow, therefore, I will attempt to identify and characterize the principal spaces and occasions where the dialogical process of the production of intersubjectivity occurs that allows for the continuation of the community as an informal interest group. These time/spaces shall be named *nodules of community*, in order to indicate that they endow with relative systematization that network of amity (a large network of interpersonal identification) that forms the foundation of this ethnic community.[11]

Nodules of Community: The Family

One of the principal characteristics of the Macanese families that today are considered 'traditional families' is that they used to be very large. During the second quarter of our century, it was common to find couples with 9 and 10 surviving children. After the Pacific War this fertility tended to decrease. During the 1950s and 1960s, couples tended to have 3 to 5 children. After the 1970s, however, very few couples have more than 2 children. This gradual process of reduction is openly recognized by the Macanese, but is also clearly visible from the numerous family histories that I gathered in the course of research (cf. Pina-Cabral and Lourenço 1993).

A number of reasons were given for the earlier high rates of fertility. Principal among them was the availability of domestic service. A Portuguese lady who met her husband at university in Coimbra and followed him to Macao immediately after the end of the Pacific War described to me with vividness the domestic situation she came to encounter in her father-in-law's extended family. It was a patriarchal home, where it was expected that each son would bring his wife to live in the parental household. Apart from the older house servants, each young couple was assisted by their own maid. When she and her husband arrived, she was surprised to find that her own personal maid had already been chosen in preparation for her arrival. On top of that, each new-born child received an *ama*, who would serve him or her exclusively until schooling age, and often after that. These *amas* taught the Macanese how to speak Cantonese and to be familiar with Chinese domestic habits. In those days, however, before the mid-1970s, most of these elite families forced the children to speak Portuguese with everybody but the servants, in order to ensure that they would acquire the necessary capital of Portugueseness, which in those days was so central for their elite status. An old man reported to me that he used to be punished each time he used a Cantonese word in front of his parents.

I have received documented reports of household compounds that were very akin to those of wealthy Chinese families at the end of the Qing Dynasty. Around his own house, the father would construct houses for each son and their respective families. The compound that Pedro José Lobo built for his children in Mong Há and that of the Jorges near the Lilau are instances of this. So long as the father was alive, the children continued to eat together, so that the culinary practices were marked by these large communal meals. 'Macanese cuisine', writes a lady from the Jorge family, 'was born of the need to satisfy large families and justify constant conviviality, two circumstances that are no longer part of our way of life.'[12]

Such families constituted a powerful base of support for their members. These patriarchs personalized a family project. As was the case with the wealthy families of Imperial China, the death of the patriarch constituted a moment of rupture, which normally terminated the familial communality. Nevertheless, powerful links of *continued identity*[13] survived that allowed the members to benefit from the family's prestige and from the large network of kindred.

The lists of names of traditional families that I have asked people to produce have a high level of overlap: names such as the Senna Fernandes, the Jorges, the D'Assumpção, the Nolascos, the Batalhas, are always present. Other names tend to be absent from the lists provided by younger people - for example, the Melos, descendants of the Baron of Cercal, whose home is today the Government Palace, but whose descendants no longer live in the city. Others, for a number of reasons, have a slightly less 'traditional' status: for example, the Leitão or the Lobos.

It is important to stress that, when the Macanese cite one of these names, they are by no means referring to a group of persons all of whom are equally identifiable or even who form a corporate group. These names are no more than *continued identities.* In certain cases, profound bitterness has developed between different branches of the family, resulting from events of such insignificance that even the descendants find it hard to recount them.

I can cite as an example the case of a man who gave me a detailed genealogical tree of his family. Starting in the mid-nineteenth century with a man who purchased a nobility title, this genealogy included people currently living all over the world, some of whom had left Macao two generations ago. Nowhere, however, in that detailed genealogy could I find one of the principal branches of the family, some members of which are today Macao notables. The cause for this, I later found out, was an inheritance conflict that none of them could now clarify and that had taken place in the 1940s!

In spite of these quarrels, and even after the death of the patriarch, these continued identities constitute a social referent of major symbolic importance for their members, both because of the vast networks of relations that they provide and because they pave the way for a claim to elite positioning. Talking to a journalist, a member of one of these families who returned to Macao after many years of absence abroad explained that his 'respectable family name has frequently helped to open a number of doors'.[14]

Yet another distinguishing feature of traditional families is their relations of marriage alliance. Marrying a member of one of these families is a considerable advantage if one has the ambition of assuming an elite role. A number of the most influential political figures of the community in the 1980s and 1990s fit into this mould. A Macanese man once said to me in a joking mood that he was thinking of forming an 'Association of the Spouses of the Xs', as it would be the most powerful association in the city. For the people that establish an alliance with such a family, the access to the prestigious name and the correlative network of relations is of the utmost importance. For the members of the family, however, and especially for the less successful ones, these elite allies constitute indispensable assets.[15]

Traditional families are not the only ones whose large numbers of children produced vast networks of relations. There were some couples economically less well endowed and socially less prestigious that gave rise to families whose importance in the Territory is recognized by all. Even though few of their members achieve elite status, these families are known by everyone, for their members are widely placed throughout the various branches of the Administration. I have in mind cases where the father was a police agent or a clerk at the Department of Finances or in the Inspectorate of Games. In a number of these instances the father was from Portugal and the mother was either a lower-class Chinese woman or a Macanese with low claims to prestige. Their children and grandchildren and their respective spouses came to form a veritable web of connectedness throughout the Administration. This network allows them to compile information gathered from very diverse sources, thus enabling them to reap a number of informal benefits - from achieving small clerical privileges (such as jumping queues and tapping limited resources) to more clandestine types of activities that need not be detailed here. In some of the families I studied, it became clear to me that this strategy of spreading people as widely as possible throughout the various services of the Administration was actively and consciously pursued.

These networks of siblings, brothers- and sisters-in-law and cousins are further extended by the bigamy of the father. The practice of maintaining more than one house has never been uncommon in Macao, among both the Macanese and the Chinese, among whom it is generally taken as a claim to prestige. The family histories compiled indicated that there is not a unique pattern to these types of bigamous relations. Some are so informal that they hardly correspond to a kind of marriage, being limited to the *perfilhação* (legal recognition of paternity) of the offspring; while others assume the nature of fully public lifelong concubinage. In either case, they have the consequence of enlarging the sibling group at a later moment in time. I have found out that, after the death of the mothers, most of these 'siblinghoods' operate as favoured networks of relations, even in cases where, before the death of the official wife, there was an avoidance relation between the different households.

Finally, as has been said, the cohabitation that characterized the large patriarchal houses and compounds terminated, largely because of the population growth that started in the late 1970s. The construction boom of the following decades meant that these large sprawling houses situated in the older parts of the city acquired incalculable value. For the majority of families, rather than keeping their outdated family mansions in Macao, it seemed more sensible to rent flats and invest in real estate in Portugal, Australia or Canada. Most of the houses bought overseas were left empty, awaiting the moment at which political conditions might force the owners to flee the Territory. At the same time, the Administration's policy of offering rent-free apartments to its civil servants meant that the majority of young couples could expect to receive an apartment from the Administration.

In fact, by the mid-1990s, when this policy was significantly reduced, the Macanese came to develop a sense of grievance in relation to the expatriate Portuguese personnel. A Macanese lady from the Administration once voiced this to me:

The people who come from Portugal are not especially qualified, they have no place, so they trample on the ones that are already here, taking their homes. People are in the housing queue. The married people from here ... just married. They can be waiting for up to five years for the right to receive a rent-free apartment, because they are civil servants. But along comes another person from Portugal, who is a friend of so-and-so, and there goes the apartment! They - the Portuguese - stay in the apartments! And they stay in the apartments with rights to everything for free, even toilet paper. ... My brother-in-law, for example, in order to get a flat had to go around complaining loudly and showing his clout, because otherwise he would have got nothing, just because he did not go and get some sort of university degree. So, that's it.

In spite of the fact that domestic servants remain cheap (by the mid-1980s this sector of employment was largely in the hands of Filipino women), the apartments in the new high-rise blocks did not allow for large numbers of servants. Furthermore, most women who entered came into adult life in the 1970s and 1980s took on salaried jobs in the Administration, and to smaller extent in commerce. This also means that there are no longer enough housewives with free time on their hands to run that 'society of ladies' to which our older female interviewees refer so nostalgically. Nor could the new professional women afford to look after such large and intense domestic arrangements. All this means that, after the second half of the 1970s, the domestic environment tended to reduce itself to the conjugal family - with extensive support from the grandparents' houses in raising the children.

If we further took into account the facts that the number of children per couple was reduced drastically, that divorce came to be a regular event, and that the domestic establishment is now numerically slimmed down, we might be led to conclude that Macanese families lost their effectiveness as nodules of community. The study of twenty families that I undertook, however, shows beyond any doubt that such a conclusion would be completely mistaken.

Macanese families remain an important network of integration into the community and one of the bases for the functioning of the ethnic collectivity as a structure of authority and, consequently, of collective action. As the laborious process of collecting family histories developed, I became increasingly aware that new practices had come to substitute for the domestic socialization around the famous *chás-gordos* or the large meetings on Catholic feast days. For example, the Macanese organize with intensity and regularity family reunions in restaurants. Typically, the family hires a 'private room' for a whole day (generally a Saturday or Sunday) and spends the entire day lunching, speaking, singing karaoke and playing mah-jong. Note that the principal form of entertainment, in which everyone participates actively, is gambling. This is always played with real money, as the Macanese on the whole partake of the Chinese notion that otherwise the game would lose all its appeal. Such a practice, which would be deeply criticized in Portugal, is here taken for granted.

When I tried to establish the regularity of these meetings in each family, I obtained very varied responses. The regularity reflects the relative vitality of each specific 'family project'. The more alive the project, the more frequent and varied are the meetings. It is common for parents to bring together their married children with their associated grandchildren once a week or once a month on a predetermined day. Further on along the family development cycle, when the widowed mother or father is still alive, it is expected that a reunion will be organized for the day of his or her birthday - people come from abroad specially to be present at such meetings. In some cases, the children and grandchildren continue to meet yearly on the same date, or on the date of his or her death.

Each person participates in a number of cycles of such reunions. Now it's the parents and the siblings; then it's the parents, their siblings and the siblings' descendants (both on the paternal and on the maternal side); then it's the parents and siblings of the spouse; or again the parents-in-law and their respective siblings and descendants (both on the paternal and on the maternal side). Thus, once we account for patrilateral and matrilateral extension, as well as for alliance relations, it is easy to see that the network of meetings could be vast if it were not for the fact that not all family identities have the same capacity for the mobilization of potential members. As is the case probably everywhere, neither are all family projects equally strong,[16] nor do family projects retain the same vitality as time passes.

It does happen that, as a response to the visit to Macao of a long-absent family member, sporadic family reunions are organized for members who have long been dispersed and whose family project in the Territory had little vitality. At those occasions it is said that *reuniram-se todos os Fulanos* ('all the X's have met'). This does not mean that all of the people that have a formal right to claim that name were present - in fact, normally, old family quarrels tend to prevent the achievement of this ideal. Often too, people that do not have a right to the name, but are closely associated either by marriage or by uterine descent, play a central role.[17]

Today, these family reunions constitute the primary nodule of community that grants coherence to Macanese ethnic belonging. They are essential for the way in which a Macanese person's professional life develops, and they are the principal vehicles for the management of the ethnic monopoly. They allow for, on the one hand, the spreading of information and opinion - 'reality projects' - and, on the other hand, they reproduce the particularistic links that are essential for the community's survival in the face of the universalistic demands of the administrative and legal structure of the Territory. Each person participates in several of these cycles of reunions. There, in contexts of great intimacy, he or she meets regularly a substantial large number of kinsfolk, who, in turn, by participating in other such reunions, meet a yet wider range of people. In this way, a cycle of intimacy is silently created that ranges throughout the whole of the community, reaching to its furthest extensions abroad.

Nodules of Community: Friendship

One of the most common phrases for identifying group belonging among the Macanese is the expression *nós' malta* ('our folk'). The expression has connotations that associate it to male youth gangs and stresses the importance of the friendships made at the time of high school for the integration of the Macanese ethnic community as a whole.

The fact that the Macanese have co-opted a number of people whose familial past may not have granted them automatic belonging to the community is often the result of such an insertion into school friendship groups. I have found with some surprise that the importance that these connections assume for people who are today in the middle of their professional careers cannot be exaggerated. It is something to which I was not attuned at the outset of the research. Slowly, however, as the evidence of the functional relevance of these links mounted, I became aware that the sporadic reports of reunions of old school friends that I kept receiving, amply illustrated by photographs, were extremely significant. Far more than they would have been, for example, in Portugal, where they do take place, but do not mark quite so definitely a person's connection to the power structure of the community. These class reunions or youth group meetings turned out to be a major nodule of community. Although this cannot be proved beyond doubt, I came to hazard the hypothesis that such meetings were held with greater intensity at times when a response to particular community challenges was required. In my supposed capacity as an expert on Macanese identity, I myself was asked to participate in one or two of these meetings.

Much like the family reunions, they tend to be realized in private but not domestic spaces, such as the private rooms of restaurants or religious premises, loaned for the purpose. They assume different formats with varying intensity: from the small closed group that meets once or even twice a month; to the less close-knit groups that meet once or twice a year; to the mammoth meetings, sporadically organized to welcome or to say goodbye to someone who is arriving back in or leaving the Territory. The most all-encompassing reunion of which I had notice was not even held in Macao. It was the grand meeting of all the old students of the Macao Portuguese High School, which took place in Lisbon at the Hotel Penta.

On the most intense side of the gamut - the weekly or monthly meetings - we are dealing with an exclusively male sociability. The feminine counterpart - that *sociedade de senhoras* ('society of ladies') whose meetings used to be domestic - was dispersed from the moment the majority of wives became working women. As a matter of fact, in the conversations I held about this in the Territory, a clear conceptual opposition emerged between, on the one hand, male sociability (accompanying a kind of 'old boy' spirit) and, on the other hand, domestic sociability.

Women's social life is more permanently marked by the family - such extra-familial contexts tend to be subsumed by family connectedness.

Women who meet with their old school girlfriends tend to do so in contexts that are either domestic or more open to familial participation. Thus the attitude of wives towards this aspect of the social life of their husbands was on the whole ambiguous. On the one hand, they felt excluded and vaguely threatened, but on the other hand, they were perfectly aware that this was a matter of the utmost importance, on which depended both the economic survival of their family and the political survival of their ethnic group.

A wife once told me:

> In the old days great friendships [were made in High School]. So my husband is also one of those that ... You see, this thing one hears of the thirty-year-olds who meet all the time? They were the last. But the ones that are fifty, like my husband, they also have their group. They have their group, but sometimes they link up with the wives and the children. They make one of those parties. Otherwise, there is a day ... I do not know if it is monthly or what ... some kind of day, that they put aside to be together. ... It's like they were boys again. They need that to refurbish themselves. It is a kind of search for identity; because they have a bit of a lost identity. This is important, so that they get it back again, at least once in a while. Perhaps it is not all that efficient, but ... But, you know, it cannot be denied that, in fact, in these meetings sometimes discussions come up that are really, really useful, attitudes that are taken, etc. So, the thing is, they continue to meet each other.

On the less intense side of the gamut of variation, one finds the irregular meetings that bring together both men and women. This is not surprising, considering that the present generation of working people integrates a large number of professional women whose levels of scholarly and professional achievement are at least as high as those of the men. While looking at photographs of these events and listening to the reports that accompanied them, I became aware that a number of these meetings had been central to the efforts leading to the re-launching of the ethnic monopoly in the wake of the challenge posed by Almeida e Costa's governorship. In these photographs, I could see people who, in the public arena constituted by the Portuguese-speaking newspapers, assume opposing positions and present themselves as political opponents.

Meetings of this nature were responsible for the return to the Territory in the course of the 1980s of a significant number of elite members who had set up home in Portugal or elsewhere. Called to visit Macao by family members and old friends, they found that they had a ready position into which to fit by simply reviving these available networks. In some cases, some associations were created that had some permanence. A man I interviewed who had been in this situation explained:

> I was abroad for seventeen years. It was a great surprise to me to discover that, as I passed people in the street, they called out 'So-and-so!' That was great! The second thing I noticed is that they said 'So-and-so, how are you? We must meet!' And then ... well, it was not like that in all cases (there was a good number of

more intimate friends that never forgot it), but the 'we must meet' was often forgotten. ... From there came the idea of founding an association of old school friends. It was a way of trying to bring people closer together. This association has developed a number of regular activities, among them a radio programme - a small thing of twenty minutes where we present weekly one old schoolmate.

This is an interesting example because it points to the role played by the Portuguese-speaking mass media as nodules of community for the Macanese. Their role is by no means univocal. In particular in the case of newspapers, there is a marked difference between the writers whose sensibility approaches them to the Macanese civil servants and those who represent more the views of the Portuguese expatriates. In spite of that, Portuguese-language newspapers have functioned as the principal means of divulging publicly community decisions, political reactions and complaints concerning the protection of the ethnic monopoly. The newspapers are one of the principal means for the personal legitimation of a Macanese elite position. This explains the peculiar practice of these newspapers and radio programmes of publishing and broadcasting curricula of people who have no specific connection to any current news event, or of publishing long curricular-type interviews. This seems to be done especially when the people in question are changing their status in some way or their employment, and it is by no means limited to top-ranking leaders.

Conclusion

In spite of being grounded in a historical past, ethnic identity is never simply a given fact. Macanese community, therefore, was here presented as an ethnic project: that is, a collectivity in constant mutation, whose very continuity depends on the existence of agreement between its members concerning how to construct the future in terms of an inheritance that is constantly being reassessed, and in terms of desires that are constantly being renegotiated.

This ethnic project, however much it is shared, is never univocal or fully consensual. It depends on a dynamic correlation of forces among the members of the group. This dynamic correlation, in turn, depends on an accounting of interests that each individual member unconsciously performs within him- or herself. His or her interests as member of this ethnic group are quite as present as other interests resulting from a highly diversified number of other types of personal and collective identifications. The ethnic project gets constructed, altered and refurbished according to the complex evolution of this process.

In the case of the Macanese, the ethnic monopoly is essential for the survival of the community. But its survival depends on the existence of an informal structure of authority. The community constitutes and defines itself by reference to an elite nucleus. In this chapter, evidence has been provided concerning the processes of internal communication that allow for the transformation of individually conceived projects into a more or less coherent ethnic project.

The change in interethnic relations that occurred in Macao during the 1970s created a situation in which it was not possible for the Macanese to maintain public arenas of community. Under the increasingly felt hand of a Chinese majority, these would have been read as exclusivist and would have become dangerous to the survival of the group. So other processes of communication and constitution of intersubjective experience were created that I called *nodules of community*. These explain how the Macanese managed to achieve the necessary coherence for reconstituting their ethnic monopoly in the face of considerable challenges.

The nodules of community were identified as times/spaces that, remaining essentially private, nevertheless allow for the constituting of intersubjectivities and consensus, which then are reflected in the public actions of the Macanese. Two main types were specially explored: one, around families; the other, around the sociability of old school friends. There are also association-type entities that, while not formally having an ethnically exclusive character, wind up in practice functioning primarily as a means of systematizing the ethnic project. But these were not very strong or very numerous.

The aim of this chapter was to show that, while this ethnic community has no formal positions of leadership to which anyone can succeed, the Macanese have managed to produce an elite and have managed to reproduce it in the face of an almost complete redrafting of their ethnic project.

Notes

1. This chapter corresponds to part of an argument presented in *Em Terra de Tufões* (Pina-Cabral and Lourenço 1993; Chinese version, 1995), a project originally undertaken in collaboration with Nelson Lourenço and financed by the Instituto Cultural de Macao.
2. The Portuguese-language original allows for a formulation that does not specify the gender of the subject in this passage. Even although the author is a woman, I have opted for a translation in the male gender, as to feminize the subject would have altered the author's original intentions even further.
3. Cecília Jorge, *O Clarim*, 7/6/91, p. 18.
4. For a study of how this process functioned at the turn of the eighteenth to the nineteenth centuries, when the British attempt to take over Macao was countered by Chinese military resistance, cf. Guimarães 1996.
5. 'The deficit of social citizenship resides in the areas of frustrated socio-juridical demand (namely the domains of housing and personal statute) as well as in the areas of social rights and labour rights, where social demands are supressed or merely emergent' (B. S. Santos 1991:

142.)

6. In *The Politics of Elite Culture*, he provides us with two definitions that are close but interestingly divergent: in the Preface, he defines elite as 'a collectivity of persons who occupy commanding positions in some important sphere of social life, and who share a variety of interests arising from similarities of training, experience, public duties, and way of life' (1981: xvi); whilst, in the Conclusion, the definition appears in altered form - 'a collectivity of people who occupy commanding positions in some sphere of social life, *who do not overtly form a distinct group, cooperating and coordinating their strategies of action informally*' (1981: 233, my emphasis).

7. Cf. Callon and Latour, 1981: 279. I am grateful to João Arriscado Nunes for having called my attention to this concept.

8. With the exception of Hong Kong, of course.

9. The 1991 official census of the city estimated the population as 403,038 persons; all realistic indices point to a considerably higher figure.

10. 'The self-regulation of community is dependent on dense, multiplex bonds' (Calhoun 1980: 115).

11. Thus we may attribute to these *nodules* the functional characteristics that Abner Cohen applies to his 'informal interest groups' (1974: 65ff.): the definition of distinctiveness; the communication of information; decision-making; the legitimation of authority and the production of leadership; the elaboration of ideologies; and the socialization conducive to a symbolically integrated collective action. I am grateful to Monica Chan for the suggestion of this term.

12. Cf. Jorge 1992, where she reports on the cuisine practised in the house of her grandfather - José Vicente Jorge, the locally famous sinologist and collector of Chinese ceramics.

13. Cf. Pina-Cabral 1997 for a discussion of this concept.

14. In *Ponto Final*, 30/7/93, p. 13.

15. Once again the example of the Creole elite of Sierra Leone studied by Abner Cohen is relevant: 'In Sierra Leone it is possible for a non-Creole to dress, worship, behave, eat, etc., like a Creole but he will not partake of the privileges of being a Creole unless he succeeds in grafting himself onto the Creole cousinhood network.' (1974: 124)

16. It should be further noticed that, in the cases where the mother was Chinese but the family adopted a Macanese identity, the connection to the matrilateral side of the family tended to vanish. For a number of reasons that have been identified elsewhere (cf. Pina-Cabral and Lourenço 1993, Ch. III and V), this tendency to cut links with Chinese matrilateral relatives is disappearing among the more recent interethnic marriages.

17. Family names pass along the agnatic line, cf. Pina-Cabral 1994.

11

Uncanny Success: Some Closing Remarks

Michael Herzfeld

What makes an elite? Clearly the question becomes more rather than less complex in the course of reading these chapters, and it may be that the very concept now faces dissolution or at least reorganization. Inasmuch as questions of succession reveal striking similarities as well as differences between groups claiming elite status and those in a politically marginal position, the very notion of elite succession arguably contains the seeds of its own collapse.

In the 1960s, especially, anthropologists were much given to exercises in what we would now call the deconstruction of the key terms of their discipline (cf. for example Needham 1971, on kinship and marriage). At times such exercises seemed to have become an end in themselves, and, as such, risked producing sterile and even destructive work. But where they resulted in a credible realignment of ethnographic data, producing novel insights and provoking further research, they were both productive and useful. Anthropologists should be especially aware of the dangers of allowing the classification of their perceptual world to drift into passive stagnation. If nothing else, the authors who present chapters here have posed some serious critical issues for rethinking a concept that has long enjoyed prominence, not only in social anthropology, but also in sociology, political science, and history. By examining elites ethnographically - by probing their intimate spaces rather than relying on their formal self-presentation - these scholars have offered an ethnographically and sometimes historically rich source of ideas to discommode the received images we currently entertain of what constitutes an elite. Elites often use such images as part of their technology of self-perpetuation, a technology that is most obviously embodied - in a literal sense - in the principles and personnel of succession itself.

Thus a chapter about (for example) Fijian chiefs may fit uncomfortably into a collective analysis of elite succession; but that discomfort then prompts us to ask what are the sources of the historical specificity of 'modern elites'. The industrialists of George Marcus's Galveston both resemble the aristocrats of Nuno Monteiro's seventeenth-century Portugal in their concern with self-perpetuation and yet depart from the latter in their ideological insistence on personal autonomy - a social sentiment that, precisely because it is social, not only turns out to be a great deal less autonomous than its adherents fondly imagine, but also links them to non-elite as well as elite groups in other places and times. As João de Pina-Cabral notes in his opening remarks, what began as a discussion of succession soon revealed the importance of choice; but choice is itself, neoliberal ideologies notwithstanding, not uniquely the product of modern Western rationalism, and the evidence that elites share with the common weal certain peculiarities of political process reveals how fragile their ascendancy may often be. While I thus remain unpersuaded of the uniqueness of modern American individualism, the seepage of such claims into our own intellectual discourse is perhaps the best evidence that a discussion of elite succession has been long overdue, as a valuable corrective to the forms of exceptionalism to which academics themselves are especially prone.

In addressing these chapters, I shall not provide an after-the-fact reader's report. I was present at the conference, greatly enjoyed the give-and-take of the discussions that took place there, and feel that such a procedure now would be both disrespectful to the authors and boring for readers who already, at this final moment in the book, will have formed their own assessments. If as a result I do not seem to give equal weight to all the chapters, this certainly does not mean that they have not all, in various ways, contributed to my understanding of the subject. Instead, I propose to focus on several major areas in which groups of chapters converge to illuminate the nature - conceptual, pragmatic, and temporal - of elite succession, in the hope that the relationships between specific chapters and these necessarily rather generic remarks will emerge clearly for attentive readers of both.

The first of the key topics is the relationships among knowledge, identity and the constitution of power. This is a complex arena in which we see immediately how elites can both depart from and yet also aggressively reproduce practices characteristic of the cultures within which they claim their special status. A common instance of such yoking of disparity with common concerns is the translation of kinship solidarity into other kinds of organizational practice, as in family firms. This may even work to the advantage of an ethnographer using the traditional anthropological approach of emphasizing areas of difference from one's informants: Antónia Pedroso de Lima, for example, found herself especially able to enter the secretive world of business succession because, as a non-member of the key families, she lacked any status that could threaten the interests of any one of these families, and this experience itself richly illuminated her understanding of their *modus operandi.*

In similar vein, the affectations that Jean Lave describes for the self-consciously English port producers of Oporto suggest the persistence, in a modernist rhetoric, of ideas that lie deeply within the emergence of ideas about status and birth in early European cultures, and that become contemptuously exclusionist in its present-day manipulations of wealth. The status of the ethnographer then becomes a sort of litmus test of the reality of that wealth: the genuinely powerful new international business elite condescends, sometimes quite kindly, to admit the ethnographer, whose prying is just so much scratching on the granite rockface of its empires, while those whose only remaining capital is the symbolic capital of past glories are diagnostically defensive.

Kinship and descent thus provide a common basis for elite exclusivity. No anthropologist would find that surprising, although, as Sylvia Yanagisako notes, we should beware of confusing the formal rules of 'structure' with the social organization of affect and sentiment - or, as I prefer to call it (in order to avoid psychologistic implications), intimacy. Such notions may be extended, as in nationalism, to large, supralocal entities; among elites they may reappear in self-rationalizing guise as 'character' (whether national or personal) and even 'race'. More generally, however, the relationship between knowledge and succession throws into relief a key tension of virtually all claims to elite identity: a tension between the notion of knowledge as acquired and that of knowledge as immanent - as residing in categories of person by divine right. And that tension seemed to play through many of the chapters. It perhaps reaches its most recognizably postmodern form in George Marcus's notion of the 'dynastic uncanny'. But there are many variations of it, and some of these are more commonly encountered in non-elite contexts as well: consider, as an especially apposite example, the tension between immanent skill and learned technique that bedevils the transmission of craft knowledge from artisans to their apprentices. For the artisans, claims to a mystique in which crafts cannot really be learned but only reveal themselves through innate ability, very much in the (elite) idiom of the attribution of 'talent' in schools of classical music (Kingsbury 1988), may mask a very deep preoccupation with ensuring some form of succession, albeit one that may as often exclude as include immediate kin. In the same way, knowledge of an arcane business or of court protocol can be used to define membership in an elite, but also to contest it, from within as well as from outside. But we should also duly note that this is not a feature limited to those groups we would ordinarily recognize as elites, except in the sense that artisans may constitute a kind of elite within a class of workers. The mystique affected by port-wine producers resembles that claimed by skilled woodcarvers in at least one important respect: both are invocations of the uncanny, of something as irreducible to description as it is alienable outside whatever is viewed as the acceptable range of successors (who presumably, because they share in this mystique, have no need to describe it).

My second point concerns methodology. How can we study elites? The idea of 'studying up' (that is, studying those who are socially considered our equals or superiors), eloquently advocated by Laura Nader (1972) many years ago and clearly instantiated in much of the work presented here, offers an important counterweight to the elitism of anthropology itself - an elitism that paralleled the racism of a discipline that focused exclusively for so long on exotic 'others'. But it also raises another issue:

whether we are not in danger of falling into a new dualism by making the distinction between studying up and studying down. Who are ordinary folk? Even keeping studying up and studying down in dialectical tension with each other does not resolve that particular problem, since it perpetuates the underlying dualism. How can we study elites without contributing to that tendency? And, conversely, if elites do succeed in acquiring distinction in Bourdieu's (1984b) sense, and if they use it to keep others out (and so perpetuate the sense of their superiority), how do we gain sufficient intimacy to be able to say anything about these people that they would not say for themselves? Was not Pedroso de Lima's inclusion itself a form of exclusion? As a member of the inner circle instead, would she have learned more or less?

Here the crucial methodological caution seems to be the importance of insisting that elites form parts of encompassing cultures. Their failure to engage that entailment would result in a complete loss of meaning for everything that constituted their vaunted superiority. This is the dilemma of the port-wine producers: should they lay claim to a Britishness now shorn at 'home' of its imperial authority, or do they dispose of sufficient distinction within the local context to maintain a separate identity in that arena more effectively? It seems that they have largely opted for the latter strategy: their rhetoric, as grandiloquent as it ever was, may be virtually all that keeps the mirage of power from imploding. Elites are in this sense like bureaucracies: if there are no clients to affirm their superiority, that superiority has no grounds; and that affirmation requires a recognition of common cultural links with the larger context, with the accompanying and ever-present threat of corrosion from such hobnobbing with ordinary people - from 'contamination'. This is the dilemma that - for the moment, at least - the Macanese described by João de Pina-Cabral seem to have negotiated much more successfully: by both moderating their exclusivism and retracting its forms to the private sphere, they have placed themselves in a relatively advantageous position in anticipation of Macao's union with China. Like the British of Oporto, they probably would not do very well 'at home', since their skills - like those of the Parsis of India - were honed on the very hybridity that, created by colonialism, seems to falter in the wake of colonialism's collapse. It remains to be seen whether, like the Parsis, they will prove to have 'lost their gamble with history' (Luhrmann 1996: 22). On Pina-Cabral's showing, at least, they seem to be facing the future buoyantly. They have moved from using Portugueseness as cultural capital to a much more China-directed position - unlike the Parsis, who pursued a path of virtue defined by their identification as the agents of the colonial power. Moreover, their engagement in the allegedly rational business of bureaucracy allows them, at least for the time being, to act as the agents, not of a faded colonial empire, but of the Weberian modernity that China clearly wishes to be thought to possess.

Methodologically, it is important to trace the areas of cultural and symbolic commonality shared by parasitic elites with those of lesser status than themselves, if only to determine how, and with what materials, difference is constructed. Is the rationality of Michel Bauer's informants an identifiable attribute, or is it rather something that gets attributed - not the same thing at all? What kind of performance does it take to secure such an attribution? This is a key question, even harder to address in the historical than in the ethnographic record.

When Portuguese aristocrats used the notion of the 'house' to define a conceptual unity far more durable and far more redolent of social authority than a mere residence, that specificity depended on a more general cultural reading of what made a house; José Manuel Sobral shows us that property was crucial here, even though - for a time - it could also be converted into other kinds of cultural capital. The Portuguese rural bourgeois he describes lost their gamble with history, it seems: they made some bad choices in the conversion process, although a few seem to have done reasonably well. They acquired university degrees and professional identities in a society where such things attract admiration (but also, therefore, envy); but in the process they moved away from the rural base that constituted quite literally the grounds of their authority. And they lost the last shreds of their distinction with the 1974 overthrow of the dictatorship: unlike elite Americans, republicans all, who have found ways of merging their status symbolism to the point where they can even exploit democratization for their own ends (using monarchical-sounding numbers to indicate lines of male succession, for example), these Portuguese squires have had to contend with a situation in which their class identity sets them apart. They have not emerged from the people and 'earned' their marks of distinction; and that, in a democratic system, strips them of significance. (Things could have been worse, as the wealthier peasants of pre-Revolutionary Russia and China could have taught them.)

Claims on property would have availed them little. But what else did they have? It is clear that their performance, in the dual sense of self-presentation and competent management, allowed them to survive quite successfully in a more or less democratic meritocracy; but, in their home contexts, performance seems to have played a greater (and in this case more negative) role in the evaluation of their social practices than perhaps the theorists invoked by Sobral actually help us to understand. How did they comport themselves as their power slipped away? What reactions did they elicit from their once underprivileged neighbours, now possessed of the same voting power as themselves (and more, if we count numbers). The Macanese, by contrast, have clearly paid very close attention indeed to the niceties and contingencies of comportment. And those Macanese who were ill-advised enough to leave their networks and their wealth behind as they disappeared in the smoke and fire of family disputes have virtually vanished from memory. Here again, one wonders whether what they squandered was their reputation for self-control, rather than, in the first place, material property. The problem is that the archival records are incomplete in ways in which sensitive ethnography often is not.

Performance is important because the position of elites is always an ambiguous one, responses to them being potentially fraught with irony. Elites may claim permanence - Helms (1998: 173) identifies this as, in effect, their defining vanity - but the permanence of any social arrangement is contingent by definition and in historical experience. When Britons speak of the 'House of Windsor', they are playing on models of dynastic succession as well as of domesticity, the latter lending an ironic potentiality to the ambiguous place of the royal family - not usually seen as a model of domesticity - in the affections of the people. This kind of uncertainty is often, as several contributors have noted, a feature of the social position of elites generally, and it means that the position of elites may be considerably more dependent on effective performance (again in the double sense) than their attempts at self-perpetuation allow them to admit.

Popular affection is no guarantee of permanence, to be sure, and may be quite fickle. It is also not clear that elite status necessarily depends on prospects of permanence, even in supposedly 'traditional' societies, although Helms seems to suggest that elites are generally composed of those who have been more successful than most at gaining a toehold in eternity or something very like it. Society is not so obliging, however, and, as Carola Lentz points out, successional struggles were sometimes expected to entail conflict - with the seemingly counterintuitive corollary that the British colonialists' attempts to suppress conflict and 'restore' order were in fact an innovation, and not a welcome or necessarily a desirable one. This is one instance in which stabilization did not automatically mean a perpetuation of the status quo ante. On the contrary, it interfered with the local construction of authority because it removed the agonistic basis on which that authority was predicated - a convenient outcome for a colonial power that practised the principle of 'divide and conquer'. In such instances, historical context is clearly vital to understanding current readings of the terms in which elite identity is conceptualized, conferred, and transmitted.

A related methodological issue to that of 'studying up or down' is that old chestnut of whether the insider or the outsider is likely to produce better ethnography. Here, too, one can argue in favour of a dialectical retention of both perspectives; but here, too, such a tactic also partially reproduces the taxonomic rigidity that it is intended to dispel. The distinction itself begs the important question: outsider or insider to what? For example, urban scholars studying rural populations in their own countries may be more disturbingly foreign to their informants than a true foreigner, who lacks their inhibitions about speaking dialect (and is less likely to sound condescending when doing so) and who lacks their association with a familiar idiom of often hostile power. On the other hand, someone who is located within a particular social group may be able to operate at a level of intimacy denied the outsider, not for reasons of cultural similarity, but because that kind of insiderhood entails a freedom of access that might actually be denied a local outsider even more strenuously than it would be a total foreigner (on this point, see especially Panourgiá 1995). Thus, dramatically, Nana Arhin Brempong provides a wonderful demonstration of how somebody who knows this material from within can nonetheless give a dispassionate account that is also an exercise in self-externalization. In using the language of the anthropologist, however, he also provides us with a means of identifying the relationship between chiefly succession and principles active in the larger Akan and indeed Ghanaian context. On the other hand, even as an outsider, João de Pina-Cabral sensed the importance of intimacy as defining the 'cycles of reunions' in which the Macanese elite does its supposedly rational and disinterested administrative business - the real nature of which is precisely what its members have every reason to hide. (Parenthetically, I would speculate that their gambling - in Pina-Cabral's account, a disapproved practice in Portugal but common among Chinese - may provide them with both avenues of intimate access to their new Chinese masters and a social context for defining the boundaries of their own intimate sphere.)

A further point, at once methodological and theoretical, concerns the ethical dimension of our field. How much consideration do elites deserve? Partly in some sense because we are also members of educational elites, we may at some point be less willing to be tolerant, or may perceive that we are right to be less tolerant, of situations in which we feel elites exercise and abuse the exercise of overwriting power. But there is also the issue of the power that they exercise over us and the extent to which we feel constrained to respect their privacy: is this because, more than other groups we study, they now 'read what we write' (Brettell 1993)? Is it because the consequences of offending them are more likely to reach right back into our professional lives? Or is it empathy rather than fear that guides our sense of restraint here, because their forms of intimacy are so much more like our own?

These are not questions to which I would presume to suggest an answer. They are intended, rather, as goads to an examination of what, for want of a better term, we might call the political and moral economy of respect. Elites command respect: when they lose it, they are no longer elites. Our own responses to the constraints they set on our work are thus something of a gauge of the limits of their power as well as of the resources on which they draw in order to maintain it. When we defamiliarize their world - when, for example, we recognize in Texas industrialists' concern with the parallels between the transmission of physical and psychological properties of the person on the one hand and material property in the form of real estate or money on the other the very similar concerns of peasants in southern Europe (compare Marcus 1992: 173-87 with Vernier 1991) - we also potentially threaten that power, so that the extent of their defensiveness in response to our probing presence may actually be an effective measure of the fragility of their grasp of status. That may be a poor compensation to the ethnographer who has been shut out of their lives; but it is nonetheless a useful ethnographic nugget in its own right.

One of the major ways in which elites perpetuate their grasp of the present and future is by monumentalizing the past. (Nationalism is in this sense a mass popularization of elite tactics.) Establishing the age of the 'house' is a means of representing its lien on immortality - again, one step on the road to what Benedict Anderson (1983: 18) has noted as a particular feature of nationalism, the submersion of individual mortalities in a collective, permanent, and ageless resurrection of the body politic. The emergence of deep unilineal clan structures, for example, is often, and in many parts of the world, tied to the consolidation of noble status (cf. for instance Shryock 1997): the reproduction of an underlying sameness in the midst of generational change is the foremost proof of that fundamental claim to perpetuity. As we conducted our deliberations in a hall decorated with portraits of the present Marquis de Fronteira's illustrious ancestors, several of us were struck - apparently to his pleasure - by a recognition of the dynastic uncanny in our midst: the conjuring trick of monumental portraiture overlays the passage of time with the paradox of an unchanging temporality. And only the present Marquis's own generosity and intellectual curiosity made it possible to discuss this cogent illustration of the workings of the uncanny - an invasion of his house to which he was genially responsive, but of which one felt that at least some of the frowning portrait busts must have disapproved. Let us note, however, that resemblance is to some extent culturally constructed: thus, the rules for perceiving dynastic continuity in the phenotypical representation of successive generations are themselves part of a larger cultural context that simultaneously validates and challenges elite pretensions.

The relationship between elites and their surroundings is thus fraught with paradox; and that paradox is perhaps best illustrated by the idea that they are the 'elect'. As George Marcus noted in discussion, etymologically the terms 'elite' and 'election' are related. But elites are not usually elected by popular mandate (although there are exceptions). Christina Toren shows us, in a Hegelian mode she derives from her Fijian informants rather than from her own intellectual training, that equality and hierarchy can be dialectically related to each other. This is especially interesting in that it reveals the tension that lies at the roots of the huge semantic swathe cut by 'election', with its intimations of both popular participation and exclusivity. Her insistence on recognizing her own informants' contribution to her theoretical formulation, moreover, is both instructive and exemplary.

We are indeed beginning to get to the point in anthropology where we are much more comfortable about acknowledging that the people we study are often the sources of our theories about them. We must be prepared to extend that generosity to the discussion of elites, as Toren does here. But we must also remember that, to the extent that we (or our informants) find it useful to acknowledge the existence of a distinction between elites and others, non-elite members have theories about elites. This dimension perhaps deserved greater exploration than it has received in these chapters, because - aside from the issue of intellectual acknowledgment - it would have revealed a great deal more about the ways in which elites maintain their status, or lose it.

But such omissions are revealing in themselves. As academics we are, willy-nilly, participants in an elite culture ourselves. Moreover, our own elite culture is riddled with inequalities inherited from other domains of social life - race, gender, class, and many other factors. Our workshop was, for example, a somewhat heavily one-sided conversation from a gender perspective, in one direction in terms of who participated, but strongly in the reverse direction in terms of the people discussed. Women may dislike their subordinate status, as is clear from the Macanese case, but they have little choice if they are to continue to belong to an elite - a situation that is likely to be reinforced by new patriarchal structures, we may surmise, with the arrival of the new administrative arrangements. The reasons for such imbalances, however, do not only reside in the cultures we study; they also reside in our methodologies. Indeed, Sylvia Yanagisako's paper is an exception to the general rule in an important sense, for, although she primarily talks about male succession, she does so in order to show how under conditions of legal liberalization the 'cherished projects' of women not only mount a credible challenge to those of men but also offer a potentially more effective means of achieving family solidarity under the new conditions of life.

Conversely, however, the overall gender imbalance in the human population of these chapters should prompt questions about how the exclusion of women from some areas of power in some societies, or men's control of women as symbolic resources in others, provides models of political organization that actually become exaggerated when a particular group attains great authority. Equally, where this does not appear to happen, we might use this circumstance to open up questions about professions of equality as a symbolic resource - as evidence of 'rationality' and 'development', not unlike the preservation of non-Western monuments by Western town planners as evidence of their liberal superiority over the despotic, oriental creators of those monuments. It is clear from Sylvia Yanagisako's account, for example, that some deployments of *la liberazione delle donne* can provide manipulative men with a rhetoric for asserting their own authority on the grounds of an assumed modernity. That, in turn, should lead us to re-examine persistent disparities between our own rhetoric and the actual direction of our conceptual energies. Why do these otherwise fine chapters appear so slanted in terms of gender and other 'internal' hierarchies? Jean Lave offered excellent advice: to imagine everyone in the ethnographic frame as equally important. That we have failed to do so is disturbing, but it can now be turned to good account: it should move us to ask what such exclusions tell us about the ways in which elite exclusivity parades its internal hierarchies as models-of, and also as models-for (Geertz 1973: 93-4), hegemony in general?

Ultimately, however, we can only do this if we return to the peculiar insistence on intimacy that is the hallmark of good ethnography - on exploring those private spaces in which, for example, our informants recognize explicitly that the marginalization of women from positions of authority, or the dismissal of the observations of children, actually happens. What we seek is not so much the basis of the dynastic uncanny as some understanding of what it is used to support: the uncanny success, as it were, of elites in perpetuating themselves. (That is, to be sure, something of a truism: as the more historical chapters presented here demonstrate, it is the capacity for self-perpetuation that, over time, creates a sense of elite identity, and thus creates elites themselves.) When we succeed in achieving the necessary level of intimacy, our own practices become a subversion of elite exceptionalism, opening it up to the realization of its human - indeed, its common - properties. It is not only in remote places that we can appreciate how the very act of ethnographic observation necessarily contaminates the imagined (and sometimes carefully constructed) purity of the observed. If it is 'contamination' that elites fear, they have a great deal to fear from anthropological examination. But if we fail to study them and to recognize that their means of self-perpetuation are not, after all, so very far removed from those we encounter in the more traditional stamping grounds of our profession, we shall merely perpetuate the exoticism that, in our predecessors' work, we have already dismissed as a betrayal of our common humanity.

Bibliography

Abercrombie, Nicholas, Hill, Stephen and Turner, Bryan S. (1994), 'Power', in *The Penguin Dictionary of Sociology*, London: Penguin Books.

Abu-Lughod, Lila and Lutz, Catherine (1990), 'Introduction: Emotion, Discourse and the Politics of Everyday Life' in L. Abu-Lughod and C. Lutz (eds), *Language and The Politics of Emotion*, Cambridge: Cambridge University Press.

Almeida, Miguel Vale de (1991), 'Leituras de um Livro de Leitura', in Brian O'Neill and Joaquim Pais de Brito (eds), *Lugares de Aqui*, Lisbon: D. Quixote.

Anderson, Benedict R. O'G. (1983), *Imagined Communities: Reflections on the Origin and Spread of Nationalism*, London: Verso.

Anthias, Floya (1990), 'Race and Class Revisited: Conceptualising Race and Racisms', *Sociological Review*, Vol. 38 (1):19-42.

Arhin, Kwame (1985), *Traditional Rule in Ghana: Past and Present*, Accra: Sedco Ltd.

—(1986), 'The Asante Akonkofo: A Non-Elite', *Africa*, 56: 25-31.

—(1991), 'The Search for Constitutional Chieftaincy', in Kwame Arhin (ed.), *The Life and Work of Kwame Nkrumah, 1909-1972*, Accra: Sedco Ltd.

—(1992), *The City of Kumasi Handbook: Past, Present and Future*, England: Cambridge Faxbooks.

—(1994), 'Sanctions Against Abuse of Authority in Precolonial Africa', in D. Brokensha (ed.), *A River of Blessings: Essays in Honour of Paul Baxter*, Syracuse, NY: Syracuse University.

Atouguia, Condessa de (1916), A *Última Condessa de Atouguia. Memórias Autobiográficas*, Lisbon: Pontevedra.

Augustins, Georges (1982), 'Esquisse d'une Comparaison des Systèmes de Perpétuation des Groupes Domestiques dans les Sociétés Paysannes Européennes', *Archives Européennes de Sociologie*, Vol. XXIII (2): 39-69.

Barth, Fredrik (1966), *Models of Social Organization*, London: Royal Anthropological Institute.

Bloom, Harold (1973), *The Anxiety of Influence: A Theory of Poetry*, New York: Oxford University Press.

Bluteau, Rafael (1712-1729), *Vocabulario Portuguez e Latino*, 1712-29, Coimbra-Lisbon, 10 vols.

Boone, James (1986), 'Parental Investment and Elite Family in Preindustrial States: A Case Study of Late Medieval-Early Modern Portuguese Genealogies', *American Anthropologist*, 88: 898-907.

Bosman, W. (1705), *Description of the Coasts of Guinea*, London.

Bottomore, T. B. (1964), *Elites and Society*, London: C. A. Walts and Co. Ltd.

—(1965), *As Elites e a Sociedade*, Rio de Janeiro: Zahar Editores.

Bouquet, Mary (1993), *Reclaiming English Kinship. Portuguese Refractions of British Kinship Theory*, Manchester: Manchester University Press

Bourdieu, Pierre (1961), 'Célibate et Condition Paysanne', *Études Rurales*, 5-6: 31-135.

—(1977), *Outline of a Theory of Practice*, trans. Richard Nice, London: Cambridge University Press.

—(1979), *La Distinction*, Paris: Les Éditions de Minuit.

—(1980), 'Les Stratégies Matrimoniales dans Le Systéme de Reproduction', in Pierre Bourdieu (ed.), *Le Sense Pratique*, Paris: Les Éditions de Minuit.

—(1984a), 'Espace Social et Genèse des Classes', *Actes de la Recherche en Sciences Sociales*, 52-53.

—(1984b), *Distinction: A Social Critique of the Judgement of Taste*, Cambridge, MA: Harvard University Press.

—(1994), 'L'Esprit de Famille', in *Raisons Pratiques*, Paris: Éditions du Seuil.

— and Wacquant, Loïc D. J. (1992), *Réponses*, Paris: Éditions du Seuil.

Bowdich, T. E. (1873), *Mission from Cape Coast to Ashantee*, London: Griffith & Farran.

Braga da Cruz, Manuel (1992), 'O Estado Novo e a Igreja Católica', in Fernando Rosas (ed.), *Portugal e o Estado Novo (1930-1960)*, Lisbon: Presença.

Branfman, Joan (1987), 'The Experience of Inherited Wealth: A Social Psychological Study', Ph.D. dissertation, Department of Sociology, Brandeis University.

Brettell, Caroline (ed.) (1995), *When They Read What We Write: The Politics of Ethnography*, Westport, CT: Bergin & Garvey.

Busia, K. A. (1951), *The Position of the Chief in the Modern Political System of Ashanti*, London: Oxford University Press.

Calhoun, Craig J. (1980) 'Community: Toward a Variable Conceptualization for Comparative Research', *Social History*, Vol.5 (1):105-29.

Callon, Michel and Latour, Bruno (1981), 'Unscrewing the Big Leviathan: How Actors Macrostructure Reality and How Sociologists Help Them To Do So', in Karin Knorr-Cetina and Aaron V. Cicourel (eds), *Advances in Social Theory and Methodology - Toward an Integration of Micro and Macro-sociologies*, London: Routledge and Kegan Paul.

Capell, A. (1973 [1941]), *A New Fijian Dictionary*, Suva: Government Printer.

Clavero, Bartolomé (1989a), *Mayorazgo. Propriedad Feudal en Castilla 1369-1836*, 2nd edn, Madrid: Siglo XXI Ed.

—(1989b), 'Del Estado Presente a la Familia Pasada', *Quaderni Fiorentini per la Storia del Pensiero Giuridico Moderno*, 18.

Cohen, Abner (1974), *Two-Dimensional Man: An Essay on The Anthropology of Power and Symbolism in Complex Society*, Berkeley, CA: University of California Press.

—(1981), *The Politics of Culture: Explorations in The Dramaturgy of Power in a Modern African Society*, Berkeley, CA: University of California Press.

Coombe, Rosemary J. (1998), 'Contingent Articulations: A Critical Cultural Studies' in Austin Sarat and Thomas R. Kearns (eds), *Law in The Domains of Culture*, Ann Arbor, MI: University of Michigan Press.

Cooper, J. P. (1976), 'Patterns of Inheritance and Settlement by Great Landowners from the Fifteenth to Eighteenth Centuries', in Jack Goody et al. (eds), *Family and Inheritance. Rural Society in Western Europe*, Cambridge: Cambridge University Press.

Crapanzano, Vincent (1980), *Tuhami: Portrait of a Moroccan*. Chicago: University of Chicago Press.

Cunha, Mafalda Soares da (1990), *Linhagem Parentesco e Poder. A Casa de Bragança (1384-1483)*, Lisbon: F. C. Bragança.

Dakubu, M. E. Kropp (1988), *The Languages of Ghana*, London: Kegan Paul International for the International African Institute.

Davis, John (1973), *Land and Family in Pisticci*, New York: Humanities Press.

Delaforce, John (1982), *Anglicans Abroad, the History of the Chaplaincy and Church of St. James Oporto*, London: SPCK.

—(1989), *The Factory House at Oporto: Its Historic Role in the Port Wine Trade*, Bicentenary edition, London: Christopher Helm Publishers Ltd in association with Christie's Wine Publications.

Der, Benedict (unpublished manuscript), 'The "Stateless Peoples" of North-west Ghana: A Reappraisal of the Case of the Dagara of Nandom', Department of History, University of Cape Coast.

Dicks, Anthony R. (1984), 'Macao: Legal Fiction and Gunboat Diplomacy', in Göran Aijmer (ed.), *Leadership on the China Coast*, Scandinavian Institute of Asian Studies, Studies on Asian Topics, 8, London: Curzon Press.

Dikötter, Frank (1992), *The Discourse of Race in Modern China*, Stanford, CA: Stanford University Press.

Duguid, Paul and Lopes, Teresa Silva (forthcoming), 'Ambiguous Company: Institutions and Organizations in the Port Wine Trade, 1814-1834', in Mary Rose and Sverre Knutson (eds), *Scandinavian Journal of Economic History*, 1999(1) Special issue on Institutional Theory and Business History.

Faria, Manuel Severim de (1740 [1655]), *Noticias de Portugal*, Lisbon.

Ferguson, Phyllis and Wilks, Ivor (1970), 'Chiefs, Constitutions and British in Northern Ghana', in Michael Crowder and Obaro Ikime (eds), *West African Chiefs: Their Changing Status Under Colonial Rule and Independence*, pp. 326-69, Iie-Ife: University of Ife Press.

Firth, Raymond (1960 [1957]), *Man and Culture*, London: Trowbridge and Esher.

Flandrin, Jean-Louis (1976), *Familles: Parenté, Maison, Sexualité dans L'Ancienne Société*, Paris: Éditions du Seuil.

Fortes, Meyer (1938), *Oedipus and Job*. London: Oxford University Press.

—(1940), 'The Tallensi', in M. Fortes and E. E. Evans-Pritchard (eds), *African Political Systems*, Oxford: Oxford University Press.

—(1950), 'Kingship and Marriage Among the Ashanti', in A. R. Radcliffe-Brown and A. Forde (eds), *African Systems of Kinship and Marriage*, London: International African Institute.

—(1957), 'Malinowski and The Study of Kinship', in Raymond Firth (ed.), *Man and Culture: An Evaluation of The Work of Bronislaw Malinowski*, London: Routledge and Kegan Paul.

—(1958), 'Introduction', in Jack Goody (ed.), *The Developmental Cycle in Domestic Groups*, Cambridge: Cambridge University Press.

—(1970), *Kinship and the Social Order: The Legacy of Lewis Henry Morgan*, Chicago: Aldine.

Foucault, Michel (1972), *The Archeology of Knowledge*, London: Tavistock.

—(1978), *The History of Sexuality*, trans. Robert Hurley, New York: Pantheon Books.

Foulkes, Christopher (ed.) (1992), *A Celebration of Taylor Fladgate Port: Published to Mark the 300th Anniversary of the Foundation of the House*, London: Published by the author.

Freire, Anselmo Braancamp (1973), *Brasões da Sala de Sintra*, 2° edition, Lisbon: Imprensa Nacional.

Fuller, F. (1920), *A Vanished Dynasty: Ashanti*, London: John Murray.

Garfinkel, Harold (1967), *Studies in Ethnomethodology*, Englewood Cliffs, NJ: Prentice-Hall.

Geertz, Clifford (1973), *The Interpretation of Cultures: Selected Essays*, New York: Basic Books.

Gersick, Kelin, Davis, John, Hampton, Marion and Lansberg, Ivan (eds) (1997), *Generation to Generation. Life Cycles of the Family Business*, Boston: Harvard Business School Press.

Giddens, Anthony (1979), *Central Problems in Social Theory*, London and Basingstoke: The Macmillan Press.

—(1985), *The Nation-state and Violence*, Vol.II of *A Contemporary Critique of Historical Materialism*, Cambridge: Polity Press.

Goody, Esther N. (1982), *From Craft to Industry: The Ethnography of Proto-Industrial Cloth Production*, Cambridge and New York: Cambridge University Press.

Goody, Jack (1956), *The Social Organisation of the Lowiili*, London: HMSO.

—(1962), *Death, Property and the Ancestors: A Study of The Mortuary Customs of the LoDagaa of West Africa*, Stanford, CA: Stanford University Press.

—(1966), *Succession to High Office*, Cambridge: Cambridge University Press

—(1976), *Production and Reproduction: A Comparative Study of the Domestic Domain*, Cambridge: Cambridge University Press.

—(1983), *The Development of the Family and Marriage in Europe*, Cambridge: Cambridge University Press.

Gubrium, Jaber F. (1990), 'Describing Home Care: Discourse and Image in Involuntary Commitment Proceedings', in Jaber Gubrium and Andrea Sankar (eds), *The Home Care Experience - Ethnography and Policy*, Newbury Park, CA: Sage.

Guimarães, Ângela (1996), *Uma Relação Especial: Macau e as Relações*

Luso-Chinesas (1780-1844), Lisbon: Edição CIES.

Hall, Peter D. (1982), *The Organization of American Culture, 1700-1900: Private Institutions, Elites and Origins Of American Nationality*. New York: New York University Press.

—and Marcus, George E. (1997),' "Why Should Men Leave Great Fortunes to Their Children?" Class, Dynasty and Inheritance in America', in Robert K., Miller Jr. and Stephen J. McNamee (eds), *Inheritance and Wealth in America*, New York: Plenum.

Hamabata, Matthews Masayuki (1990) *Crested Kimono: Power and Love in the Japanese Business Family*, Ithaca, NY and London: Cornell University Press.

Hann, C. M. (1998), 'Introduction: The Embeddedness of Property', in C. M. Hann (ed.), *Property Relations: Renewing the Anthropological Tradition*, Cambridge: Cambridge University Press.

Harvey, David (1989), *The Condition of Postmodernity*, Cambridge, MA: Basil Blackwell.

Helms, Mary W. (1998), *Access to Origins: Affines, Ancestors, and Aristocrats*, Austin, TX: University of Texas Press.

Hocart, A. M. (1913), 'On the Meaning of the Fijian Word *Turanga*', *Man*, 13: 140-3.

—(1952), *The Northern States of Fiji*, Occasional Publication, 11, London: The Royal Anthropological Institute.

—1970 (1936), *Kings and Councillors*, Chicago and London: University of Chicago Press.

—(Unpublished manuscript), *The Heart of Fiji*, Canberra: Australian National University Library, microfilm.

Hooper, Steven (1982), *A Study of Valuables in the Chiefdom of Lau*, Fiji, Ph.D. Thesis, Cambridge: University of Cambridge.

Horn, David (1994), *Social Bodies: Science, Reproduction and Italian Modernity*, Princeton, NJ: Princeton University Press.

Hsu, Francis L. K. (1981 [1953]), *Americans and Chinese: Passage to Differences*, Honolulu: University Press of Hawaii.

Jorge, Graça Pacheco (1992), *A Cozinha de Macau de Casa do Meu Avô*, Macao: Instituto Cultural de Macau.

Kaplan, Martha (1987), 'The Coups in Fiji: Colonial Contradictions and the Post-Colonial Crisis', *Critique of Anthropology*, 8: 93-116.

Kelly, John D. (1988), 'Fiji Indians and Political Discourse in Fiji: From the Pacific Romance to the Coups', *Journal of Historical Sociology*, 1: 399-422.

Kingsbury, Henry (1988), *Music, Talent, and Performance: A Conservatory Cultural System*, Philadelphia: Temple University Press.

Kondo, Dorinne (1990), *Crafting Selves: Power, Gender and Discourses of Identity in a Japanese Workplace*, Chicago: University of Chicago Press.

Kuper, Adam (1990), 'Psychology and Anthropology: The British Experience', *History of the Human Sciences* 3 (3): 397-413.

Ladouceur, Paul A. (1979), *Chiefs and Politicians:The Politics of Regionalism in Northern Ghana*, London: Longman.

Lal, Brij V. (1992), *Broken Waves: A History of the Fiji Islands in the Twentieth Century*, Honolulu: University of Hawaii Press.

Lamb, Christina (1997), 'Grape Britain', *London Times Sunday Magazine*, 3 August, pp. 42A-46.

Lasch, Christopher (1979), *The Culture of Narcissism: American Life in an Age of Diminishing Expectation*, New York: Norton.

Lash, Scott and Urry, John (1984), *The End of Organized Capitalism*, Madison, WI: University of Wisconsin Press.

Laslett, Peter and Wall, Richard (eds) (1978 [1972]), *Household and Family in Past Time*, Cambridge: Cambridge University Press.

Latour, Bruno and Woolgar, Steven (1979), *Laboratory Life: The Construction of Scientific Facts*, Beverly Hills, CA: Sage Publication.

Lave, Jean (1999), 'Getting to be British', in Dorothy Holland and Jean Lave (eds), *History in Person: Enduring Struggles and Practices of Identity*, Santa Fe: SAR Press.

Lears, T. J. Jackson (1982), *No Place of Grace*, New York: Pantheon.

Lefebvre, Henri (1974), *La Production de L'Espace*, Paris: Éditions Anthropos.

Lentz, Carola (1993), 'Histories and Political Conflict: A Case Study of Chieftaincy in Nandom, Northwestern Ghana', *Paideuma*, 39: 177-215.

—(1998a), *Die Konstruktion von Ethnizität: Eine Politische Geschichte Nord-West Ghanas*, 1870-1990, Studien zur Kulturkunde 112, Cologne: Köppe Verlag.

—(1998b), 'The Chief, the Mine Captain and the Politician: Legitimating Power in Northern Ghana', *Africa*, 68: 46-67.

—(1998c), 'Staatenlose Gesellschaften oder Häuptlingstümer? Eine Debatte unter Dagara Intellektuellen', in Heike Behrend and Thomas Geider (eds), *Indigene Ethnographien*, Cologne: Köppe Verlag.

Lessard, Suzannah (1996), *The Architect of Desire: Beauty and Danger in Stanford White Family*, New York: The Dial Press.

Lessico Universale (1979), *Successione*, Roma: Instituto della Enciclopedia Italiana, Vol.XXVIII.: 198-9.

Lévi-Strauss, Claude (1963a), *Totemism*, Boston: Beacon Press.

—(1963b), 'The Effectiveness of Symbols,' in C. Lévi-Strauss, *Structural Anthropology*, New York: Basic Books.

—(1977 [1958]), 'Structural Analysis in Linguistics and Anthropology', *Structural Anthropology*, New York and London: Penguin Books.

—(1978 [1973]), 'Reflections on the Atom of Kinship', *Structural Anthropology 2*, New York and London: Penguin Books.

—(1984), 'La Notion de Maison', in *Paroles Données*, Paris: Plon. Lisón-Tolosana, Carmelo (1983 [1966]), *Belmonte de los Caballeros. Anthropology and History in an Aragonese Community*, Princeton, NJ: Princeton University Press.

Lobo, A. de Sousa Silva Costa (1903), *Historia da Sociedade em Portugal no Seculo XV*, Lisbon.

Loewenthal, David (1993 [1985]), *The Past is a Foreign Country*, Cambridge:

Cambridge University Press.

—(1998), *The Heritage Crusade and the Spoils of History*, Cambridge: Cambridge University Press.

Luhrmann, T. M. (1996), *The Good Parsi: The Fate of a Colonial Elite in a Postcolonial Society*, Cambridge, MA: Harvard University Press.

Lukes, Steve (1978), 'Power and Authority', in Tom Bottomore and Robert Nisbet (eds), *A History of Sociological Analysis*, London: Heinemann.

Maine, Sir Henry (1861), *Ancient Law*, London: Murray. Mara, Ratu Sir Kamisese (1997), *The Pacific Way. A Memoir.* Honolulu: University of Hawaii Press.

Marceau, Jane (1989), *A Family Business? The Making of an International Business Elite*, Cambridge: Cambridge University Press; Paris: Maison des Sciences de l'Homme.

Marcus, George E. (1989), 'Chieftainship', in Alan Howard and Robert Borofsky (eds), *Developments in Polynesian Ethnology*, Honolulu: University of Hawaii Press.

—(1990), 'The Production of European High Culture in Los Angeles: The J. Paul Getty Trust as Artificial Curiosity', *Cultural Anthropology*, 5(3): 314-30.

—(1992), 'Dynastic Endgame: Sallie Bingham and The Fall of The House of Bingham,' in Peter D. Hall and George E. Marcus (eds), *Lives in Trust: The Fortunes of Dynastic Families in Late Twentieth Century America*, Boulder, CO: Westview Press.

—(1993), *Elites: Ethnographic Issues*, Albuquerque, NM: University of New Mexico Press.

—(1995), 'On Eccentricity', in Debbora Battaglia (ed.), *Rhetorics of the Self*, Berkeley, CA: University of California Press.

— and Hall, Peter D. (1992), *Lives in Trust: The Fortunes of Dynastic Families in Late Twentieth Century America*, Boulder, CO: Westview Press.

Marx, Karl and Engels, Frederick (1976), *The German Ideology*, Moscow: Progress Publishers.

McCaskie, T.C. (1980), 'Office, Land and Subjects in the History of the Manwere Fekuo of Kumase: An Essay in the Political Economy of the Asante State', *Journal of African History*, 21 (2): 189-208.

—(1995), *State and Society in Pre-Colonial Asante*, Cambridge: Cambridge University Press.

McDonogh, Gary (1982), *The Good Families of Barcelona*, Princeton, NJ: Princeton University Press.

—(1988 [1986]), *Las Buenas Familias de Barcelona. História Social de Poder en la Era Industrial*, Barcelona: Editiones Omega.

Melcafe, G. E. (1964), *Great Britain and Ghana: Documents of Ghana History*, London: University of Ghana by Thomas Nelson and Sons Ltd.

Mengoni, Luigi (1961), *Sucessioni per Causa di Morte*, Milan: Guiffre Editori.

Mills, Wright (1956), *The Power Elite*, New York: Oxford University Press.

Milner, George (1997), 'An Elder Statesman', Review of Ratu Mara's *The*

Bibliography

Pacific Way, *Times Literary Supplement*, September 12: 30.

Monteiro, Nuno Gonçalo (1993a), 'Casa e Linhagem: O Vocabulário Aristocrático em Portugal nos Séculos XVII e XVIII', *Penélope. Fazer e Desfazer a História*, 12: 43-63.

—(1993b), 'Casamento, Celibato e Reprodução Social: A Aristocracia Portuguesa nos Séculos XVII e XVIII', *Análise Social*, 123-124: 921-50.

—(1995), *A Casa e o Património dos Grandes Portugueses* (1750-1832), Institute of Social Sciences, Lisbon: Universidade de Lisboa.

—(1998), *O Crepúsculo dos Grandes. A casa e o Património da Aristocracia em Portugal* (1750-1832), Lisbon: Universidade de Lisboa. Nadel, S. F. (1990), 'The Concept of Social Elites', in John Scott (ed.), *The Sociology of Elites, Vol. I, The Studies of Elites*, Brookfield, VT: E. Elgar Publisher.

Nader, Laura (1972), 'Up the Anthropologist - Perspectives Gained from Studying Up', in Dell Hymes (ed.), *Reinventing Anthropology*, pp. 285-311, New York: Pantheon Books.

Needham, Rodney (ed.) (1971), *Rethinking Kinship and Marriage*, London: Tavistock.

Norton, Robert (1990), *Race and Politics in Fiji*, Brisbane University of Queensland Press.

Olival, Fernanda (1986-1991), 'O Dispositivo Linhagístico e a Atribuição das Comendas de Avis (1551-1670): Perspectivas de Análise', *Primeiras Jornadas de História Moderna*, Lisbon.

Ong, Aihwa (1991), 'The Gender and Labor Politics of Postmodernity', *Annual Review of Anthropology*, Vol. XX: 278-309.

Panourgiá, E. Neni K. (1995), *Fragments of Death, Fables of Identity: An Athenian Anthropography*, Madison, WI: University of Wisconsin Press.

Pereira, Francisco Gonçalves (1995), *Portugal, a China e a 'Questão de Macau'*, Macao: Instituto Português do Oriente.

Pina-Cabral, João de (1991), *Os Contextos da Antropologia*. Lisbon: Difel.

—(1994), 'Personal Identity and Ethnic Ambiguity: Naming Practices among the Eurasians of Macao', *Social Anthropologist 2* (2): 115-32.

—(1997), 'Houses and Legends: Family as Community of Practice in Urban Portugal', in Marianne Gullestad and Martine Segalen (eds), *Family and Kinship in Europe*. London: Pinter.

—(1998a), 'A Composição Social de Macau', in F. Bettencourt and K. Chaudhuri (eds), *História da Expansão Portuguesa*, Vol. 5, Lisbon: Círculo de Leitores.

—(1998b), 'The Threshold Diffused: Margins, Hegemonies and Contradictions in Contemporary Anthropology', in Patrick MacAllister (ed.), *Culture and the Commonplace: Essays in Honour of W. D. Hammond Tooke*, Johannesburg: University of the Witwatersrand Press.

—and Chan, Mónica (1997), 'O Parasita do Mandarim: A Lotaria dos Exames Imperiais (*vaeseng*) em Macau e Cantão', *Oceanos. Olhares Cruzados*, *32*: 151-63.

—and Lourenço, Nelson (1993), *Em Terra de Tufões: Dinâmicas da tnicidade Macaense*, Macao: Instituto Cultural de Macau (Chinese version, 1995).

Piore, Michael and Sabel, Charles F. (1984), *The Second Industrial Divide*, New York: Basic Books.

Radcliffe-Brown, A. R. (1950), 'Introduction', in A. R. Radcliffe-Brown and D. Forde (eds), *African Systems of Kinship and Marriage*, London: Oxford University Press.

—(1952), *Structure and Function in Primitive Society*, New York: The Free Press.

Rattray, R. S. (1927), *Religion and Art in Ashanti*, London: Oxford University Press.

—(1929a), *Ashanti Law and Constitution*, London: Oxford University Press.

—(1929b), *Tribes of the Ashanti Hinterland*, Vol. 2, London: Oxford University Press.

Reiter, Rayna (1975), *Toward an Anthropology of Women*, New York: Monthly Review Press.

Ricouer, Paul (1970), *Freud and Philosophy*, New Haven, CT: Yale University Press.

Rieff, Philip (1969), *The Triumph of the Therapeutic*, Boston: Beacon Press.

Robertson, A. F. (1973), 'Histories and Political Opposition in Ahafo, Ghana', *Africa*, 43: 41-58.

Rosa, Maria de Lurdes (1995), *O Morgadio em Portugal nos Séculos XIV e XV: Modelos e Práticas de Comportamento Linguístico*, Lisbon: Estampa.

Rosaldo, Michelle Z. (1984), 'Toward an Anthropology of the Self and Feeling', in R. Schweider and R. LeVine (eds), *Culture Theory*, Cambridge: Cambridge University Press.

Rosas, Fernando (1992), 'As Grandes Linhas da Evolução Institucional', in Fernando Rosas (ed.), *Portugal e o Estado Novo (1930-1960)*, Lisbon: Editorial Presença: 86-143.

—and José Maria Brandão de Brito (1996), *Dicionário de História do Estado Novo*, Vol. I and II, Lisbon: Bertrand Editores.

Sahlins, Marshall (1985), *Islands of History*, London and New York: Tavistock Publications.

—(1991),'The Return of the Event, Again; With Reflections on the Beginnings of the Great Fijian War of 1843 to 1855 Between the Kingdoms of Bau and Rewa', in Aletta Biersack (ed.), *Clio in Oceania. Towards a Historical Anthropology*, Washington and London: Smithsonian Institution Press.

Saint-Martin, Monique de (1993), *L'Espace de La Noblesse*, Paris: Métaillé.

Salaff, J. (1981), *Working Daughters of Hong Kong*, Cambridge: Cambridge University Press.

Sampaio, António Vilas Boas (1725 [1676]), *Nobiliarchia Portuguesa. Tratado da Nobreza Hereditaria e Politica*, Lisbon.

Santos, Boaventura Sousa (1991), 'A Justiça e a Comunidade em Macau', *Revista da Cultura*, 15, Macao.

Sarbah, J. M. (1897), *Fanti Customary Laws*, London: W. Clowes and Sons.

—(1906), *Fanti National Constitution*, London: W. Clowes and Sons.

Sayes, Shelley Ann (1984), 'Changing Paths of the Land: Early Political

Hierarchies in Cakaudrove, Fiji', *Journal of Pacific History*, XIX: 3-20.

Schneider, David M. (1965), 'Some Muddles in the Models', in *The Relevance of Models for Social Anthropology*, London: A.S.A. Monographs.

Scott, Ian (1989), *Political Change and the Crisis of Legitimacy in Hong Kong*, Hong Kong: Oxford University Press.

Shils, Edward (1981), *Tradition*, London: Faber and Faber.

Shostak, Marjorie (1981), *Nisa: The Life and Words of a !Kung Woman*, New York: Norton.

Shryock, Andrew (1997), *Nationalism and the Genealogical Imagination: Oral History and Textual Authority in Tribal Jordan*, Berkeley, CA: University of California Press.

Silbert, Albert (1968), *Le Problème Agraire Portugais à L'Époque des Premières Cortès Libérales*, Paris: PUF.

Simmel, George (1986 [1908]), 'El Espacio y la Sociedad', *Sociología: Estudios Sobre las Formas de Socialización*, Vol. 2, Madrid: Alianza Editorial.

Sobral, Jose Manuel (1999), *Trajectos: o Presente e o Passado na Vida de uma Freguesia da Beira*, Lisboa

Sousa, Manuel de Almeida e (1814), *Tratado Prático de Morgados*, 2nd edn, Lisboa: ICS

Staniland, Martin (1973), 'The Manipulation of Oral Tradition: Politics in Northern Ghana', *Journal of Development Studies*, 9(3): 373-90.

Strathern, Marilyn (1980), 'No Nature, No Culture: The Hagen Case', in C. McCormack and M. Strathern (eds), *Nature, Culture and Gender*, Cambridge: Cambridge University Press.

—(1988), *The Gender of the Gift: Problems With Women and Problems With Society in Melanesia*, Berkeley, CA: University of California Press.

—(1992), *Reproducing the Future: Essays on Anthropology, Kinship and New Reproductive Technologies*, New York: Routledge.

Tordoff, William (1965), 'Economic and Social Change', *Ashanti Under the Prempehs, 1888-1935*, London: Oxford University Press.

Toren, Christina (1989), 'Drinking Cash: The Purification of Money Through Ceremonial Exchange in Fiji', in J. Parry and M. Bloch (eds), *Money and The Morality of Exchange*, Cambridge: Cambridge University Press.

—(1990), *Making Sense of Hierarchy. Cognition as Social Process in Fiji*, School of Economics, Monographs in Social Anthropology, London: Athlone Press.

—(1994a), 'Transforming Love: Representing Fijian Hierarchy', in Penny Harvey and Peter Gow (eds), *Sex and Violence: Issues in Representation and Experience*, London: Routledge.

—(1994b),'All Things Go in Pairs or the Sharks Will Bite: The Antithetical Nature of Fijian Chiefship', *Oceania*, 64: 197-216.

—(1995), 'Cosmogonic Aspects of Desire and Compassion in Fiji', in D. Coppet and A. Iteanu (eds), *Cosmos and Society in Oceania.* Oxford: Berg.

—(1998), 'Cannibalism and Compassion: Transformations in Fijian Concepts of the Person', in Verena Keck (ed.), *Common Worlds and*

Single Lives, Oxford: Berg.

—(1999), *Mind, Materiality and History: Explorations in Fijian Ethnography*, London: Routledge

Turner, James West (1986), 'The Sins of the Father: Rank and Succession in a Fijian Chiefdom', *Oceania*, 57: 128-94.

Vernier, Bernard (1991), 'La Genèse Sociale des Sentiments: Aînés et Cadets dans l'île Grecque de Karpathos, *Recherches d'Histoire et de Sciences Sociales, 50*, Paris: Editions de l'Ecole des Hautes Etudes en Sciences Sociales.

Visceglia, Maria Antonietta (1988), *Il Bisogno di Eternitá. I Comportamenti Aristocratici a Napoli in Età Moderna*, Naples: Guida Editori.

Walter, Michael A. H. B. (1978), 'An Examination of Hierarchical Notions in Fijian Society: A Test Case For The Applicability of The Term "Chief"', *Oceania*, 49: 1-19.

Weber, Max (1922), 'Class, Status, Party', in H. H. Gerth and C. Wright Mills (eds), *From Max Weber: Essays in Sociology*, London: Routledge.

—(1947), *The Theory of Social and Economic Organization*, ed. Talcott Parsons , trans. A. M. Henderson and Talcott Parsons, New York: Free Press.

West, Bob (1985), *Danger! History at Work: A Critical Consumer's Guide to the Ironbridge Gorge Museum*, Stencilled Occasional paper no. 83, Birmingham: Centre for Contemporary Cultural Studies, University of Birmingham.

Wilks, Ivor (1975), *Asante in the Nineteenth Century: The Structure and Evolution of a Political Order*, Cambridge: Cambridge University Press.

—(1979), 'The Golden Stool and the Elephant Tail: An Essay on Wealth in Asante', *Research in Economic Anthropology*, Vol. 2: 10-11.

—(1989), *Wa and the Wala. Islam and Polity in Northwestern Ghana.* Cambridge: Cambridge University Press.

—(1993), 'Founding the Political "Kingdom". The Nature of the Akan State', in Ivor Wilks (ed.), *Forest of Gold: Essays on the Akan and the Kingdom of Asante*, Ohio: Ohio University Press.

Wright Mills, C. (1956), *The Power Elite*, New York: Oxford University Press.

Yanagisako, Sylvia (1979), 'Family and Household: The Analysis of Domestic Groups', *Annual Review of Anthropology*, 8: 161-206.

—(1991), 'Capital and Gendered Interest in Italian Family Firms', in David Kertzer and Richard Saller (eds), *The Family in Italy. From Antiquity to the Present*, New Haven/London: Yale University Press.

—and Collier, Jane (1987), 'Toward a Unified Analysis of Gender and Kinship', in J. Collier and S. Yanagisako (eds), *Gender and Kinship: Essays Toward a Unified Analysis*, Stanford, CA: Stanford University Press.

—and Delaney, Carol (1995), *Naturalizing Power: Essays in Feminist Culture Analysis*, New York: Routledge.

Yarak, L. W. (1990), *Asante and the Dutch 1744-1873*, Oxford: Clarendon Press.

Yee, Albert (1989), *A People Misruled: Hong Kong and the Chinese Stepping-Stone Syndrome*, Hong Kong: API Press/UEA.

Young, Michel (1983), *Magicians of Manumanua*, Berkeley, CA: University of California Press.

Index

Abercrombie, Nicholas, 149
Abrempong, 87
academic training, 43
Accra, 79
Adae festival, 81
Almeida, Miguel Vale de, 33
Akan, 75-7, 79, 81, 85, 87
American upper classes, 22
amity, network of, 208, 212, 215
Anderson, Benedict, 234
Anthias, Floya, 204
antithetical duality, 116, 118, 120-1, 124
Arhin, Kwame, 75, 79, 80, 88, 106
Asante, 4, 75-9, 85-9 *passim*
    Tradicional rules 77, 81-2, 85-89
Atouguia, Condessa de, 133-4
Augustins, Georges, 137
authority, 1, 3, 76, 202, 204-7, 212, 215, 219, 223
    parental, 14, 15
    dynastic, 15, 18, 20, 25
autobiography, 19-21, 25

Barth, Fredrik, 66
Bauer, Michel, 231
birth order, 33
Bloom, Harold: the anxiety of influence, 16, 25
Bluteau, Rafael: definition of successor, 133
Boone, James, 136
Bourdieu, Pierre 66, 149-50, 153, 156, 160, 230
Braga da Cruz, Manuel, 44
Busia, K. A., 79-81, 88

Calhoun, Craig J., 204, 207, 214
Capell, A., 117
capital
    economic, 150, 158
    educational and cultural 150, 158, 160, 162
    human, 12, 25
    social, 150, 158

symbolic, 26-7
chief, 76, 88, 113, 115, 117-8
    chieftaincy: introduction of, 91
    election 100-5
    and lineal succession, 115, 118, 120
    and installation, 114-115, 118-119, 122-123
    and ritual, 116-120 *passim*
Christian missions, 80
choice, 2, 4, 144-5, 227
citizenship *versus* sovereignty, 205-6, 224
Clavero, Bartolomé, 135, 137
Cohen, Abner, 43, 204-5, 207, 212
collective action 201-2, 205, 207, 214, 219
Colonel Sanders, 195
colonial, 4, 202, 205, 230
    regime 91, 97-101 *passim*
    rule, 79-81
commodification (ghosthood and self-coomodification), 193-5
community, 204-5, 207, 212-215, 225 n10
    ethnic, 201, 204, 221
    arenas of, 213, 215
    bounderies, 213
    nodules of, 215
Como
    silk industry, 54, 68-9n3, n4
    bourgeois fractions, 54, 69-70n5
continued identity, 216-17
constituing process, 32, 41
corporate (corporate group, corporateness), 1, 201
    property, 76
cross-cousins, 115, 118-22

Davis, John, 57-58
decontextualization
    practices of, 170, 175-81, 195
Delaforce, John, 172-174, 182, 185
Delaney, Carol66
descent, 38, 40, 43, 47, 76